KT-528-006

(OsL)

CAR

WITHDRAWN

TEACHING FOR CITIZENSHIP

WITHDRAWN

CARLISLE LIBRARY
ST MARTINS SERVICES LTD.

TEACHING FOR CITIZENSHIP IN EUROPE

edited by Audrey Osler, Hanns-Fred Rathenow and Hugh Starkey

Trentham Books

First published in 1995 by Trentham Books Limited

Trentham Books Limited
Westview House
734 London Road
Oakhill
Stoke-on-Trent
Staffordshire
England ST4 5NP

© Audrey Osler, Hanns-Fred Rathenow and Hugh Starkey

All rights reserved. No part of this publication may be reproduced in any material form (including photocopying or storing it in any medium by electronic means and whether or not transiently or incidentally to some other use of this publication) without the prior written permission of the copyright owner, except in accordance with the provisions of the Copyright, Designs and Patents Act 1988 or under the terms of a licence issued by the Copyright Licensing Agency, 90 Tottenham Court Road, London WlP 9HE. Applications for the copyright owner's written permission to reproduce any part of this publication should be addressed in the first instance to the publisher.

British Cataloguing in Publication Data
A catalogue record for this book is available from the British Library
ISBN: 1 85856 052 7

Designed and typeset by Trentham Print Design Ltd., Chester and printed in Great Britain by Bemrose Shafron (Printers) Ltd., Chester.

Contents

Acknowledgements

We wish to thank a number of individuals and organisations who have supported us in the preparation of this book.

The European Commission for its support of the ERASMUS curriculum development project, *Education for Citizenship in a new Europe: learning democracy, social justice, global responsibility and respect for human rights*, which enabled many of the contributors to this book to meet together from 1992-1995 to exchange ideas and develop courses on human rights education and citizenship in their universities.

The European Academy in Berlin for hosting the symposium in September 1995 where most contributions to this volume were first presented. We should like to thank the director and staff, particularly Marc de Jong and Heike Dörrenbächer. Thanks also to Barbara Munske who acted as interpreter at the symposium.

The Council of Europe and particularly the Director of Human Rights, Pierre Imbert, for providing bursaries to colleagues from Eastern and Central Europe to enable them to attend the Berlin symposium.

Martin O'Shaughnessy for translating chapter twelve, and Judith Wilson and Dennis Beach for assisting with that of chapter two and eighteen respectively.

Finally we would like to express a special debt of gratitude to Judy Dandy who has taken on much of the administrative work behind this book, keeping in touch with 22 contributors in 11 different countries and assisting with the preparation of the manuscript.

List of Contributors

Irina Ahmetova is Vice Principal of Moscow School No. 199, Russia.

Jean-Pierre Branchereau is Lecturer in Geography, with responsibility for International Relations, at the Institut Universitaire de Formation des Maîtres, Nantes, France.

Nick Clough is Senior Lecturer and leader of the Primary Undergraduate Teacher Training Programme in the Faculty of Education, University of the West of England, Bristol, UK.

Ian Davies is Lecturer in the Department of Educational Studies at the University of York, UK.

Roman Dorczak is a Research Assistant in the Department of Developmental and Educational Psychology, Jagiellonian University, Kraków, Poland.

Carmen Gonzalo is Lecturer in Human Geography at the Faculty of Education, Universitat Autònoma of Barcelona, Spain.

John Halocha is Principal Lecturer in Geography and Teaching Studies at Westminster College, Oxford, UK.

Mirjam M. Hladnik is Lecturer in Sociology at the Faculty of Education, University of Ljubljana, Slovenia.

Alison Jolly is a Research Officer at the Human Rights Centre, University of Exeter.

Gitte Kragh is Senior Lecturer at Haslev College of Education, Denmark, where she teaches psychology.

Ian Menter is Director of Studies for Research and Staff Development in the Faculty of Education, University of the West of England, Bristol, UK.

Vilgot Oscarsson is Lecturer in the Teacher Department, Institute of Didactics at Göteborg University, Sweden.

Audrey Osler is Lecturer with responsibility for the Human Rights and Equality in Education programme of study at the University of Birmingham, UK.

Ekaterina Rachmanova is Lecturer in Law at the Moscow State Pedagogical University, Russia.

Hanns-Fred Rathenow is Professor of Education with a special interest in political education and Director of the Institute for Social Studies at the Technical University of Berlin, Germany.

Teresa Ravazzolo is Specialist in Institutions and Techniques for the Protection of Human Rights, at the Centre for Training and Research on Human Rights, University of Padua, Italy.

Hugh Starkey is Principal Lecturer and Co-ordinator of European Affairs at Westminster College, Oxford, UK.

Jane Tarr is Senior Lecturer in Primary Education in the Faculty of Education, University of the West of England, Bristol, UK.

Sue Thorne is Headteacher at Chad Vale Primary School, Birmingham, UK.

Stephen Thornton is Lecturer in Philosophy and Media Studies at Mary Immaculate College, University of Limerick, Ireland.

Maria Villanueva is Lecturer in Human Geography at the Faculty of Education, Universitat Autònoma of Barcelona, Spain, and editor of the journal Documents d'Anàlisi Geogràfica.

Norbert H. Weber is Professor of Education at the Technical University of Berlin, Germany, with a special interest in holocaust education and peace education.

PART 1

Concepts of Citizenship and Human Rights

Chapter 1

Introduction: Citizenship, Schooling and Teacher Education

Audrey Osler

> Our education programmes should encourage all young Europeans to see themselves not only as citizens of their own regions and countries, but also as citizens of Europe and the wider world. All young Europeans should be helped to acquire a willingness and ability to preserve and promote democracy, human rights and fundamental freedoms (Council of Europe, 1983).

This recommendation of the Council of Europe's Committee of Ministers presents a challenge not only to teachers but also to those engaged in teacher education across Europe. The contributors to this book have responded to this challenge in a wide variety of ways through their analysis and research and through work with student teachers, experienced teachers and children in schools. Our understanding of what it means to be a citizen is constantly evolving and therefore the nature of citizenship education must remain under review.

Post 1989 changes in Europe have increased interest in how we might prepare young people for European citizenship and most effectively confront racism, xenophobia, sexual inequality and other challenges to social justice. The contributors to this volume present a rich mixture of ideas and activities which reflect not only the different contexts and cultures in which they are working, but also the range of academic disciplines which they represent. Many of these projects have developed in direct response to recent socio-economic and political changes in Europe, as teachers and students acknowledge the inadequacy of existing curricula in preparing students for active citizenship.

3

The nature of citizenship and citizenship education

Lynch (1992) suggests that education for democratic citizenship needs to recognise three interdependent *levels* of citizenship, local, national, and international, operating across four *domains* (social, cultural, environ- mental and economic). He argues that in teaching for citizenship these levels and domains are in reality indivisible and should address cognitive, affective and conative or action-orientated *objectives* in two international *dimensions*, human rights and social responsibilities. He reminds us that much of what has, in the past, been classified as citizenship education has in fact been teaching for national citizenship. The challenge remains of developing approaches to citizenship education which meet the needs of a multicultural Europe, in which members of minority communities are often struggling to claim their rights.

I have argued elsewhere that an appropriate education for the twenty-first century is one which:

> encourages the development of an inclusive rather than exclusive understanding of national identity and citizenship. This revitalised view of education would promote an understanding of the rights and responsibilities of democratic citizenship not dependent on ethnic affiliation or identification but recognising and supporting diversity both within and between societies. This view of education for active, participative citizenship might therefore acknowledge diversity, interdependence and differences in perception, and might approach areas of study from a variety of cultural perspectives, encouraging students to recognise shared values (Osler, 1994).

The development of inclusive, rather than exclusive, understandings of citizenship and national identity are further explored in this volume. Gitte Kragh has a psychological perspective, suggesting that we need to understand that, although young people need to define their identity in ways that will inevitably bring them to make judgements about who is not like them, they can also accept difference. They can operate at the level of either/or and also both/and. Nick Clough, Ian Menter and Jane Tarr provide a concrete example of how these issues are dealt with in Latvia, where since independence from the Soviet Union was declared in 1990, debate on citizenship has focused on the relationship between the state and nationality, ethnicity, language policy, and the position of the significant Russian minority. Whilst there is heavy institutional pressure to opt for either/or the educational task is essentially to promote both/and.

European education systems have tended to remain monocultural, and where forms of intercultural education have been introduced they have often been restricted in practice to minority communities or to those urban areas which have undergone population changes as a result of immigration. Tragically, exclusive understandings of national identity and citizenship are more commonly promoted in schools, either through the explicit curriculum or through school organisation and teacher attitudes. One notorious and symbolic example, cited by both Mirjam Hladnik and Alison Jolly, is the French case where Muslim girls have been prevented from attending school wearing the *hijab* or headscarf. There is evidence that some young Muslim women in France and in other European countries are choosing to wear the *hijab* as an affirmation of their religious and cultural identity (Gaspard and Khosrokhavar, 1995); these young women reject the (western) feminist interpretation of the veil as a symbol of oppression. Where such a choice has been made it may be seen as a courageous one, for it can frequently provoke racial harassment (Osler, 1995: 188-189). While schools seek to impose a conformity on their students which denies religious or cultural diversity and interdependence, they re-affirm a narrow exclusive notion of citizenship and establish a climate where it becomes difficult to recognise shared values and impossible to acknowledge differences in perception or to approach studies from a variety of cultural perspectives.

Examples of exclusive interpretations of national identity and citizen- ship through education are also to be found among those European countries which have undergone recent political change. Mirjam Hladnik observes that in the newly created state of Slovenia current debates focus on the introduction of religious teaching, and suggests that there is a fear that socialist indoctrination will be simply replaced by religious indoctrination, by the Roman Catholic Church. This is a theme which is also explored by Roman Dorczak, who argues that in Poland schools have always been an instrument of ideological struggle and indoctrination. After the overthrow of the communist government in Poland conservative Roman Catholic political parties quickly established Catholic religious instruction in schools. Although in theory there is a choice between religious instruction and courses of ethics, in practice students are unable to exer- cise this choice; schools lack alternative curriculum materials and teachers the incentive to develop alternative courses.

In the development of an inclusive national or European identity and an inclusive understanding of citizenship the issue of choice is clearly a central theme. Hladnik suggest that the way a state educates refugees is a limiting case. As she puts it:

> perhaps the answer to the question of education for refugees is the answer to education in general, and thus the responsibility of the state itself.

Members of refugee communities often long to return to their homelands, but for many this proves to be a impossible dream. Refugee children have the right to special protection and assistance, they have the right to enjoy their own culture and practice their own religion and culture. Like all other children they have the right to preservation of identity. At the same time they have various rights of participation which will depend on access to the official language of the state in which they are living, and on access to mainstream cultural, economic and political life. The realisation of participation rights are likely to be determined largely by the quality of education they receive. An education which permits children to maintain their own culture but which does not exclude them from the majority culture will guarantee participation, and permit the adoption of multiple identities. Such an education is one which secures choice for the individual. The way a state educates members of any minority community is perhaps the touchstone of its commitment to a democratic and peaceful future.

Recommendation R (83) 4 (cited above) suggests that education should encourage young Europeans to see themselves as citizens at local, regional, national, European and global levels. This demands an education which recognises and accepts that young people may wish to adopt multiple identities rather than be confined in the strait-jacket of a narrow identity which has often traditionally been imposed through schooling. It also requires teachers to act in accordance with the UN Convention on the Rights of the Child and to acknowledge that children have the right to participate in decisions about their own lives, including their own education. Children, as well as adults, have citizenship rights, and schools have a responsibility to recognise these rights, and not merely accept the task of preparation for citizenship sometime in the future.

Concepts of citizenship and human rights

This first section of the book, 'Contexts of citizenship and human rights', explores the changing contexts in which debates about citizenship and citizenship education have taken place. In the next chapter Teresa Ravazzolo traces the development of these rights over the past two centuries. She reminds us that the precise formulation of citizenship cannot be universal since a citizen is generally subject to the laws of a particular country. She points out some of the difficulties of European citizenship where a number of rights are clearly defined but others, such as social rights, are not guaranteed. Nor are the duties of the European citizen explicit. In the twentieth century questions have been raised about the universal nature of human rights by some philosophers who have found it increasingly difficult to speak about an objective moral system. In the ethical field this has led to relativism. Following the second world war, the urgent need to prevent further wide scale violations of human rights caused those who drafted the Universal Declaration to put such philosophical problems aside. Ravazzolo argues for a new concept of citizenship to meet the needs of modern global society where people of different cultural and ethnic backgrounds require a common ethical system. She argues that human rights as shared values present us with a new basis of citizenship; individuals educated in human rights seek to respect life, peace, equality, solidarity, democracy and non-violence. As the

United Nations Secretary-General put it at the World Conference on Human Rights in June 1993:

> To be sure, human rights are a product of history. As such they should be in accordance with history, should evolve simultaneously with history and should give the various peoples and nations a reflection of themselves that they recognise as their own. Yet, the fact that human rights keep pace with the course of history should not change what constitutes their very essence, namely their universality (UNHCR, 1994:7).

From a philosophical perspective, Stephen Thornton examines the tension between universalist and cultural relativist interpretations of human rights which are highlighted in Teresa Ravazzolo's account. He argues that a society which promotes policies of multiculturalism (commonly perceived as the prioritisation of cultural or group rights) may endorse the infringement of individual human rights, and consequently reject the claim that human rights have universal validity. For example, the practice of female circumcision may be endorsed by a society which prioritises the rights of a community to follow their traditional cultural practices over the rights of individual women to be free from discriminatory treatment or harmful practices. Thornton rejects such a position and seeks to demonstrate that cultural relativism is, in fact, damaging to multiculturalism; he concludes that if multiculturalism is to have either moral or political impact and universal relevance it must root itself in a universalist interpretation of human rights.

Mirjam Hladnik poses a key question: who defines education for citizenship in a new Europe? She highlights how nation states have made citizens of their inhabitants by denying them their language and other aspects of their culture, and draws attention to the tensions which exist between citizenship and (narrow) definitions of national identity: 'where do the borders of tolerance exist between different cultures and when does tolerance become a tool for the production of second class citizens?'

Gitte Kragh argues that education for human rights, democracy and global responsibility, although usually dominated by political issues, has much to gain from a Jungian psychological perspective; educators need to recognise the importance of self-development, as part of the process of understanding patterns of identity, strengths and weaknesses, possibilities and limitations. She sees the political and psychological dimensions of human experience as complementary in promoting social justice.

In the final chapter in this section Alison Jolly examines the concept of tolerance, and considers its relevance to educators concerned to challenge discrimination and promote equality and human rights. She defines tolerance as minimum standards of treatment for everyone, suggesting that it is prerequisite for establishing a society in which diversity may be secured. Furthermore, she argues that a society must do more than merely accommodate different ethnic and religious groups; tolerance must recognise that rights belong to all, without discrimination. The chapter goes on to consider the limitations of tolerance. While there are examples of situations when human rights might be limited on the grounds of public safety, health or morals, or to protect the fundamental rights and freedoms of others, she urges caution in restricting the rights and freedoms of those groups whose views we might find repugnant or distasteful. She concludes that intolerance around the world is growing, and that educators have a direct responsibility to address this problem, through the curriculum, by example, and by a willingness to confront the 'unacceptable' with clear, strong, arguments as to why it is wrong.

Citizenship and the education of teachers

In this second section teacher educators working in Britain, Germany, Latvia, and Spain present a number of projects designed to raise human rights and citizenship issues with student teachers and experienced teachers. One of the difficulties encountered by teacher educators wishing to work in this field is that, more often than not, initial teacher education courses are planned around traditional subjects, and cross-curricular issues such as citizenship are seen as the responsibility of all. This often means that they are given low priority in overall course design. Hanns-Fred Rathenow and Norbert H. Weber describe how they have worked within the framework of a traditional three-year initial teacher education programme in a German university to develop an elective six-month course on peace education. This course adopts a range of methods to promote independent student learning, through cooperative project-based work. The approach is inter-disciplinary and the topics are of direct relevance both to the students' immediate social context and to their future work. Such project-based work demands a high level of commitment from students beyond regular classes, and the authors describe a number of initiatives in which their students have participated, including workshops on history textbook analysis and street theatre. They also describe students' experiences of visiting concentration camp memorials. The visits, which are set within a series of seminars dedicated to the pedagogical problems of Holocaust Education, are designed to enable both students and teachers to confront their own history, through the biographies of individual victims.

In the following chapter I present a research and curriculum development project which examines human rights and citizenship issues in a local context. The project involved a university course for experienced teachers. It developed out of a concern about how the media represent inner city communities and particularly how they choose to represent urban protest. One outcome of the project was the development of a teachers' handbook for human rights and citizenship. They examine policing, exploring both the role of the police in protecting rights how they are sometimes seen as violators of rights. Among the barriers to human rights and citizenship they identify poverty, housing and homelessness. The material considers a number of structural inequalities which can serve to deny the rights of individuals and groups, particularly racism. It also considers how teachers and students can challenge injustice and inequality, through a critical analysis of schooling.

Carmen Gonzalo and Maria Villanueva consider the potential of their subject specialism, geography, to promote democracy and human rights, through an examination of the processes of migration and the multicultural nature of modern Spain. Their students, who are future primary school teachers, engaged in a research project focusing, first on the migratory experiences of their own families to Catalonia from various parts of Spain, and then on the experiences of those who have migrated to Spain from other parts of the world. The method adopted was interviews conducted by the students. The individual life histories of migrants then provide a basis for the analysis of migration from the perspective of the migrants themselves. Students discover that the causes of migration remain quite similar over time and that the degree to which migrants are accepted is likely to depend on a range of socio-economic factors. Most importantly, the project encourages learning which is both conceptual and affective, and invites students to consider their own role as future teachers in promoting equality and social justice.

Hugh Starkey, also working with future primary school teachers, considers the extent to which a French language and culture course can enable them 'to be supportive of the fundamental European values of liberty, democracy and respect for human rights'. Within the course is a unit on modern French history which takes human rights as the linking concept. Students study the 1789 Revolution, the Declaration of the Rights of Man and the Citizen and also the origins and status of twentieth century human rights texts. Another element of the course emphasises popular culture; students learn about the production of media products and are encouraged to develop those critical skills which are an impor-tant part of learning for a democratic society. Student evaluation of the course reveals that they appreciate the opportunity to study human rights and are able to link their learning to current political events. Interestingly, study of French culture and a period spent abroad reinforces many students' sense of their own British identity; while some students feel 'more European' others reject the notion of a European identity. Starkey notes that schools have largely neglected language teaching as a means of promoting social justice, democracy and human rights. He argues that students' increased awareness of their own values will equip them to improve their understanding of liberty, democracy and respect for human rights.

In the final chapter in this section Clough, Menter and Tarr examine citizenship education programmes in Latvia which have been developed by teacher educators there, with support from Danish and British colleagues. These programmes have been developed in the context of a programme of thorough restructuring in Latvian teacher training over the past few years. As well as focusing on the central issues of Latvian citizenship and national identity, mentioned above, the chapter outlines how various subject specialisms, including history, sociology, philosophy and geography are contributing to citizenship education. The authors also provide an example of how the issue of women's rights has opened up debate on human rights. They discuss appropriate pedagogy for democratic citizenship, and the implications of their work in Latvia for teaching and learning about citizenship in Britain. They explore the concepts of freedom and security, inclusivity, and solidarity as key values in any democratic citizenship education programme.

Children, citizenship and the school curriculum

This final section explores children's understanding of citizenship issues and reports on various initiatives to develop citizenship education in both primary and secondary schools across a range of European countries. Jean-Pierre Branchereau discusses a research project which explored children's understanding of international conflict and war, and particularly television coverage of war, through a study of schools in Heidelberg, Montreal, Nantes and Oxford. Through a questionnaire, children aged eight to 12 years old were invited to explain the causes of the Gulf War, present their images of events, and to explain the sources of their knowledge. A single television channel formed the source of news that was broadcast around the world and one aim was to discover how children in different countries interpreted the pictures to which they all had access and the various commentaries on the war. Branchereau discovered that television, perhaps not surprisingly, was children's major source of information, and that children were able to name the main political personalities, with boys showing more 'technical' knowledge about weapons used. He notes that although a significant number of children also claimed to have learnt something of the war from their parents, the majority felt they had learnt nothing or very little at school. He concludes that we should not underestimate the geo-political awareness that children acquire through television and that teachers have a responsibility to enable children to re-contextualise, structure and enrich it.

History is often presented as the school subject which has the greatest contribution to make to citizenship education. In his chapter Ian Davies describes a small scale project which explored the potential of history to contribute to European citizenship in the framework of the National Curriculum of England and Wales. Working with history teachers in five secondary schools he explored appropriate teaching materials and methods European citizenship. He concludes that students' understandings of the rights and responsibilities of European citizenship are unlikely to be met by the history curriculum. He explains that this is due in part to lack of clarity among policy makers concerning these rights and responsibilities and also to teachers' uncertainty about the most effective ways of teaching about rights. While the project team had originally decided that the focus of the work should be issues of human rights, drawn from legal case histories, this focus was lost as teachers sought to consider the broader aims of history education. Davies concludes that for teaching for citizenship through history teaching to be effective, more explicit work is needed on the relationship between history and citizenship education, particularly on the question of identity.

In the following chapter Roman Dorczak reports a small scale project in Poland, which has the aim of introducing a new model of moral education into Polish schools. This project explores an alternative to the approach adopted by the majority of schools; in these the Roman Catholic Church has assumed full responsibility for moral education through the medium of religious instruction. Arguing that a new form of indoctrination has replaced the old, and recognising the dangers to democracy inherent in the system, Dorczak is involved in an initiative which seeks to democratise schools by dealing with whole school organisation and management, teaching styles, and decision-making processes as well as curriculum content. He remains optimistic about the potential of schools to promote such changes, observing that students, while subject to the pressures of commercialism and academic achievement, are often readier than their teachers to adapt to new methods of teaching and learning.

Sue Thorne, writing from the perspective of a primary school headteacher, discusses the widespread problem of bullying. She describes a school-based project which explored children's understandings of bullying and involved them in developing a whole school behavioural policy. The project developed out of a desire to provide a learning environment where all children are guaranteed the right to achieve their potential, and where there are effective measures to challenge discriminatory behaviour such as bullying, racism and sexism. Children were given the opportunity of presenting their experiences to parents, and developed, with their teachers, a number of effective strategies for countering bullying. Not only have their ideas been adopted, their priorities have also been observed in the preparation of the school's budget. Money has been allocated to the improvement of the play environment and children are working with a landscape architect to put their ideas into practice. Sue Thorne concludes that in acknowledging children's right to participate in decision-making and in giving them responsibility for identifying problems and finding appropriate solutions, the children have been helped to 'consider the rights of others and to take a shared responsibility for their future'. She sees this as an important step in involving children in democratic processes and developing the school as a human rights community.

The chapter on civic education in Russia, written by a lawyer and a teacher, demonstrates how those with complementary skills and expertise are working together to bring about changes in education to meet the needs of a developing democracy. Irina Ahmetova and Ekaterina Rachmanova highlight the new freedom of educators in universities and schools to develop an awareness of human rights and an understanding of the mechanisms of legal protection, which they identify as one of the essential conditions of any modern democratic society. To this end the Moscow State Pedagogical University, which is responsible for the training of both school teachers and teacher educators, has introduced core courses in human rights education. They stress the important role which non-governmental organisations have played in the development of civic education in Russia. A teachers' association for civic education has been formed and members have been quick to recognise the importance of developing new textbooks to support teachers in their work. The authors describe the impact of changes on one secondary school, including the development of international school links to study environmental issues and human rights education projects. Problems encountered include conflict between teachers and students and between students and their parents as students become aware of their human rights; lack of legal awareness among school administrators, teachers and parents; and student scepticism.

John Halocha develops the theme of citizenship education through international links, in this case between an institution of higher education and its partner schools. Within the project, *School on Site*, primary school children come into the college for a number of weeks and seminar rooms are transformed into classrooms by the students. In such an environment the students take greater responsibility for planning children's learning than they would normally be able to do within a school context. They also have scope to develop the European dimension, for example, through the management of information technology to communicate between countries. Halocha describes how links were developed with a cluster of Italian primary schools, enabling teachers, students and children to discover something about their partners' way of life, first through the exchange of photographs, and later through fax messages and the making of a video. Through such activities students gain first-hand experience of planning and working democratically and are able to confront issues related to the development of democratic teaching methods. They also have the opportunity to develop skills in working with children on stereotypes, identities and nationalisms. The chapter emphasises how teachers and children can engage in such activities and develop skills for democratic citizenship and at the same time meet rigorous curriculum requirements.

The final chapter reports on a research project which set out to investigate young people's attitudes to the future. As Vilgot Oscarsson argues, since 'every new generation must be won over to democracy ... it is important to examine if pupils feel they can influence their situation, if they have a desire to, and if they know what they need to accomplish this'. The research also sought to explore the extent to which students judged their learning in school to be an appropriate preparation for the future, in line with the aims of the Swedish National Curriculum. It was found that students who responded to the questionnaire were more optimistic about the global future than those surveyed in the 1970s and 1980s. The research also found students to be more positive about their personal futures than they were about Sweden's or the global future. Those who held the most optimistic views were those who scored most highly on an index of *social reliance*. Girls obtained higher ratings in *social reliance* than boys but tended to be less self-confident, whereas boys tended to score more highly in *political reliance*. Oscarsson concludes that schooling needs to foster the self-confidence of girls, the holders of democratic values, while encouraging the development of social competence amongst boys: 'In this way schools can improve their capacity to prepare for a positive and democratic future'.

Teaching for a democratic future

Governments and non-governmental organisations in eastern and central Europe have a new democratic agenda and are recognising the central role of education. The new emphasis on democratic political development in global politics has also increased debate about education for human rights and democracy in western Europe.

Teaching for citizenship and for a democratic future requires both schooling and teacher education to develop in a more democratic direction. Democratic values need to be learned and to be learned they need to be experienced. Various contributors to this book have discussed how this might be achieved and have offered case studies of how we might promote respect for human rights and develop more participative and democratic ways of working with children, student teachers and experienced teachers. There is today a widespread international consensus on the need for greater democracy; the key role of education in achieving a more democratic political culture was recently re-affirmed by the Director-General of UNESCO:

> Education for human rights and democracy in the last analysis means the empowerment of each and every individual to participate with an active sense of responsibility in all aspects of political and social life. It is the continuing process of fostering attitudes and behaviour conducive to that 'art of thinking together' which is at the heart of the democratic ethos and which is antagonistic to discrimination and injustice. ... The entire school system

should constitute an initiation to democratic living — to the assumption of responsibilities, to the challenges of participation, to learning about the linkage between rights and duties, knowing and caring (UNESCO, 1993).

Such an initiation to democratic living is critical to our future development:

> The purpose of human development is to increase people's range of choices. If they are not free to make those choices, the entire process becomes a mockery. So, freedom is more than an idealistic goal — it is a vital component of human development. People who are politically free can take part in planning and decision making. And they can ensure that society is organised through consensus and consultation rather than dictated by an autocratic elite (UNDP, 1992: 26).

References

Council of Europe (1983) *Recommendation No. R (83) 4 of the Committee of Ministers to Member States Concerning the Promotion of an Awareness of Europe in Secondary Schools*. Strasbourg: Council of Europe.

Gaspard, F. and Khosrokhavar, F. (1995) *Le Foulard et la République*. Paris: La Découverte.

Lynch, J. (1992) *Education for Citizenship in a Multicultural Society*. London: Cassell.

Osler, A. (1994) Education for Development: redefining citizenship in a pluralist society, in: A. Osler (Ed.) *Development Education: global perspectives in the curriculum*. London: Cassell.

Osler, A. (1995) *The Education, Lives and Careers of Black Teachers in Britain*. Unpublished PhD thesis. University of Birmingham.

UNESCO (1993) Opening address of the Director General to the International Congress on Education for Human Rights and Democracy, Montreal, Canada, 8-11 March 1993, *Human Rights Teaching*, 8, pp. 26-33.

UNDP (1992) *Human Development Report*. New York: UNDP.

United Nations High Commissioner for Refugees (1994) *Human Rights, the new consensus*. London: Regency Press.

Chapter 2

Human Rights and Citizenship

Teresa Ravazzolo

These reflections touch on two important humanitarian achievements: citizenship and human rights. Both these concepts were established during the Age of Enlightenment and were first defined during the French Revolution. From that moment on the rights of citizenship, and human rights — some of which were thought of as rights of the citizen — were no longer only abstract and theoretical ideals but also concrete entitlements that needed to be improved upon. Today human rights concern everyone everywhere, while citizenship is still an individual category (Lippolis, 1994).

The meaning of citizenship changes in relation to the political or juridical context (Quadri, 1959). Such differences become more relevant in the internal structures of different countries. From a general point of view citizenship refers to the legal status of an individual who is part of a country, in particular the relation between the state and the individual. Apart from citizenship, the person becomes a member of a community, a part of a larger group. What is most important at this level of interpretation is the state: it defines the conditions and what is necessary if an individual wants to be a citizen. A citizen is subject to the the laws of a particular country and therefore the precise formulation of citizenship, in this legal sense, is not universal.

In addition to this broad concept of citizenship there is a more precise one. Today when we use the terms citizen and citizenship we are at first referring to a particular condition that deals with specific rights and duties. Among these are: the right to live and work where you want; the right to elect and to be elected; the right to be protected (including diplomatic protection); the right to social assistance; the duty to serve the country; the obligation of taxation. Citizens of a democratic country are securely protected by a system that guarantees their rights (Bobbio, 1991).

Arising from this is a democratic idea of the country; within this idea is a decisive role attributed to popular sovereignty. When the concept of citizen was born with the French Revolution, the individual was considered only as a subject of the king. The subjects then declared formally that they had fundamental rights innate to all human beings (Lippolis, 1994). Since then individuals are consequently no longer subjects but also participants. Those who remain excluded are the foreigners because they are not members of a 'group' and they do not have the sovereign rights that define the others as citizens.

The foreigner is symbolic of the existing distinction between person and citizen in public law. Between these two there is a line of separation that coincides with existing borders between the rights of citizens and the rights of persons.[1] Citizenship developed as a condition that characterises the person as a part of a country and is explicit in that context. In the past, but also now, citizenship has been linked with nationality. The individual has been absorbed in the national system based on ideological authority and centralistic power. In this case, groups that are considered different are discriminated against in order to preserve a spurious unity that refuses to acknowledge differences.[2]

Any country that defines and grants citizenship, must consider both, its system of rights and protection and its capacity to face critical challenges arising from global complexity. This global complexity creates crucial problems inside the country and in international relations.

From this point of view, the European citizenship that was established after 1 January 1993 is a step ahead. A citizen from one country in the European Union is at the same time a European citizen and the second is linked to the first. However, even if some rights are specified (freedom of movement, to be elected and to elect, freedom to petition the European Parliament, to appeal to the European Mediator, and to appeal to the Supreme Court of the Union) social rights and also fundamental individual rights are only implicit.[3] The duties of the European citizen are not defined. Nonetheless, this is the first attempt at a dissolution of national borders and the creation of a supra-national citizenship. Above all, from the point of view of European citizenship, the building of the European community is linked not only to economic integration but also to strengthening people's participation in a common future.

The first official declarations of human rights were those of America and France. In these, citizens have precise rights which are the same as those innate rights understood by reason and which are a fundamental part of natural law. At that time the defining of human rights was necessary in order to defend the individual from a political situation that was a great violation of human rights (absolute monarchy). Their proclamation justified the new shape of the state based on the assumption of personal autonomy and reason which arose from the modern period.

Declarations are linked with social-political facts (the birth of the sovereign state as rule of law) and socio-economic events (the merger of social subjects as commercial, financial, industrial bourgeoisie and proletariats). However, to understand what they represent requires the philosophical approach of the doctrine of natural law. This philosophy looks at the doctrines from the past but gives them subjective and individualistic aspects; rights are at first qualified as the 'power' and 'potential' of the individual in relation to property and conditions. Within the doctrine of natural law there are different theories but all of them are unified in the concept of contractualism. This implies giving priority to the natural condition over the social and political condition. Fundamental innate rights come from this philosophical system. They are not invented and they pre-exist the social contract. The power of the state cannot be absolute as it must recognise this untouchable and original condition that belongs to every human being. Fundamental human rights are recognised by natural reasoning that is present in everyone and are universal, as opposed to specific rights conceptualised by different legislations for different groups.

The theoretical suppositions are: first, that 'human nature' is unique and from it specific rights are derived; second, that reasoning has the capacity to discover the universality of human nature and to identify the rights arising from such. In view of this, human rights are universal because human nature is universal. In their juridical translation human rights coincide with those innate fundamental rights understood in philosophical reasoning. In this way of thinking, the juridical system becomes identified with the moral system.

In the nineteenth century, at the political level, it became more common to appeal for human rights, but the roots that gave natural and universal foundations to those convictions started to weaken. The doctrine of natural law seemed abstract and unrealistic because it was shown to be extremely problematic to refer to a unique human nature considered as unchangeable and from which it was possible to identify distinct, individual fundamental rights. In the meantime, reasoning lost its capacity to be an instrument common to all human beings. On the contrary it seemed clear that human reasoning was conditioned by specific cultural, social, political, and economic habits. Thus, the first human rights were rather abstract. Human rights referred in a generic way to a theoretical human nature so they were not able to deal with the conflicts of the real society. [4]

In the twentieth century the prevalent way of thinking underlined contingency as the fundamental character of existence and reasoning. It seemed impossible to define human nature and human rights in an universal and objective way (for example existentialism, hermeneutics, and analytical philosophy). In the philosophical field it is always more and more difficult to speak about an objective moral system and also to speak about absolute human rights.

Based on the aforementioned, the consequences are that now there is a gap between philosophical perspectives, which in the ethical field has led to relativism, and juridical perspectives. At the end of the second world war it appeared clear that if people wanted to avoid new catastrophes such as those caused by nazism, it was essential to be aware of the importance of peace and human rights. Thus, all countries had to work in order to put human rights and peace as the goal to which they could aspire (Cassese, 1988). In the juridical field the new laws, arising from the 1948 Universal Declaration of Human Rights, are connected to some principles of natural law and to those social principles of the Eastern Bloc countries. The Declaration of 1948 is the final result of more ideology and different conceptions of international politics. However, this does not apply to different cultures if we mean that culture has the individual disposition to confront reality that is present because everyone is part of a historically determined society (Tentori, 1987). The people who wrote the Declaration did not intend to reconcile philosophical and cultural diversities. They decided to leave doubts aside and to go ahead because it was urgent to save and protect human dignity. An example of this is the decision by the Human Rights Commission, during the twelfth session that was held in Geneva on 2 December 1947, to refuse a report prepared by UNESCO with an introduction by J. Maritain. Included were the recommendations of many philosophers that dealt with the theoretical problems connected to the preparation of universal Declaration of Human Rights because only a few human rights were universally valid for all the different cultures.[5]

Even though there are problems arising from the philosophical and anthropological considerations of human rights, they are the point of strength of the new conception of international law. This new international law has begun to conflict with the previous traditional rules that controlled relations between national states (Cassese, 1984). According to the old system of international law, countries were not obliged to specify what they meant by national citizenship and they were not obliged to specify which rights an individual had. Citizen's rights were defined by International law. Countries, by using consuetudinary law, have always been free to treat their citizens inside their borders as they wanted.

International human rights law disrupts this situation. Human rights covenants give everyone an international identity, and so individuals have rights that before were recognised — or not — only on the basis of their national law.

Human rights laws are defined in many covenants,[6] requiring countries that sign them to respect their duties to individuals. In this way, principles such as human dignity, equality, social justice, solidarity and democracy are legitimised and oppose the principles of the old international law such as sovereignty, no intervention in internal affairs, and an international legal status reserved only for states. The strongest idea linked to all human rights is clarified in the first article of the Declaration of 1948: 'All human beings are born free and equal in dignity and rights'.

Human rights are innate in all human beings irrespective of whether they are citizens or foreigners and all are entitled to them. International recognition of human rights frees persons from territorial, legal and national conditions that sometimes relate to discrimination and privileges (Papisca, 1994).

Until now, this analysis has developed along two parallel lines. In the next section I will bring them together in order to emphasise a new relationship between human rights and citizenship.

It has already been said that citizenship is based on and is defined by nation states. But is such an entity as the nation state able to face globalisation, particularly interdependence, transnationalisation of relations and structures, and the global economy? Nation states may be thought of as knots in a larger net. The scale is so large and interconnected that it is usual to describe the world as a global village. Individuals often find themselves involved at different levels: national, transnational, and international. Global processes are opposite in logic to those within national borders. An example of the global dimension inside every state is the multicultural reality. 'Foreigners' are no longer transient or looking for jobs but may be resident over many generations and sometimes have citizenship in the country. The situation is different in northern and central Europe, where immigration has existed for a long time, and southern European countries where immigration is relatively new.[7] In both situations the identification of a particular nationality with citizenship or a spurious peculiarity provokes enormous tension between ethnic groups inside the same territory. It is urgent and it is a fundamental necessity to have ethnic and religious neutrality at the root of every democratic system. It does not imply ethical neutrality. Rather, it is necessary to discover a respectable, common ethical system in order to live together as a society. From this a new basis of citizenship is defined; human rights considered as shared values.

The status of citizen would not depend on belonging to a nation or place of birth but rather on being a member of the universal community of human beings. This could be the foundation of the multicultural society.

How can we reconcile the universality, indivisibility, and interdependence of human rights[8] while they are perceived as being the product of European culture? What does equal treatment on the basis of human rights mean if people have different cultures, religions, races and so on? How can diversity in thinking about human rights in a philosophical and anthropological way be reconciled with an international legal framework?

In the first place, it is no longer possible to define human nature as an unchangeable reality already expressed in a global and unique way. Human dignity is expressed in forms which are determined by culture. However, people may transcend their own culture and be aware of their limits.

Help in reaching these goals comes from anthropology and jurisprudence. One of its important tasks is to explain the behaviour of society. The law is not constant but is a means by which individuals have organised their relationships. In this way every society has codified certain rules and behaviours that were already included in other systems, such as religion and ethics. Due to this, inside diverse cultures there are parallels between conceptions of law and the conception of universal rules (Rouland, 1988).

In the Christian world, but also in the Islamic world, the organisation of the society is delegated to an external authority. In the beginning this was God and later it became the State. The individual is subjected to a power that arises from abroad and from which the law is also derived; the law transforms the original community within the organised society. Since the cohesion of the system is not the result of a reciprocal integration of the elements but is the result of laws imposed by authorities, individuals are autonomous and equal. This model, which is called a 'model of submission', is found within the organisation of modern society (for example, in old industrialised countries). Other models are different: individuals are responsible for themselves and there is no external authority. Anyone can change status depending on the role played in society.[10] This should demonstrate that sometimes the analysis of a traditional society using Western theories and conceptions can provoke misunderstandings.

However, in every part of the world, governments and official diplomacy appeal to human rights, but members of international civil societies do so even more. Their actions for humanity are sustained by this new International law created by the United Nations.

Undoubtedly, ethnicity may be dangerous when it leads to viewing other societies in terms of its own ideology. The anthropological perspective recognises in every culture the right to be autonomous in relations with others. In order to obtain this it is necessary to have a reciprocal agreement and respect. Human rights need to combine their universality with a more flexible and creative approach capable of change, of implementation, of building new institutions, and giving birth to a new awareness. Norbert Rouland expresses all this with the concept of *droit prospectif*. It means a kind of law able to accept a traditional organisation of society and not only the western one. By this notion it is easier to find a model law, based on a flexible and nonimperative principle, instead of a sanctioned law. The *droit prospectif* can reach a balance between the state on one side and the pluralist community on the other, not based on the submission model. All this means that the new legal procedure, even if inside the International Law of Human Rights, has to be integrated within the different societies. Its function could be changed according to cultures. It would be necessary to foresee transitional measures and work for a juridical plan which would be progressive and controlled. The final goal is to design a model of what the future society could be, starting with differences and ending with universality without uniformity.

It is obvious that the juridical plan, especially on the international level, needs to express human rights clearly and not ambiguously or evasively. Juridical jargon sounds definitive, and also it is not able to express completely all the circumstances in which human dignity is displayed. However, if it is capable of offering humanity more advantages than disadvantages, it may be a necessary instrument to translate the ethical needs of the majority of human beings.

Certainly, the current International Law of Human Rights is based on western culture and theory. However, in its instrumental character it may be accepted even if it does not reflect the conception of human dignity of different cultures. It could be the beginning of enhancing the significance of citizenship and it could put together human rights and the rights of citizens.

What contribution can education make to this process? Education is a fundamental means for putting theoretical concepts into practice and for passing from declarations to practical living.

The General Assembly of the United Nations has proclaimed, starting from 1995, a Decade for Human Rights Education and it intends to address this period to the well-being of humanity. Sustained education is a means of instilling the significance and the spirit of the new international law of human rights. From this viewpoint, education can begin to be an efficient instrument for the protection of human rights and educators can begin the first defence of them. This education is based on common values and precise thinking — found inside many covenants of human rights. Its most important goal is to help all students to be aware of their status as individuals and of their innate dignity. Human rights education is put into action and this action is accomplished through peace. This last is a condition in which all human rights are achieved.

The Decade for Human Rights Education concerns everyone because people are educated about human rights, have a strong empathy for the human condition and for the well-being of all creation. In their own lifestyle, individuals educated in this way try to respect life, peace, equality, solidarity, democracy, and nonviolence (Papisca, 1995).

Notes

1. Opinion is divided in Italy. There are those convinced that rights of freedom have to be ascribed to citizens and foreigners on the basis of Article two of the Constitution (Barile, 1984). But not everyone agrees (Pace, 1990).

2. A clear example of this is the situation of the former Yugoslavia where states are founded on the concept of Nations.

3. The 1992 Treaty of European Union guarantees in Title 1 Article F2 observance of the European Convention of 1950 on Human Rights and Fundamental Freedoms.

4. In fact the same philosophers from the Age of Enlightenment more or less consciously introduced the historical dimension when they promoted the codification of human rights.

5. See, Verdoodt, 1964: M. Dehousse, the Belgian representative, supposed the UNESCO report.

6. The principle components of the international law of human rights are: Universal Declaration of Human Rights (1948); the two Covenants on civil and political rights and on economic social and cultural rights (1966); the European Convention (1950); Inter-American Convention (1969); African Convention on Human and People's Rights (1981). The Convention on the Rights of the Child became law in 1990.

7. It would take too long to examine the ways in which citizenship is obtained in different countries. It is important to say that these diversities further weaken European citizenship.

8. These principles are stated in the final Declaration of the Second International Conference on Human Rights which took place in Vienna (June 1993).

9. See Panikkar, 1990.

10. From the different way of thinking about the relation between an individual and the group of which he is a part comes 'collective rights'. Indigenous people asked for these rights.

References

Alston, P. (1992) *The United Nations and human rights: a critical appraisal.* Oxford: Clarendon Press.

Barile, P. (1984) *Diritti dell'uomo e libertà' fondamentali.* Bologna: Il Mulino.

Bobbio, N. (1991), *L'età dei diritti.* Torino: Einaudi.

Bonazzi, T., Dunne, M. (1994) *Cittadinanza e diritti nelle società multiculturali.* Bologna: Il Mulino.

Bori, P.C. (1991) *Per un consenso etico tra culture.* Genova: Marietti.

Bouldind, E. (1988) *Building a global civic culture. Education for an interdependent world.* New York: Teachers College Press.

Callari Galli, M. (1993) *Antropologia culturale e processi educativi.* Firenze: La Nuova Italia.

Cassese, A. (1984) *Il diritto internazionale nel mondo contemporaneo.* Bologna: Il Mulino.

Cassese, A. (1988) *I diritti umani nel mondo contemporaneo.* Bari: Laterza.

De Stefani, P. (1994) *Il diritto internazionale dei diritti umani.* Padova: Cedam.

Levi Strauss, C. (1984) *Lo sguardo da lontano.* Torino: Einaudi.

Lippolis, V. (1994) *La cittadinanza europea.* Bologna:Il Mulino.

Pace, A. (1990) *Problematiche delle libertà costituzionali.* Padova: Cedam.

Panikkar, R. (1990) *E'universale il concetto di diritti dell'uomo?* Volontari e terzo mondo, 12, pp.24-48.

Papisca, A. (1994) *Democrazia e diritti nell'era dell'interdipendenza planetaria.* Pace diritti dell'uomo, diritti dei popoli, V(3), pp.12-30.

Papisca, A. (1994) *Per i diritti di cittadinanza: dallo stato confinario allo stato di diritto.* Democrazia e diritto, 2, pp.33-55.

Quadri, R. (1959), *Cittadinanza.* Torino: Einaudi.

Rouland, N. (1988), *Anthropologie juridique.* Paris: Presses Universitaires de France.

Tentori, T. (1987) *Antropologia culturale.* Roma: Studium.

Veerdoodt, A. (1964), *Naissance et signification de la Déclaration universelle des droits de l'homme.* Paris: Nauwelaerts.

Chapter 3

Cultural Rights, Multiculturalism and Cultural Relativism

Stephen Thornton

> The significance of human rights for protecting minorities against majorities is one of the most important implications of the principle of equality underlying the human rights idea (Burgers, 1990).

The tension which exists between universalist and cultural relativist interpretations of fundamental human rights concepts is universally recognised, and the literature is correspondingly extensive. In this context 'universalism' may be defined as the view that human rights are inherently immune to conditions of social, economic and cultural diversity and variability. 'Cultural relativism' by contrast, derives from the quite extraordinary heterogeneity of moral norms and social practices, and takes the view that, since culture is either the major or the sole source of human rights and values, human rights are either partially or wholly culturally relative, and therefore non-universal.

The significance of the debate has been compounded in recent years by the *de facto* establishment of conceptual connections between cultural relativism and multiculturalism. No-one with a serious interest in the protection, implementation or teaching of human rights can now afford the luxury of treating the universalist/ cultural relativist controversy about the nature of human rights as an abstract philosophical issue. In what follows I will argue that if multiculturalism is to be self-consistent, its links with cultural relativism must be severed, and it has to be associated with a universalist interpretation of human rights. Also that such an interpretation of human rights alone is compatible with the multiculturalist emphasis on the priority of cultural rights, and of establishing a social order which accords equal respect to the rights of members of minority cultures.

To begin, it is necessary to examine the considerations which have led to the association between multiculturalism and cultural relativism in the first instance, and to see what it entails.

Multiculturalism and cultural relativism

There is now a broad international consensus on the importance of multicultural educational policies in the struggle against resurgent egocentrism, socio-centrism, and ethnocentrism. As one commentator puts it:

> multicultural education has been instrumental in developing awareness, sensitivity, and the implementation of human rights and human rights education regarding ethnicity, race, religion, national origin, citizenship and such associated rights as equality before the law (McLeod, 1991, p.164).

There are therefore strong *prima facie* reasons for thinking that it can continue to fulfil this functional role.

Broadly speaking, this level of consensual agreement is not misplaced. Indeed, given the cumulative effects of the increasing Westernisation of world culture, the political and economic integration of Europe, with a global economy increasingly differentiated on a North/ South axis, and unprecedented changes in racial, cultural and religious demographics, it is not difficult to see why such a heavy emphasis should now be placed on the goals of multiculturalism by those concerned with human rights, equality and social justice. Society is becoming more and more multicultural and there has been a shift from assimilation and integration of minority cultures to acceptance, engagement and dynamic inter-action, to the point where celebration of cultural diversity has become orthodox. And it is true that, in terms of motivation and orientation at least, this celebration of cultural diversity 'is expressive of, and justified by, a belief in equality' (Harris, 1982, p.233), a belief from which springs respect and toleration for the values, belief-systems and social practices of other human beings. Moreover, some of the main international human rights instruments not only favour the multicultural approach to the education of the young, but actually require it, or something closely analogous to it (Singh, 1994, p.87). Thus, for example, Article 13 of the International Covenant on Economic, Social and Cultural Rights affirms that

> education shall enable all persons to participate effectively in a free society, promote understanding, tolerance and friendship among all nations and all racial, ethnic and religious groups, and further the activities of the United Nations for the maintenance of peace.

And Clause IV of the Declaration Regarding Intolerance adopted by the Committee of Ministers of the Council of Europe in 1981 asserts it a goal of the Council

> to promote an awareness of the requirements of human rights and the ensuing responsibilities in a democratic society, and to encourage ... the creation in schools ... of a climate of active understanding of and respect for the qualities and culture of others.

However, multiculturalism is not without its inherent difficulties, some of which would seem to call its very intelligibility into question, and to show that, so far from representing one of the most effective contemporary mechanisms for the promotion of fundamental human rights and values, it is in fact inimical to, and ultimately destructive of, the belief that those rights and values have universal validity. The difficulties can be exemplified in two related ways, which exhibit the conceptual connections which have been established between multiculturalism and cultural relativism.

Let us take first the distinction between external and internal judgements of value regarding social and cultural practices internationally. Given the very high level of transnational agreement which has been achieved since the proclamation of the Universal Declaration of Human Rights in 1948 on the values which are protected through human rights, by codification and implementation — in particular the fundamental freedoms or liberties — there is now strong support for the concept of a global or 'cosmopolitan' moral community (Donnelly, 1989, p.114). This is because any system of morality logically presupposes a reference group for whom it functions as a guide for conduct, and since human rights function as moral rights, in the strong sense of entitlements, which are inherent to human beings, such rights presuppose a moral community which is nothing less than the global human community itself (Wright, 1989, p.46). In other words, 'reference to human rights implies a global society or a society of mankind' (Hill, 1989, p.9).

In this connection, then, we may understand an internal judgement of value as one which assesses a particular cultural practice in terms of the beliefs and values-system of the society itself. It follows that, insofar as such internal judgements would take place at all, they would almost invariably be positive in their content. An external judgement of value, by contrast, would be one which would evaluate the same practice in terms of the value-system or systems of the global moral community — more specifically, by reference to the values which are protected by human rights. And it is not difficult to visualise circumstances where a commitment to the universality and inalienability of human rights would necessitate a negative external judgement of value on the practice in question. Slavery, infanticide, the caste system, child marriage, and female circumcision are practices which are sanctioned by the value-systems of some cultural communities, but which would be condemned — one wishes to say, justifiably — by the wider global moral community as constituting violations of fundamental human rights.

So tension exists between the ideals of multiculturalism and the claim of human rights to universal validity. The human global community is multi-cultural, in the most comprehensive sense possible, and the principle of respect and toleration for the cultural practices of others, which for multiculturalism is a *sine qua non*, would seem to preclude the mere possibility of negative external judgements of value on such practices. Yet a failure on the part of the global community to censure when confronted with practices which abrogate fundamental human rights, on the grounds that such practices are sanctioned by the culture in question, would be an attenuation of the claim of human rights to universal validity, and would be an abandonment of that very claim. In short, multi-culturalism can seem to demand, in this way and for these reasons, a relativist interpretation of human rights, which is strictly incompatible with a belief in their inviolability and universal validity.

This problem is, if anything, compounded when we switch our attention from international society to the state, commonly a pluralist multicultural one, sub-scribing to the principles of freedom, social justice and equal respect for the rights of all of its members, and where the latter are understood to extend, not only to *individual* members of minority cultures, but also to the minority cultures *per se*.

However cultural rights are to be interpreted, it is indisputable that there are such rights specified in the international instruments. Article 27 of the Universal Declaration of Human Rights, for example, recognises the right 'freely to parti-cipate in the cultural life of the community'. Article 15 of the International Covenant on Economic, Social and Cultural Rights recognises the right of everyone 'to take part in cultural life', and the obligation of the states parties to effect the necessary steps 'for the conservation, the development and the diffusion of science and culture.' Article 13 recognises the rights of parents to send their children to schools other than those provided by the state — which can in practice be an effective device for the preservation by minority groups of their cultural identity — while Article 27 of the International Covenant on Civil and Political Rights expressly provides that, in states where ethnic, religious or linguistic minorities exist,

> persons belonging to such minorities shall not be denied the right, in com-munity with the other members of their group, to enjoy their own culture, to profess and practice their own religion, or to use their own language.

Cultural rights, then, are an important category of human rights, and must be treated as such. Indeed, the issue of the protection of cultural rights is widespread, embracing as it does the cases of Native Americans and Cubans in the United

States, French-speakers in Canada, Bretons in France, Australian Aborigines, gypsies, and ethnic and religious minorities everywhere.

It is in relation to the preservation of cultural rights in pluralist societies that the multicultural approach, and the social and educational policies which devolve from it, is seen to embody the egalitarian ideals fundamental to liberal democracy, and to the promotion of human rights. Multicultural, social and educational policies originated as egalitarian alternatives to policies of cultural assimilation and hegemony, which — implicitly equating social concord with cultural homogeneity — effectively required a member of the minority culture 'crassly to accept the unimportance or worthlessness of the things he holds most dear' (Walkling, 1980, p.88) by surrendering to the overwhelming pressure of the dominant culture to conform.

However, precisely the same tension between the claim of human rights to universal validity and the ideals of multiculturalism which we encountered above, arises when we consider the position of an egalitarian multicultural society with a constituent minority culture which is itself discriminatory with respect to its own members. That there are cultures and sub-cultures which are discriminatory with respect to their own members is not in question — though it is only fair to add that for reasons which are themselves ironically cultural, the question as to *which* cultural practices are discriminatory is a contentious one. The position of women in certain fundamentalist Islamic, Jewish and Christian sects, the patriarchal and sexist nature of the Christian priesthood, female circumcision as practised by some African tribal cultures, and the Hindu caste system are frequently cited as culture-based discriminatory institutional practices. In such cases, what one commentator terms the 'paradox' of multiculturalism (Harris, 1982) arises.

In the first instance, how can a cultural grouping which discriminates against its own members, in the sense of denying them firm entitlements such as equality of opportunity or freedom of movement, consistently claim equality of respect for itself from the broader society of which it is a part? More fundamentally, however, there is the related question as to how an egalitarian multicultural society, fully committed to upholding the human rights of all of its members, can consistently do so in relation to such a constituent discriminatory cultural grouping. It has been argued that a society confronted with this dilemma must take one of two courses of action, and that each of these involves the infringement of human rights — though not necessarily infringements *by* the society in question (Harris, 1982; Singh, 1994). On the one hand it may choose to uphold the rights of each individual member of society equally, in which case it must be prepared to exclude, eliminate or condemn those aspects of the minority cultural practices which are discriminatory, notwithstanding that in doing so it would appear actively to abrogate the rights of the constituent minority culture which would evoke allegations of cultural imperialism. Or it may choose to adhere strictly to the precept of respecting all cultures equally, thus implicitly endorsing the discriminatory practices of the constituent minority culture, and permitting the rights of individual members of that grouping to be violated. As one commentator puts it, in such circumstances,

> if the society wishes to show each individual the same concern and respect that it accords to any, then it will be required to outlaw, frustrate or at the very least condemn, important features of a constituent and discriminatory culture. While if it respects all cultures equally, a society may find itself endorsing culturally enshrined inequalities (Harris 1982, p. 224).

This 'paradox', devolves precisely from the fact that multiculturalism is commonly perceived to give priority to cultural rights, conceived of as the rights of *cultural communities* to distinctive practices which define their cultural identity, in order to promote all other human rights within a multicultural society. Yet a society which accepts such priority is thereby logically committed to a policy of equal respect for all its indigenous cultures, irrespective of their content, again leads to radical cultural relativism. Thus once more we find multiculturalism and the human rights claim to universality, so far from being complementary, appear to be mutually subversive.

It is therefore unsurprising that strong links should now exist between multiculturalism and cultural relativism with respect to human rights, and that many of the protagonists of the ideals of multiculturalism should find cultural relativism compelling, and should consider the two positions totally congruent and compatible. Given the historical and political provenance of multiculturalism, and the appropriate emphasis which it gives to the protection of the cultural rights of minority cultures against threats from the state or the dominant culture, it is inevitable that anything which appears to imply moral imperialism will be regarded anathema by those who subscribe to multiculturalist ideals. Commitment to the equality of respect for the members of all cultures would itself appear to obviate negative social comment, much less legal exclusion or prohibition, of practices which are culturally rooted and authenticated. The multiculturalist may, when confronted with the dilemma outlined above, seek to resolve it by embracing a cultural relativist position, which may in any case seem to complement the multiculturalist approach to the establishment of mutual respect for diverse cultures in a manner in which universalism does not. Harris suggests that:

> we cannot [exclude culture-based discriminatory practices] and remain multiculturalists in that powerful sense which requires us to show equality of respect to other cultures and especially to those aspects of their culture that the members of the culture themselves value (Harris, 1982, p.227).

Such a view is deeply flawed theoretically and practically — the link between cultural relativism and multiculturalism is implicitly corrosive of the latter and generates a *genuine* paradox. If multiculturalism does indeed require us 'to show equality of respect to other cultures' then it is evident that the commitment of the multiculturalist is to preserve cultural rights as universal, and such a position clearly presupposes universality. Yet to accept cultural relativism is to adopt the view that *no* human rights are universal — that all rights and values are not only culturally variable, they are in all cases cultural *products* of particular communities. And if the latter is true then cultural rights are themselves relative, and there can be no reason for believing them to have a universal significance, or to possess a necessary trans-cultural domain of application. Such a standpoint, it should be clear, deprives multiculturalism of its very *raison d'etre*. On this view the most that could be argued in its favour is that its ideals represent a particular — admittedly egalitarian — view of the manner in which contemporary multicultural societies can seek to implement what they regard as principles of justice and equity. But such principles could themselves be justified only internally, which would not transcend or vitiate alternatives. In short, even if it could be established that multiculturalist policies and strategies are effective mechanisms for achieving the ideals to which they are directed, they could provide no justification for considering such ideals intrinsically meritorious.

Multiculturalism must be deeply rooted in a universalist interpretation of human rights to possess universal relevance. The task is to determine how the tensions between universalism and multiculturalism can be overcome. How is the 'paradox' of multiculturalism to be resolved without abrogation of either human rights universalism or multiculturalism itself? To answer this question we need to examine two related issues: the nature of cultural rights as human rights, and whether groups, as well as individuals, may be the bearers or subjects of human rights.

The nature of cultural rights

The formula 'A has a right to X against B in virtue of Y' (Gerwith, 1982, p.3) is commonly taken as the definitive statement of the principal terms and relations invoked in all assertions of rights. It identifies the subject or agent (A) to whom the right is ascribed; the right (X) which is ascribed to the subject; the feature (Y) of the subject which justifies the assertion of the right; and the duty-bearer (B) against whom the right can be asserted. Thus rights and obligations are, broadly speaking, correlative — if A has a right to X with respect to B, then B has a duty to A with respect to X. I wish to comment on some of the terms involved and governed by human rights.

First of all, on such rights: if human rights in general are to be taken, again, as just those rights which one has by virtue of the fact of existing as a human being, then it is from this that such rights derive their unique and fundamental character, which makes them 'moral rights of the highest order' (Donnelly, 1990, p.40). Persons may possess other rights by virtue of contractual or quasi-contractual agreements which they have entered into with those who have the corresponding obligations, but their human rights are strict entitlements which they possess simply by virtue of the fact that they exist as human beings or have a human nature. We should be clear also that in such contexts the term 'human nature' has itself a highly specific moral connotation — it is not human nature as described by anthropological or biological investigation, which maps the upper limits of strict human possibilities, but rather a selection of moral boundaries from within the range of these possibilities, a selection which represents the position 'beneath which we may not permit ourselves to fall' (Donnelly, 1990, p.42). Human rights are also not to be confused (as they sometimes are by positivists) with legal rights, i.e. as rights which are strictly justiciable and legally enforceable, for while they may be incorporated into, and confirmed by, positive law, as rights they are *anterior* to positive law — they are those rights which are so fundamental as to be deemed indispensable for a life worthy of a human being. Thus, encapsulating those preconditions for an existence compatible with human dignity, they constitute, in the first instance, extralegal standards as to what the law *should* be, and as such operate as implicit directives for the creation of positive law. Human rights, then, do not owe their existence to positive law or to the international instruments in which they are enshrined, nor do they originate in the actions of any authority, human or divine — they originate rather in the moral nature of human beings (Häusermann, 1992, p.47).

With regard to what is against which, and from which, human rights may be asserted, or what acts as duty-bearer correlative to the entitlements which human rights confer, the answer is, centrally and typically, the state. Indeed it is plausible to see the consciousness of human rights as evolving in this century in the face of the increasing power of the modern state, and specifically as a means of redressing the extreme asymmetry of power which has developed between the individual and the state (Burgers, 1990, p.65). This evolution is also commonly seen as an emergence of sequences or generations of rights. The first generation of human rights comprises the classical civil and political rights, which may be invoked *against* the state, and which place strict limits upon the manner and extent to which the individual can be coerced, especially by the state. Such rights entail obligations upon the state to refrain from coercing, restraining, enslaving, or otherwise infringing the fundamental freedoms of the individual. This generation of rights has found expression not only in the international instruments, but also in constitutional and positive domestic law in a great many countries.

The second generation of human rights are the right to adequate food, shelter, education, work and participation in cultural life. Such rights, unlike the first generation rights, may be demanded *of*, rather than *against*, the state, and entail positive obligations on the state, though of a rather diffuse kind — they oblige the state to take such general measures as are necessary for the promotion and realisation of the rights concerned. Second generation rights have found less widespread expression in constitutional and positive domestic law than first generation rights, but both have been given formal and simultaneous recognition in the international instruments, and are very widely perceived as being indivisible.

An important aspect which both first and second generation rights share is the fact that they are predicated upon a (minimally) latent conflict of interest between the human rights of the individual and the general welfare of the state. There has been much discussion on a 'new', third generation of human rights, generated not by such implicit adversarial relationships, but, on the contrary, 'born of the obvious brotherhood of men and of their indispensable solidarity; rights which would unite men in a finite world' (Vasak, 1979). Suggestions for classification in the proposed new category of human rights include the right to development, to peace, to communication, to a healthy environment, and to cultural identity.

Now in some respects the idea of such a third generation of human rights based upon solidarity between individuals, social communities, and states, is an attractive and intuitively plausible one; it certainly resonates with recognition of the deep interconnections which exist between all living things. However, it is an idea which has generated fierce opposition from some theorists, many of whom maintain that the very notion of solidarity rights is both conceptually flawed and politically dangerous, and that it encourages people to fall into the trap 'of calling everything good a human right, thus draining all meaning from the term' (Donnelly, 1990, p.44). It is argued that the notion is conceptually flawed because while all rights presuppose corrective obligations and while this condition is satisfied by first and second generation rights, the alleged solidarity rights are held by everyone against everyone, which effectively makes the concept of a duty-bearer correlative to such putative rights quite vacuous. The related political danger which the notion of solidarity rights poses is that 'being held against the world at large they provide a convenient basis for repressive regimes to shift the blame for their failure upon the shoulders of others' (Donnelly, 1990, p.48).

Here I must state that my sympathies lie with the critics of solidarity rights. I do not doubt that solidarity between human beings in relation to the common social, political and environmental problems which we face is highly laudable and would be enormously beneficial to the global community, but I do not think it correct to categorise such matters as *human rights*. I have to add that part of the debate about solidarity rights relates to an issue which I believe to be the key to a proper understanding of the nature of cultural rights, and to the reconciliation of multiculturalism and human rights universalism. This is whether human rights are necessarily *particular*, in the sense of being ascribable exclusively to individuals, or whether there are *collective* rights, belonging to groups, including cultural groups. The exponents of solidarity rights are necessarily committed to the view that the bearers of human rights can be groups as well as individuals, because most suggested solidarity rights are collective. By the same token, many of those who are opposed to the concept of solidarity rights base their opposition upon the conviction that human rights are possessed by individuals.

Here too the considerations argued in favour of the view that the bearer of human rights is necessarily an *individual* are both theoretical and practical. On the theoretical side, while human rights invariably have a social dimension — in that, for example, they are characteristically exercised by the individual as part of a social community — they are nonetheless rights possessed by the *individual* rather than the community:

> If human rights are the rights that one simply has as a human being, then it would seem that only human beings have human rights; if one isn't a human being, then by definition one can't have a human right. Only individual persons are human beings. Therefore ... only individuals can have human rights. And, except for the right to self-determination, the Universal Declaration and the Covenants in fact include only individual rights: economic, social and cultural rights, as well as civil and political rights, are the rights of individuals (Donnelly, 1990, p.43).

The practical corollary of this is that the view that such collective entities as the community, culture grouping or the state possess human rights which are held against the individual negates the central function of human rights claims to counteract the demands of the state where they conflict, and paves the way for a supremely ironic repression of the individual by the state in the name of 'human rights'.

It is this mistaken *collective* conception of human rights that generates the so-called 'paradox' of multiculturalism. For acceptance of this view leads, for example, to the conclusion that a state which upheld the rights of individual members of a constituent minority culture would violate the human rights of that minority culture. Clearly this conclusion is valid only if the implicit assumption that minority cultures and other collective grouping can possess human rights is *itself correct*. In other words, multiculturalism generates no paradox whatever when human rights are seen to be exclusively individual in character.

An understanding of human rights as the rights of individuals — and *only* this understanding of human rights — at once abolishes the so-called 'paradox of multiculturalism' and eliminates the apparent tension between multiculturalism and universalism. It is not denied that cultural communities possess rights to their distinctive cultural practices, merely that these rights are not *human* rights — but rather the rights *of the individual members of the cultural community* to the integrity of their culture. Definitive features of cultural life include language, religious belief and ritual, the transmission of a world-view and value-system through education, and the organisational structure of family life. These are amongst the cultural rights which are enshrined in, and the universality of which is asserted by, the international instruments. Their interdependence with other human rights, such as the fundamental freedoms, merits some emphasis. The rare cases in which a constituent minority culture is internally discriminatory represent a conflict between the universal, absolute and inalienable *human* rights of the members of that minority culture, and the non-absolute *collective rights* and interests of the cultural community itself. In such circumstances priority must be given to the human rights of the individuals concerned, who are entitled to *demand* the protection of the state, as are the members of the majority culture. To argue otherwise would be to ratify the discriminatory practice and endorse the view that membership of a minority group constitutes grounds for violation of individual human rights. In effect this forces group membership upon the individual. It is a gross distortion of multiculturalism to suggest that it sanctions such a perspective.

All human rights seek to establish minimum conditions of existence commensurate with dignity, a form of existence 'beneath which we may not allow ourselves to fall'. Particular cultural rights differ from other human rights *only* in that they are possessed by individuals in the context of their membership of cultural communities, while the right to life and liberty, for example, is possessed by individuals, irrespective of the community. Thus multiculturalists are entirely justified in attributing to cultural rights a primary role in the protection of minority cultural communities against arbitrary interference by the state. Cultural rights can play this critically important functional role only if they are genuinely *universal* human rights — it is in this sense that multiculturalism is deeply rooted in universalism. Virtually all the major human rights instruments, from the Universal Declaration onwards, are expressly universalist in both form and content, and cannot be interpreted in a relativist way without distortion.

In the context of a Europe which is becoming increasingly multicultural, the importance of the consolidation and development of multicultural social ideals and educational strategies can scarcely be overestimated. Recognition of this fact can scarcely fail to have a direct effect on the content of curricula in circumstances where a society seeks to inculcate a sense of respect for the dignity and rights of each human being, as well as that celebration of cultural diversity which is definitive of multiculturalism. More specifically, Recommendation R (85) 7 of the Committee of Ministers of the Council of Europe on 'Teaching and Learning about Human Rights in Schools' should be seen, not only as offering guidelines for the promotion of affirmative attitudes towards human rights and democratic values 'in the face of growing intolerance, racism and xenophobic attitudes', but also as encapsulating standards relating to an existence worthy of human beings. Within such a frame of reference the teaching of the universality of human rights entitlements and the advancement of the ideals of multiculturalism can scarcely fail to interconnect.

References

Burgers, J. H. (1990) The Function of Human Rights as Individual and Collective Rights, in Berting, J. et. al. (Eds) *Human Rights in a Pluralist World — Individuals and Collectivities*. London, Meckler.

Donnelly, J. (1989) *Universal Human Rights in Theory and Practice*. Ithaca, Cornell University Press.

Donnelly, J. (1990) 'Human Rights, Individual Rights, and Collective Rights', in Berting, J. et. al. (Eds) *Human Rights in a Pluralist World — Individuals and Collectivities*. London, Meckler.

Gerwith, A. (1982). *Human Rights*. Chicago University Press.

Harris, J. (1982). A Paradox of Multicultural Societies, *Journal of Philosophy of Education*. 16, (2).

Häusermann, J. (1992) The Realisation and Implementation of Economic, Social and Cultural Rights, in Beddard, R. and Hill, D. M. (Eds) *Economic, Social and Cultural Rights — Progress and Achievement*. London, Macmillan.

Hill, D. (1989) Human Rights and Foreign Policy: Theoretical Foundations, in D. Hill (Ed) *Human Rights and Foreign Policy — Principles and Practice*. London, Macmillan.

McLeod, K. (1991) Human Rights and Multiculturalism in Canadian Schools, in H. Starkey (Ed) *The Challenge of Human Rights Education*. London, Cassell.

Singh, B. R. (1994) Group Identity, Individual Autonomy and Education for Human Rights, *Educational Studies*, Vol. 20, No. 1.

Vasak, K. For the Third Generation of Human Rights: The Rights of Solidarity, Inaugural Lecture to the Tenth Study Session of the International Institute of Human Rights, 2-27 July 1979.

Wright, M. (1989) How Problematical are the Moral Foundations of Human Rights?, in D. Hill (Ed) *Human Rights and Foreign Policy — Principles and Practice*. London, Macmillan.

Walkling, P. H. (1980) The Idea of a Multicultural Curriculum, *Journal of Philosophy of Education*. 14. (1).

Chapter 4

All Different — All Equal: who defines education for citizenship in a new Europe?

Mirjam M. Hladnik

Introduction: language, culture and citizenship

At the beginning of the 1990s, Dahrendorf (1990) predicted that the coming decade would be the decade of citizenship. The validity of his prediction has become increasingly apparent in today's Europe: new states have been established, others have disappeared; the wider European context has given rise to growing problems concerning the status and rights of its restructured population; similarly, the numbers of pogrom and genocide victims are also growing, along with the number of people wandering the continent, desperately seeking a state to protect their rights and their lives.

As defined by Marshall (1950), citizenship is the status of those members of society possessing full rights, meaning each member is equal in relation to rights and duties. He warns that there exists no universal principle determining what these rights are. The fact that the ideals of citizenship and the citizen are always formed in a specific society, and that achievements are measured and aspirations are conceived according to this society, is of utmost importance for 'a new Europe'.

How to define the rights and duties of what the French in 1789 called 'a man and citizen' remains the fundamental problem of societies and states, either old or new. This problem is even more complicated if we know that every 'man' is not necessarily a citizen, which was the case when The Declaration of the Rights of

Man and of the Citizen excluded 'one half of the human race' (Wollstonecraft, 1792). It seems today that the functions of those social institutions that make the use of rights and the performing of duties possible should be re-evaluated. Among them, schools hold the most important position. As Marshall puts it:

> The right to education is a genuine social right of citizenship, because the aim of education during childhood is to shape the future adult. Fundamentally it should be regarded, not as the right of the child to go to school, but as the right of the adult citizen to have been educated (Marshall, 1950:25).

In the last century, the mass elementary education of citizens was part of the context of nation-state formation. The process was famously described by d'Azeglio: 'We have made Italy, now we have to make Italians' (quoted in Hobsbawm, 1990). The tool needed to forge members of the nation-state, its citizens, was language. The most important mechanism in implementing a common language, and the culture conveyed by that language, was education. When we speak of education we also, by definition, speak of culture. The mechanism for creating citizens remains the same today.

After World War I, part of Slovenia was annexed to Italy: the Slovene language was prohibited in public, family names were changed, and teachers taught in Italian about Italian culture. In this manner, Slovenes became Italian citizens. This remains the way that Kurds in Turkey or Albanians in Kosovo are transformed into Turkish or Serbian citizens. Likewise, some French public schools have recently forbidden Muslim women to wear veils. The legal argument behind the decision was that the veils should not be allowed because of their religious meaning, but clearly the problem is, in fact, a cultural one.

Citizenship and national identity

Habermas (1994) points out, in his vision of the future for a 'changed' united Europe, that democratic citizenship requires the socialisation of all citizens in a common, political culture no matter what the differences in cultural lifestyles. If we follow the evolution of the new European Community, which will bind together not just nations and nation-states but also a great number of immigrants, refugees and asylum seekers from all parts of the world, we witness the steadily rising tension between citizenship and national identity.

Habermas remains an optimist, however, and believes that different national cultures will be able to form a common political culture in the future. He proposes that states should not close their doors to immigrants, arguing that different lifestyles can enrich each other and coexist inside the framework of a democratic state of law. Given this condition and the fact that world public opinion is now a political reality, there is no doubt for Habermas that we are approaching world citizenship.

Nevertheless, the priority must be to coordinate the introduction of new people into existing nation-state structures. The question of the veil is highly symbolic in this respect. Whether it represents, for the French, a religious insignia (and as such to be banned in a secular public education system) or merely a different lifestyle (Eastern culture versus Western culture), it has raised passions and divided French society. This debate centres around three key questions:

- how do we define human and citizen rights and the function of the social institutions that make the implementation and enjoyment of these rights possible, and how do we (re)define the social function of education?

- whose political culture is to become the one common culture in the context of democratic citizenship, and what role must education take in this citizenship?

- should the concept of multiculturalism, which allows the ghettoisation of those whose 'different' cultures it supposedly respects, be reconsidered?

Refugees and education

At this point, I would like to focus on refugee education as an example of the education of all 'uprooted' people. If it is true that the concepts of citizenship are formed over a long span of time and in concordance with a specific political framework (Marshall, 1950), perhaps the answer to the question of education for refugees is the answer to the question of education in general, and thus the responsibility of the state itself.

The simple question of whether a human being is always a citizen requires, in specific circumstances, a sophisticated answer: the refugees are human beings, but they are not Slovene, French, British or German citizens. So, to what kind of (elementary) education are they entitled? What we must consider is whether this necessarily means that the refugee children, who as children have a right to education, exactly on the presumption that one day they will be adults, will never be Slovene. French, British or German citizens.

Here I would like to stress two points. First, during the nineteenth and twentieth centuries, the concept of citizenship evolved inside nationality to such an extent that, today, civic rights cannot be separated from being a member of a nation or different nations that form a particular state. Access is either by birth or naturalisation. A sovereign national state has been, until now, the only possible framework that can guarantee the enjoyment of rights (Dahrendorf, 1990). Of course, we have to consider the fundamental differences between the definition of the citizen as a member of a national community, in a state that is primarily defined as a national community, and the definition of the citizen as an 'identity of empty abstraction', in a state that is primarily defined as a political community (Mastnak, 1992).

Secondly, for human rights, which are defined by ambiguity and paradox, to be effective, they must be defined exactly on the abstract basis of human nature. This is also the rehabilitation of the concept of human rights by Lefort (1991). According to this view, neither naturalism nor historicism can accurately document human rights. The naturalistic concept denies the fact that, at a certain moment, people give themselves their rights and freedoms with a declaration; while historicism denies the idea of human nature. Thus, the same reason which prevents us from strengthening the concept of human nature, to turn it into nature itself, prevents us from issuing a critique of human rights. The fear is that this would, under the disguise that it is turning fiction into reality, destroy the universal scope of human rights.

But what does it mean to take the cultural roots or background of these children, that which they are born with, as their defining characteristics? Is this in compliance with or in violation of a specific right? Where do the borders of tolerance exist between different cultures, and when does tolerance become a tool for the production of second class citizens? Can the observance of one right mean the violation of another, to be or to become equal? And finally, can the nation-state, as the only guarantee of human rights, survive without education as 'the great equaliser' of the people, who are, though born equal, different?

The debate in Slovenia

Human rights education or education for democracy has made for an unusual situation in Slovenia, which only a few years ago became an independent, democratic state. Since gaining independence, the education debate has focused on the issue of national, curriculum 'values'. However, these so-called values which are to be transmitted and reproduced through the public school system have roused controversy which, surprisingly, is not structured around citizenship or democratic education.

The main educational dispute of the last five years has been whether or not to re-introduce religious instruction in Slovenian public schools. After forty years of a religiously neutral public schooling system in which private schooling did not exist, the new legislation provides the establishing of private (confessional and non-confessional) schools. For one section of Slovenian opinion, the acqui-sition of a democratic and pluralistic political system provides the opportunity for schools to educate children in the most important and necessary set of values for life in a democratic Slovene society, namely those of the Roman Catholic Church. On the other hand, this view provokes equally strong opinions against it.

For the last five years, Slovenia has seemed to be inhabited by only two kinds of people: Catholics and atheists. Many people would support the principle that children should be taught how best to live in a society rather than in a particular religion, but their views are not canvassed. Indoctrination has surfaced, once again, as a popular means through which to create good, obedient citizens; although this time, it has appeared in a slightly different mask. The so-called socialist (or communist) educational goal, to educate the 'all-rounded socialist person', has been replaced with the ambition of educating the 'all-rounded religious person', as religion is now claimed to be 'the most important dimension of the human being'.

Slovenia's recent Education Bill, based on the new concept of public education, prescribed only one aim for the school system in respect of values:

> to fully develop the human personality and respect of human rights and freedoms, to promote the understanding, tolerance and solidarity among all people, nations, racial and religious groups.

For many, however, this is insufficient and even unimportant. What matters is the result of the long battle between Church and State, deciding who will dominate the People's minds.

The cover of the White Paper on Slovene education, proclaims that Slovene schooling has descended from:

> the common European tradition of political, cultural and moral values, which can be recognised in human rights, plural democracy, tolerance and solidarity (Ministry of Education 1995).

As citizens, we can only hope that these standards will continue to find acceptance.

References

Dahrendorf, R. (1990) The Coming Decade of Citizenship. *The Guardian,* 1 August.

Habermas, J. (1994) Citizenship and National Identity, in B. van Steenbergen (Ed.), *The Condition of Citizenship.* London: Sage Publications.

Hobsbawm, E.J. (1990) *Nations and Nationalism since 1780 Programme, myth, reality,* Cambridge: Cambridge University Press.

Lefort, C. (1991) *Essais sur le politique, XIX-XX siècles.* Paris:Seuil

Marshall, T.H. (1950) *Citizenship and social class and other essays.* Cambridge: Cambridge University Press.

Mastnak, T. (1992) *Vzhodno od raja Ljubljana:* DZS

Ministry of Education (1995) *The White Paper on Education in Slovenia.* Ljubljana

Wollstonecraft, M. (1792) *A Vindication of the Rights of Women.* (reissued 1988) London: Norton

Chapter 5

Education for Democracy, Social Justice, Respect for Human Rights and Global Responsibility: a psychological perspective

Gitte Kragh

Come sit with me, and let us smoke the pipe of peace in understanding. Let us touch, let us, each to the other, be a gift as is the buffalo. Let us be meat to nourish each other, that we may all grow (Hyemeyohsts Storm: Seven Arrows).

Discussions on education for democracy, respect for human rights and global responsibility are often dominated by politics. I feel, however, that we also have much to learn from the Gaia hypothesis, which presents an organic picture of the world (Lovelock, 1979 and 1988) and from depth-psychology (Jung, 1977a, 1977b), although in my experience, such concepts may be alienating to educators with a political and sociological, as opposed to psychological background. I wish to argue that the psychological factor has to be acknowledged too, and these two features have to work together to make possible our hopes for humanising changes.

Oscarsson (1996, this volume) provides a convenient link between the political and the psychological. He concludes that the school is one important factor in helping children develop into what he calls 'active optimists', that is, citizens who feel positive about their chances of influencing future development.

41

Oscarsson describes two different aspects important for developing active optimism, namely, social competence and self confidence. 'Girls appear to have a greater social competence than boys, however they also appear to have less self-confidence'. He stresses the importance of working with these dimensions to create a more balanced state in both girls and boys.

This is a good example of the concept of polarity, itself a very important and useful tool (Bertelsen, 1988). Consider a field of energy consisting of two poles with contrasting but interdependent qualities. The energy generated between these two poles can take many forms. Oscarsson's example sets self-confidence at one pole and social competence at the other. Each of these is formed by a complex pattern of influences, biological, biographical, educational and cultural. We see a pattern with girls dominating at one pole (social competence) and boys at the other (self-confidence). Both qualities have positive, or creative and negative, or destructive, potential. The social competence pole is a state with much awareness of other people, their needs, interests and feelings. At this pole individuals will have well-developed antennae sensitive to human inter-relatedness. On the other hand it also can be a victim position if you are not able to feel, and give expression to, your own needs.

The self-confidence position can become egoistic self-assertion, with no sensitivity to other beings, but is also a fundamental necessity in claiming and defending your rights. So the ideal position would require that you are able to use both poles in a balanced and centered way.

A Romanian woman colleague told me a story which illustrates this. It is the sort of thing that happens every day in many situations, not just in Romania. A teacher told her class of ten-year olds to do a composition, using a list of words that she gave them. One of the pupils, a bright boy, was aware of the fact that words can have many meanings, and he played with that insight in his composition, finding pleasure in using his creativity. The teacher, when she saw his composition, became very angry and scolded the boy severely, telling him that he had misbehaved by failing to obey her instructions.

This is a very typical, and very painful story. It illustrates the concept of polarity, and the necessity of working with personal development in teacher training. In this painful meeting between the the teacher and the boy I see a polarity between conformity (the teacher) and creativity (the boy). It would appear that the teacher's biographical and cultural experiences had 'taught' her to prefer the conformity pole, and to renounce the creativity pole. All of us have the potential to feel comfortable with all possible polarities. However, as a result of family-norms, tradition, values, or culture, we are allowed to develop some of the many positions and neglect, suppress, avoid and reject others. This process of acceptance and rejection slowly creates what is called our pattern of identity — our ego.

Our ego consists of the conscious, developed poles; the undeveloped, suppressed poles become or remain unconscious. In Jungian terminology this is known as the shadow. According to this theory, the suppressed or unconscious poles still exist and, in fact, influence our way of reacting, feeling and perceiving. They will be projected, and we will be able to meet them in our dreams or in the outside world, for instance, in other people who are living these suppressed aspects of ourselves.

Such encounters give rise to many different feelings: hate, fear, envy, fascination, admiration or worship. As long as these relationships are unconscious, we will react to the tension created in relationship to these 'carriers of projections'. We may, for instance, persecute them, discriminate against them, segregate them, admire them, adore them or worship them. So the teacher meets her own suppressed creativity in the boy, and that frightens her, because during her own life creativity has been a dangerous kind of energy, maybe connected to punishment, loss of love, loss of life. So she reacts violently to the boy.

Another, more life-enhancing, creative way of reacting would be for her to start looking at her 'pattern of identity'. She could attempt to use the anxiety and anger that arises in this confrontation as a starting point for self-development. She could try to contact and eventually integrate her own creativity, thereby making her personality more encompassing and richer, more tolerant. But for that to happen she will need particular knowledge and tools.

This example shows why it is important for teachers to understand and learn about self-development, not necessarily by means of therapy, but as a general understanding of patterns of identity, strengths and weaknesses, possibilities and limitations. Teachers and their pupils, like all individuals. have a developmental history that can be worked with and developed.

Another example of the concept of polarity that occurs frequently in discussions of citizenship and democracy is that of exclusion and inclusion. The concept of exclusion can deepen our understanding of the ego. We might say that exclusion is a necessary prerequisite for the formation of the ego, our pattern of identity. As an illustration, one of the first fundamental distinctions each of us have to make is 'me' as opposed to 'not-me'. This awareness and selection can be extended indefinitely: my family, my home, my car, my country.

The ego, it appears, structures in either/or. It is a necessary condition for building up concepts. We have to be able to separate, to differentiate. Our mental structures depend on creating boundaries, borders, walls, both inside and outside, conscious and unconscious. We are forced to choose one pole of the polarities.

That said, we still have choices. We can choose to see 'the other', 'the stranger', 'them' either as fascinating and enriching or as frightening and dangerous. The concept of inclusion in fact describes the concept 'the Self' in a Jungian sense. Self, as a concept, includes the totality of the psyche, and amazingly complex patterns of polarity. The Self is also a utopian ideal for a process of individuation, a living journey of discovery, where a person tries to work to raise awareness of their pattern, and to transform and integrate polarities, in order to attain a centered state from where they can use both poles according to the situation.

If the ego is structured around either/or then we can say that the Self is structured around both/and. The title of the Council of Europe's anti-racist campaign of 1995 expresses this: all different — all equal. Rey (1995) makes a distinction between ' mono thinking' (as in monocultural) and 'inter thinking' (as in intercultural). We are used to thinking in one dimension, the mono, but we need to learn to think in a new way, an inter way. To learn this it is necessary that we work both with the knowledge dimension (Logos) and the experience dimension (Eros — the inner world of symbols and feelings) .

We need to be aware of two overlapping factors: the social construction of reality (Berger and Luckmann, 1971) and the ego, also seen as a construction. We always experience what we know as 'the world' through a filter of interpretation formed by biology, culture and biography. We may be aware of this, but we must also be aware that the map is not the territory (Bateson, 1973).

The Gaia hypothesis also suggests that this is a special time in history, where there seems to be a major change of paradigm (Sahtouris, 1989). This is a time of crisis, meaning both danger and possibility. At this point in the history of human consciousness, we may feel that the time is ripe for a major change of consciousness, a development from ego towards Self.

> Journeys in space and to the moon are an expression of an immense mobilisation of the yang-forces (Logos) of the superpowers — the huge lifting rockets with their overwhelming potency of fuel, technology and power are the paradigm of yang force in a brilliant extreme — and from this masculine ego-competition of the superpowers emerges, as a soft, gentle yin-point (Eros) this moving, highly meditative image of the luminous, blue planet in the black cosmic void (Bertelsen, 1988).

In this age where mainstream scientific research, chaos theory, tells us that the wings of a butterfly can influence the global meteorological situation, the consciousness of global interrelatedness becomes more clear. We have become aware that all our acts have consequences for the global future.

Educators need to remember that they are working with young people who are in the process of developing their ego and their sense of self, what we might call personal development individuation. As educators we need to provide differentiated tasks, within a group and between different age-levels. With children's development as a major aim, the focus of our work is to help them create a strong ego, a secure sense of identity and self-acceptance. Later, as grown-ups, they can work on relativising the ego.

It remains the case, however, that we also need to change the balance between the knowledge (cognitive) dimension and the experience (emotional) dimension in all levels of education. We need to enhance an awareness of and respect for the symbolic, emotional content, which until now has been largely undervalued, neglected and even suppressed in our culture. We might say that instead of building high, impenetrable walls inside the psyche, we must try to build in windows and doors.

Is depth psychology a new way to self-knowledge? In a sense it is a new way, because the methods practised previously took no account of the existence of the unconscious. Once we admit and understand the fact of the unconscious, our view of the world is fundamentally altered. We now understand human beings to have a dual nature, a conscious side which we know of and are aware of, and an unconscious side of which the individual knows nothing but of which our friends and colleagues may be very much aware. How often do we make all sorts of mistakes without being conscious of them in the least, whilst their consequences are borne by others, all the more painfully for us being unaware of the damage we may be doing!

So long as we ignore our unconscious we live as creatures whose one hand does not know what the other is doing. The recognition that we have to allow for the existence of an unconscious is a fact of revolutionary importance. Conscience as an ethical authority extends only as far as consciousness extends. When people lack self-knowledge they can do the most astonishing or terrible things without calling themselves to account and without ever suspecting that what they are doing is hurtful or wrong. Unconscious actions are always taken for granted and are therefore not critically evaluated. We are then surprised at the incomprehensible reactions of our neighbours, whom we tend to blame. We fail to see what we are doing ourselves and we seek in others the cause of all the consequences that follow from our own actions.

References

Bateson, G. (1973) *Steps to an ecology of mind.* London, Paladin

Berger, P. and Luckmann, T. (1971) *The social construction of reality.* London: Penguin

Bertelsen, J. (1988) *Selvets virkelighed.* Copenhagen: Borgen

Jung, C.G. (1964) *Man and his symbols.* Garden City N.Y.: Doubleday

Jung, C.G. (1977a) *Psychology and Religion.* London: Routledge and Kegan Paul

Jung, C.G. (1977b) The Symbolic Life in H. Read et.al. (Eds) *Collected Works Volume 18.* London: Routledge and Kegan Paul

Lovelock, J. (1979) *Gaia: a new look at life on earth.* Oxford: Oxford University Press

Lovelock, J. (1988) *The Ages of Gaia: a biography of our living earth.* Oxford: Oxford University Press

Oscarsson, V. (1995) Pupils' Views of the Future, in: A. Osler, H-F. Rathenow, and H.Starkey, *Teaching for Citizenship in Europe.* Stoke-on-Trent: Trentham

Rey, M. (1995) *D'une Logique Mono à une Logique de l'Inter: pistes pour une éducation solidaire.* Paper presented at the symposium 'Education for citizenship in a new Europe', European Academy, Berlin 29 August-3 September.

Sahtouris, E. (1989) *Gaia — the human journey from chaos to cosmos.*: Pocket Books

Chapter 6

Tolerance: implications for educators

Alison Jolly

In the United Nations Year for Tolerance it is essential to define the concept of tolerance. In one sense, that is easy, because every day we are faced with situations that require us to permit things we do not like and to bear things we do not like. Our everyday experiences are played out on a larger scale at national and international level in rampant nationalism, xenophobia, racial or religious hatred, or suppression of political opposition. It may be difficult to connect these large scale examples of intolerance with what happens to us every day, but the principles are the same. While international campaigns are important, the best defence against intolerance is always in the minds of individuals, and for educators, the task must be to make concepts of tolerance and intolerance clear in the thoughts and actions of us all.

At the United Nations, the idea of tolerance is linked to

> faith in fundamental human rights, in the dignity and worth of the human person, in the equal rights of men and women and of nations large and small.

When tolerance is linked to human rights we can get a clear idea of what we must and must not tolerate. There are three key linked ideas, namely: tolerance, human rights, and equality of treatment. This chapter focuses on definitions of tolerance and on two aspects of tolerance for educators .

Shades of tolerance

Tolerance has many meanings, but essentially it refers to minimum standards of treatment for everyone. Beyond tolerance, we might talk of welcoming diversity, or understanding various cultures, but such welcoming and understanding is more than tolerance, and the short term aim is to build the foundation on which diversity may one day be safe in a given society.

The dictionary provides two definitions of tolerance. First, to permit without protest or interference, and second, to bear. Those are not separate ideas. Sometimes in permitting something, we must bear offence, dislike, distrust, anger or annoyance. We have to learn when our behaviour and the behaviour of others is appropriate, and when it is not. And we must also understand that there will be situations that we cannot, will not or should not tolerate.

Tolerance has a positive and a negative aspect. Commonly, it is said that to be tolerant, we must first have the urge to be *intolerant*. It is only in suppressing our feelings of intolerance, or forbearing from acting on them, that we are tolerant.

Say we live in a street full of young families with children who play happily but loudly in the street. If we are happy to listen to the sound of children playing, then we are not 'tolerant' of them, we are simply listening to something we enjoy. If, however, the noise annoys us and we rush into the street and demand the children play quietly indoors, we are being intolerant. But if the noise annoys us and we do nothing, perhaps for the sake of good neighbourly relations, then we *are* being tolerant. We are putting up with something we dislike, we are keeping our anger at bay, and we are putting others before ourselves.

This is the stuff of everyday tolerance, and we are often faced with situations that set off our intolerant impulses. At this level, teaching tolerance is about give and take. It is also about teaching that some behaviour is not appropriate, so that while it may be tolerable for those children to play noisily at home, if they sing at the top of their voices in the middle of a maths lesson, we would rightly say that 'we will not tolerate this behaviour'. In saying that, we would have what lawyers would call a 'legitimate purpose': by putting limits on people's behaviour, we ensure that everyone benefits from the maths lesson.

A second thing to note is that there are two parts to tolerance or intolerance: the impulse to be intolerant, and how we act on that impulse.

This is a basic, working definition of tolerance. But it is not as simple as that and I now want to look at what tolerance means for us as individuals, as communities and as a society if we have a commitment to human rights.

Human rights as minimum standards

Human rights and fundamental freedoms can be described as minimum standards of treatment. Most importantly, they are owed to everyone Article 2 of the Universal Declaration of Human Rights puts it:

Everyone is entitled to all the rights and freedoms set forth in this Declaration, without distinction of any kind, such as race, colour, sex, language, religion, political or other opinion, national or social origin, property, birth or other status....

This is the 'equality' or 'non-discrimination' article of the Universal Declaration, and it underpins all human rights. Equal respect for human rights is one basis for building tolerance.

Tolerance as non-discrimination

Tolerance and intolerance are about how thought translates into action, and when we are talking about respect for human rights, intolerance is translated into discrimination against individuals or groups in society.

To illustrate this, I shall return to our noisy street. Let us say that one of the noisy children comes from a family we do not like. If we go into our street, grab that one child, and drag him or her home to demand that he or she plays quietly indoors, but leave the other children outside playing happily, then we are discriminating. We are not applying the same rules to that child as to the others, we are limiting one child's freedom and at the same time giving in to our own prejudices about the child's family. In human rights terms, this is not what tolerance is about, and this principle works not only in individual situations, but also on a larger scale, in communities and societies.

In any society, there will be degrees of what we might call 'toleration'. There may be groups that are simply allowed to live in society, but with wide scale denial of their rights and freedoms. In Sierra Leone, for example, Christian children tend to have better access to good schools, and from there they go on to good jobs, they go into the civil service and government, and their lives are better because of good education. It might be said that this society is 'tolerant' in that it *contains* different ethnic and religious groups, but tolerance without respect for human rights is negative because rights belong to all without discrimination.

Another type of 'tolerant society' is one which is tolerance with strings attached. An example of this comes from France, where Muslim girls were not allowed to wear the veil to school. This requirement to conform to standards of dress laid down by the school may seem unimportant in the grand scheme of things, but it is highly significant and symbolic, which is why the question of the veil has aroused such passions in France. Why are those children singled out for wearing the veil, which may be, for them, an essential expression of their Islamic religion, when others are not singled out for wearing, say, the colours of a football team, even though this may be an equally important expression of identity? These Muslim girls were given a clear message from the school authorities, supported by certain political parties, that their presence in school and in society is tolerated only if they modify specific behaviours.

49

Legitimate discrimination

It is clear that we do not have to tolerate everything. So when is discrimination, or the expression of intolerance, allowed? Human rights standards include clauses which, in fact, allow discrimination but only in certain closely defined situations. These are generally on grounds of public safety, health or morals, or the protection of the fundamental rights and freedoms of others.

If as an expression of identity a child wished to wear knuckle dusters to school, there would be a good case for saying 'we will not tolerate that', and for insisting that the knuckle dusters are not brought into the school, because they may threaten public health or safety. If a child is selling computer disks containing pornographic images in the school, and claims freedom of expression, we could argue that his or her free expression affects public morals, and legitimately claim that we will not tolerate that. Nor would we have to tolerate bullying, or rowdiness in the classroom, or aggression in the school yard.

But to return to France and the Muslim girl who is not allowed to wear the veil; we might question the purpose of that ban. Does wearing the veil threaten safety, or health, or morals, or rights and freedoms? If the child has chosen freely to wear the veil, then I would say that it does not. And if it does not, then it is outright, illegitimate discrimination and more than this. It probably masks prejudice which is translated into action by the denial of the right of that child to wear religious clothing.

One argument supporting such bans says that the veil represents the repression of women, and denial of their rights. In response, we should note that many Muslim women and girls choose freely to wear the veil to express their identity as Muslims.

Tolerance with respect for human rights

Pulling these strands together, we can reach a definition of tolerance that is inextricably linked to respect for human rights, and to non-discrimination. Simply, it is this. Unless we have a clear and legitimate reason for proscribing some forms of behaviour, we must respect all people's rights equally, and tolerate their behaviour equally. The converse of this is that we must be intolerant of violations of human rights whether we like the victims or not, and whether we agree with them or not.

How would a tolerant society that respects human rights work? First, this tolerant society should realise that non-discrimination might mean, in some cases, taking affirmative action. In Britain, for example, in order to ensure that the disabled are able to enjoy their right to take part in the cultural life of the community, as stated in Article 27 of the Universal Declaration of Human Rights:

Everyone has the right freely to participate in the cultural life of the community, to enjoy the arts and to share in scientific advancement and its benefits,

we might have to enact legislation to make some people improve access for the disabled to their premises or to their facilities. In educational institutions, it might mean enacting a policy against bullying or harassment, preferably drawn up in consultation with staff and students.

It is important to explode the myth that action on behalf of one group necessarily discriminates against other groups. Legislation for the disabled, or any disadvantaged group, may be said to 'discriminate' in the sense that it costs money and affects profits. Now, of course, expenditure can have real implications for jobs and profits, and in the real world we cannot deny this, but such ostensibly good reasons for not doing something to ensure respect for human rights justify a good, long look. Properly formulated, affirmative action should aim to bring disadvantaged groups up to the same level of treatment as the rest of society. It would be an entirely false argument to claim that we could not have anti-bullying policies because they discriminate against bullies, and we should not be misled by similar false reasoning in other areas.

A second quality of a tolerant society is that where two sets of rights appear to clash there must be compromise. Recently, we have seen in Northern Ireland a solution to the problems of the marching season. Protestant, or Unionist, Orange-men wishing to march through Portadown claimed they had the right to do so. Local Catholics wanted to stop the march. The solution, in consultation with both sides, was to allow the march to take place without the usual pipes and drums and noise, while the Catholics stood on the pavements with their backs to the marchers.

Now, we may think this solution bizarre. Yet, in that time, at that place, it worked. Neither side 'won', neither side 'lost', and, most importantly, the dignity of both sides was upheld.

Disputes such as this, where two sets of rights apparently collide, are often mediated by reference to three little words of dispute resolution: time, manner, place. If the British National Party wants to hold a march, and claims that it has the right to freedom of association, then the authorities might look to time, manner and place in deciding whether or not to let the march go ahead. It might be possible to allow such a march at a time when racial tension is not high. It might be acceptable if the march proceeds in a quiet manner. It might be all right to march through an area where the local residents will not feel threatened. It would clearly, though, not be acceptable for a far right party to march at a time when racial tension is high, particularly if they intended to shout racist slogans and provoke a riot. It might not be all right to march through an area with a very mixed population like the London Borough of Tower Hamlets. But it is conceivable that a march of some sort could go ahead in an appropriate time, manner and place, so that, in a free and tolerant society, freedom of expression, albeit limited by concern for the effects on others, is preserved.

Tolerating views that we find repugnant, such as fascism, is problematic for most of us, and we might want to ban fascist organisations outright, but human rights are owed to all regardless of political or other opinion, subject only to the same restrictions faced by us all. Also, not everyone wants to ban the same groups. There are those who would wish to ban the expression of gay and lesbian sexuality, for example, or the right to peaceful public protest. It is not always necessary to ban every activity of a group in order to protect the rights and freedoms of others. Driving some groups underground and allowing them to see themselves as an oppressed minority does not tackle the root causes of the problem. While looking always to protect everyone's rights and freedoms, it may be better to face those views we find repugnant, to discuss them openly, and to trust that we can defeat views such as fascism, without violating human rights.

Teaching tolerance

Tolerance and human rights in the school have the same principles of compromise, appropriate behaviour and equal treatment as demonstrated earlier. Intolerance requires motive and opportunity. Motive is our intolerant impulse, our prejudice, our selfishness and, often, our mental or physical strength in relation to others. Education for tolerance must work both on motive and on opportunity, and I shall finish with some short examples of how this works in school.

First, opportunity. A tolerant school will have rules which make it clear to all members of the school what behaviour will be tolerated and what will not. The rules must be open and understandable to all, and if possible, should result from discussion with students. The United Nations Convention on the Rights of the Child in Article 12 (1) states that children's views should be taken seriously, in accordance with their age and understanding:

> States Parties shall assure to the child who is capable of forming his or her own views the right to express those views freely in all matters affecting the child, the views of the child being given due weight in accordance with the age and maturity of the child.

An anti-bullying policy, for example, will show that it is fine to throw someone over your shoulder in a martial arts class with a crash mat but it is not fine to throw someone on a tarmac playground. Internationally, it is paralleled by rules banning the use of force or aggression, except in clear cases of self-defence. Such rules will also have clear guidelines on what to do if you are being bullied or if you suspect someone else is being bullied.

Again, internationally, the United Nations Charter lays down guidelines for various methods of settling disputes. There should be proper guidelines so that both bully and victim can explain their case in a calm atmosphere, a rule which equates to fair trial in international law. And there must be rules about appropriate punishment. There is one area in which international law is relatively impotent. How far have aggressors been punished for their crimes in former Yugoslavia, or Rwanda, or Chechnya? Yet international impotence must not be an excuse for individuals and organisations to do nothing.

Of course, underlying this anti-bullying policy must be the rule that every person brought to answer a case should be treated without respect to their race, religion, language, sex, or any other status.

Working on restricting *opportunities* for bullying in the school is not enough. If the long term aim is that bullying should be eradicated as far as possible, it is essential also to look at what motivates bullies, and to examine their motives.

Beyond the school gates, teachers cannot control pupils' opportunities for bullying, and this makes it doubly important for schools to try to tackle motive, whether it be racial, religious, gang rivalry, or simply a matter of the strong preying on the weak. Students should be taught about equality of treatment, about standing up for others, about peaceful conflict resolution, and that force and violence are bad ways to solve disputes. Even if a school has no outward signs of racial tensions, it does not mean that its pupils will not one day find themselves faced with issues of racial discrimination. The issues tackled in each school may have a different focus, but the lessons learned from teaching for tolerance through equality and human rights, can be applied to racial intolerance, or gender intolerance, wherever they arise.

Conclusion

Intolerance around the world is experiencing a comeback. Since the 'old enemy' of communism has fallen, so new 'enemies' have risen, and we have seen an increase in ethnic and religious hatred. Before we seek easy solutions, we should note that some skills that help to promote tolerance are already taught in schools through the current curriculum. For instance, critical evaluation of what we read, learning to see both sides of an argument, learning what is appropriate and where, and learning that others may find certain words or actions hurtful, even if we do not.

Even where time is limited, staff should express their attitudes to intolerence. Grandiose international initiatives and specialist materials apart, every time a teacher says 'I will not tolerate that behaviour', every time a rule is invoked, every time teachers spend time listening to students' problems, they are expressing what is appropriate and what is not.

Promoting tolerance does not mean only presenting those things that are acceptable. It is demonstrating what is unacceptable with good, clear, strong arguments.

The best defence against intolerance is in the mind of each individual. If, as a minimum, individuals learn at school not to act on intolerant impulses, something will have been achieved. If they can learn about equality, about compromise, and about respect for others, more will have been achieved. In this educational process teachers will work against students' prejudices, against parental prejudice, and against their own prejudice. Teaching about tolerance is equipping people to live together.

PART 2

Citizenship and the Education of Teachers

Chapter 7

Education for Peace, Justice and Human Rights in the Context of Teacher Training:
some methodological reflections

Hanns-Fred Rathenow and Norbert H. Weber

I feel that our educational institutions are in a desperate state; and that unless our schools can become exciting, fun-filled centres of learning, they are quite possibly doomed (Carl Rogers)

Introductory remarks

Most of the courses at German universities are structured so as to offer a traditional understanding of the academic discipline. Research and teaching are often divorced from a social and political context. Moreover, courses often follow the subjects of the school curriculum. Such variety may give breadth but little opportunity to deepen understanding.

Our experience described here, however, shows that methods using project-orientated work are better suited for revealing the complex structure of education and also the problems of education for peace, justice and human rights.

At present German teachers in training are normally required to take six courses which last one semester (six months) each. The first two of these courses are compulsory, namely: Introduction to Education and Preparation for School Experience. For the remaining four courses students have a free choice from a variety of topics on education. There is no requirement that any of these elective

57

classes should focus on society-related problems. Much as we are convinced that peace education should be a core element of teacher training, as lecturers we have no influence upon the amount of time students devote to peace education topics.

Peace education can be defined as teaching people how to 'make peace' (Nicklas, 1982, p. 19). According to Galtung (1975) peace means more than just an absence of war (the negative definition of peace), but also the establishment and preservation of basic human rights. Thus peace education has the significant responsibility of transmitting those skills and attitudes needed to establish and preserve a state of peace.

In Germany, as in most countries, teacher training still does not equip students to teach subjects with a political dimension. However, citizenship education, which is widely accepted as a legitimate element of education and which covers education for democracy, peace, social justice, human rights and global responsibility, inevitably has a political dimension. It provides knowledge which can be applied in social contexts. What a university course can do is to help students to organise independent study within a social and local context.

Project-orientated work

Project-orientated work, as we have practised it for years, demands, on the one hand, long-term motivation and additional commitment from the students beyond their usual classes (Pike and Selby, 1988; Hicks and Steiner, 1989; Rathenow, 1993) and, on the other hand, requires that the tutors be confident in experiential learning. It leads the participants towards a common process of learning and experiencing and is characterised by the following elements:

- Co-operative planning, carrying out and evaluating on an inter-disciplinary basis.

- Reference to real social problems and to the future profession of students.

- Activity-based learning.

- The results should have an impact on the social surroundings (universities, schools, the public) and demonstrate the commitment of the students. This is much more motivating than an exam (Valk, 1984).

- The process of co-operative project work is practising peaceful means of problem solving.

The successful collective production of results must be based on a reflective process. Students and teachers should talk about the process of their work, the solving of problems that arose during the work, the way conflicts between group members developed and how they were overcome. In this way students develop abilities such as understanding their role, empathy, tolerance of ambiguities and the development of an identity (Krappmann, 1971; adapted by Wulf, 1992). If students succeed in achieving these qualities and a satisfactory result in an atmosphere of social and emotional security (Loewer, 1984) in the group, they are better prepared for conflicts in society. When teachers plan to do project-orientated work, they should be capable of working with techniques (Gestalt therapy, global education approach, group training methods) which make it easier to sensitise students to problems of communication and interaction. In this context it seems important to us that tutors, too, get involved with the group. The following four projects were designed according to these criteria.

Project 1: Workshop

1. Notes concerning the term

Though workshops are well-known outside school, in schools and universities the method has largely been restricted to the fields of art and music. Our experience of workshops at international meetings convinces us that this way of learning is particularly suitable for education for peace, justice and human rights at university level. In co-operation with two colleagues from the Netherlands, the late Léon Valk and Robert Aspeslagh, we developed the concept of the International Workshop on Peace Education which was designed for student teachers and students of social education. Since then we have organised seven workshops on education for peace, justice and human rights between 1982-1994 in co-operation with our colleagues from different countries: Denmark (1982), Great Britain (1984), The Netherlands (1986), Germany (1988), Hungary (1990) Poland (1992) and Lithuania (1994).

These workshops which have brought together almost 400 dedicated teachers, educators, students and social workers from different countries have focused on a series of key issues and primary problems. They were aimed at the presentation and discussion of the basic problems of peace education, peace research and the peace movement from the countries that sent students.

One of the primary regular issues was the East-West conflict. After the collapse of the communist system in Eastern Europe, topics such as economic problems in East and West, the forces of nationalism, ethnic minorities seeking political independence or the annexation of one state by another, have become more important.

Workshops on peace education make the participants aware of the stereotypes, clichés, prejudices and 'enemy images' they have. In one amusing but thought-provoking exercise we portray auto-stereotypes and hetero-stereotypes of the participating nations, such as paprika, the Puzta and Lake Balaton as a description for Hungary; clogs, tulips and windmills as stereotypes for the Netherlands; and soccer, punctuality, cleanliness, sauerkraut and beer for Germany.

2. *Characteristics of workshop teaching methods*

Through our experience with workshops we have discovered a number of basic features which characterise the workshop as a method in teacher education:

- To improve communication among the participants of the workshop, communication exercises such as the ones that are described in the global education approach (Pike and Selby, 1988) are useful at the beginning and during the workshop. These experiential exercises not only serve the getting-to-know each other process, but also help to overcome language barriers at the beginning.

- It is essential that all the participants have a basic knowledge of the topics of the workshop. Furthermore, central terms like peace, war, violence, nationalism, ethnocentrism as well as prejudices and 'enemy images' should have been discussed in the preparatory meetings, because they tend to have various meanings. Communication among the participants can be made easier by the prior exchange of written material on school systems and teacher training.

- The planning should always be flexible enough to allow the integration of current political events into the work. Participants value working on crisis situations, such as the Gulf War or the War in former Yugoslavia that are of immediate interest and concern.

- By definition, workshops involve the preparation of topics as the basis for the work of the international groups. The results are presented and discussed, then they merge into a new product, fixed by the participants of the working groups. In this respect the workshop is also a method. The understanding of democracy which we as a group are trying to achieve within this international context is based upon autonomy, whereby each participant is both independent and a full partner in the co-determination process. For this reason students from the participating universities are always included at preparation meetings.

- The teacher of the workshop can be described as a 'facilitator', as a competent or an expert helper, in contrast to a lecturing authority. Process-oriented work requires sensitivity, rather than a traditional leadership role. It is a risky thing for a person to become a facilitator of learning rather than a teacher. It means uncertainties, difficulties, set-backs — and also exciting human adventure, as students begin to blossom. (Rogers, 1983, p.137).

In this learning environment, which is applicable to all areas of citizenship education, teachers should not dominate because of their knowledge, views or age but rather assume the role of partner in the dialogue, also hoping to learn something.

• The production of results can be documented in different ways. At our workshops we publish written results on notice boards and posters, and interim conclusions are published immediately in the workshop newspaper, updated every morning. By publishing our results in this way, the participants are able to keep themselves informed of the work of the other teams. The results are then made public at a 'market stall', where they are received by a critical and interested public. After the workshops the results have been published in booklet form in German and/or Dutch.

Project 2: textbook analysis

During the International Workshops on Peace Education there is usually one group that works on an analysis of history textbooks. History textbooks are one of the most important sources in class as well as for the teacher's reference in Germany and in other countries. The advantage of these textbooks is that historical information, which is based on the political and ideological aims of the different countries, is presented in a concise way. While in Germany various groups (political parties, trade unions, churches) have their own set of values and decide which books are to be allowed in class, history textbooks from the former communist states of Eastern Central Europe have, until recently, reflected only the official view of historical events. History textbooks are, whatever the political system, an expression of a political consciousness in a society.

The following account based on a workshop report by Doug Clark from the 1990 International Workshop attempts to describe both the content and the process employed in the workshop as the group proceeded from stage to stage.

1. Introduction and selection of topic
Of the ten members of the group, seven were students and three were instructors. Four members of the group were from the East Bloc which provided an important balance for the investigation of the tentative topic, which was initially 'East-West Relations in the Era of Gorbachev as Reflected in Textbooks'.

First a general overview of the twenty-six textbooks was made to evaluate the material. Each member selected up to three texts according to language proficiency. Surprisingly, none of the texts made reference to the Gorbachev era. Finally the decision was made to select an earlier historical event. The final topic was: the East-West Perspectives of the Hungarian Crisis as seen in National Textbooks.

Once the texts had been searched for the topic, the books were narrowed down to nine, from Poland, Hungary, East- and West-Germany and the United States. The years of publication ranged from 1977 to 1989; grade levels ranged from grade 7 to 12 and college.

2. A Hungarian account of the 1956 crisis

One of the students in the workshop was Hungarian. And although she was born after the 1956 Crisis, she had studied the crisis in school and heard about it from stories told to her by her father. It was decided that she and several other Hungarian students would reconstruct an oral history of the crisis. It was interesting to see which historical figures and institutions, what policies, which mechanisms would be mentioned in such an account. In a sense, it would give a kind of measuring stick, a place to begin. The following is a summary of the account as recorded by the student participants:

On the 3 October, 1956 there was a demonstration of students in Budapest. They went to the radio (station) and a lot of people joined them who were disappointed with the way of living and with the policy of the Hungarian Workers Party. It all began as a demonstration but later turned into a revolution because of the great number of people who wanted change. Imre Nagy was appointed Prime Minister by the Supreme Presidium. He belonged to the progressive wing of the Hungarian Workers Party. The leader of this party at that time was Erno Gero.

The next important step was the demonstration in front of the Parliament (building). There was a big crowd waiting for Imre Nagy, and some unidentified troops machine-gunned into them. Starting at this time, we call the events a battle. It should be mentioned that at that time Russian troops were stationed in Hungary. The people of Hungary didn't like this system. They wanted the Russian troops to go home. They didn't like the troops in general, nor did they like the Russian soldiers as individuals. The Russian troops were ordered to oppose the uprising, but most of them joined the Hungarian people. On the 31 October, the Party Office Building in Budapest was attacked and hundreds of people were killed in this battle.

3 November is a very important date because the Hungarian Revolutionary Workers Peasants Government was formed. It was led by Janos Kadar. They had Russian troops to help them, because the Russians promised to help if a new government were formed, but only in that case. At the same time, Imre Nagy made his famous speech on the radio, asking the UN for help because the Russian troops had invaded Hungary. But there was no response. So, the newly-formed government (of Kadar) managed to demolish the 'counter-revolution' and they began to arrest people who took part in the events. The leaders and a lot of other people who had connection with 1956 were killed.

Until last year, the events were called a 'counter-revolution' to indicate that (the uprising) was against socialism. But like in the other Eastern European countries, changes began in Hungary, too. A committee was set up which was allowed to officially announce that it was not a counter-revolution, but a revolution or uprising. Of course, most of the people were well aware of this, but it had never been announced officially. The new interpretation changed the role of the leaders and people taking part in the revolution. Imre Nagy was buried again as a symbol recognising his positive role, and as the symbol of the new interpretation of events. This was on 16 June 1989, and we can say that this event also marked the burial of the old regime.

3. Establishing criteria for the analysis

It was decided to have both a qualitative and a quantitative analysis of the texts. As a result, it was necessary to establish some measurable criteria. The account described the causes, the course, and the effects of the crisis. Causes could be subdivided into long-term (such as Cold War struggles) and short term (specific events like the demonstration in front of Parliament). The course of the conflict was subdivided into eight categories, which included mention of:

- the student revolt
- the role of Imre Nagy
- the role of the Hungarian Army
- the number of people involved
- the extent of the hostilities
- the number of victims
- the role of Janos Kadar
- the reactions of the western powers

Finally, effects were subdivided into long-term (such as the establishment of a government for more than 30 years) and short-term (emigration, internal terror).

4. Analysis

For purposes of the qualitative analysis, the nine texts were put into three general categories, East Bloc books, western European books, and US books. East Bloc books, it was felt, gave a relatively broad spectrum of information, but some facts seemed manipulated and the authors referred to these events as riots and counter-revolution. West European books, on the other hand, provided less information, primarily from the perspective of Eurocommunism. Finally, books from the United States provided little information about the course of the crisis, emphasising the events in Hungary as merely part of the larger Cold War struggle between the US and USSR.

5. Teaching controversial topics with existing biased textbooks

Texts are a mixed blessing. Although they are readily available in most class-rooms, they are, by their very nature, out-of-date and often biased in their per-spective. And though woefully incomplete and partial as they may be, they do provide a wealth of information.

Although any work in the classroom takes place in a specific historical context (such as the Hungarian Crisis of 1956), teachers need to emphasise the transferability of skills. Thus, the focus might be on historical skills and concepts rather than on the events themselves. Other cognitive skills could be stressed, such as comprehension, analysis, judgement, interpersonal communication, and advocacy. Certain concepts might be presented as well, such as substantive concepts (revolution, communism) and procedural concepts (change, continuity, use of evidence, empathy). Finally, certain values might be promoted such as respect for reasoning, fairness, and justice.

The following is a possible scenario: with a brief written explanation, students are introduced to the events. Then, a number of carefully selected primary and secondary sources could be present. All sources should be easy to read. These sources might include:

- both primary and secondary sources
- sources presented in different ways: written (speeches, poems) and pictures (photos, cartoons)
- sources designed to focus upon different perspectives, for example party political or feminist viewpoints
- a source which reveals the evidence has been constructed using intentional and unintentional bias; emotive and factual language; bias by inclusion and omission; the difference between fact and opinion.

Questions and activities must relate to aims. Most questions should be open ended. Questions might either be presented in an ascending order of difficulty or it may be possible for each pupil to apply varying levels of sophistication to each question.

Small group problem-solving might be used as the basis for role play or for the provision of raw material for a debate. The teacher might also use different teaching strategies, adopting the position of a neutral chairperson in one situation, committed to one perspective in a second situation, presenting a 'balanced' approach with several conflicting positions in a third situation. The strategies should be employed after full consideration of the pupils' backgrounds.

6. Criteria for selection of new textbooks
Because teachers sometimes need to choose textbooks, here are some helpful criteria:

- sources from different points of view, with reference to the past (history) and application to the present
- up-to-date, with a variety of material such as pictures, illustrations, lyrics, propaganda posters. A selection of texts rather than a single text, might include reporting, describing, presentation of stories, verbatim speeches

- didactic questions which require interpretation of the many sources and points of view.

- social history, which tends to personalise information and include background information on key figures, historical context, ideology.

Project 3: street theatre

1. Notes concerning the term

Since the 1920s, street theatre, developed particularly in the Soviet Union and the Weimar Republic, has been political theatre. Erwin Piscator, who was very active in the Proletarian Theatre, founded in 1920, related it in the beginning, to the concept of class struggle. Without applying the standards of bourgeois art, they played on the streets, in assembly rooms and local pubs, in the working class areas of Berlin, with the intention of explaining political problems to people in a lively manner (agitproptheatre). In that respect street theatre was originally theatre for workers by workers.

Agitation and propaganda in the sense of Piscator's Confessional Theatre prompted students at the end of the sixties to rediscover this form of theatre. In contrast to the agit-prop-campaigns of the Weimar Republic, in Germany street theatre became a means of propagating the goals of the student movement at the end of the sixties. In this context the Socialist Street Theatre of Berlin (West), which became popular far beyond the city limits, has to be mentioned.

- Street theatre as we know it from the student movement is characterised by a number of elements of style which are mentioned here briefly (Arbeitsgruppe Friedenspädagogik, 1982):

- Street theatre is marked by a lively presentation on the one hand and stylisation on the other; abstract concepts and real-life situations are portrayed with the help of character types who are merely representatives of their class or of respective objects (the capitalist, the worker, the housewife, force, fear).

- Language is the most effective means of expression. It consists of repetitions, enumerations, parallelisms, thesis and anti-thesis, parodies and puns and is directed towards the audience. First of all the subject is presented. Only thereafter are they expected to think.

- Music is another important factor: on the one hand it functions as background, on the other hand, independent songs are worked into the programme. Its purpose is also to attract spectators and listeners and to create an atmosphere.

- The distribution of leaflets during and after the performance is an essential part of the street action. Thereby the spectators become involved in the play(ing) and get the opportunity to discuss the content with the players. Play and reality merge.

2. The content of the workshop

The preceding elements of street theatre were the basis for the student project that, among others, took place in a course on peace education which was carried out in co-operation with Achim Hellmich of the Institute of Elementary School Education at the Technical University of Berlin. Controversial public discussion about the adoption of new armaments by NATO caused a sense of fear in many students. It was the main motivation for the students' commitment on that course. As the discussions during the course illustrated, many fears such as the fear of suffering, death, rape, inhumanity, callousness, loss of love, loss of beloved people, boundless injustice and oppression, were concealed behind their commitment. Turning these fears into productive energy was the aim of the group. The 20 minute play, which the students developed under their own direction, places a scenic dialogue with the title: 'I am frightened' (*Ich habe Angst*) or 'Awake from your apathy' (*Erwacht aus eurer Gleichgültigkeit*) at the centre of the play:

> People with white plaster masks follow stylised activities. The occupations are repeated in a stereotyped fashion so as to create a sense of paralysis, indifference and isolation. After one to two minutes a woman without a mask steps among the masked persons. She is hectic and agitated.
>
> Woman: I've got a problem! I have to talk with somebody! Won't anybody listen to me? (She addresses single people.) Can I talk to you? Will you listen to me? Stop doing that, listen to me, please. What's the matter with you? I have to talk with you. I've got a problem. Why doesn't anybody listen to me? Won't you listen to me?
>
> Man: (with a half-mask, joining her) What's the matter here? What kind of problem have you got? If you have a problem, just go ahead and talk about it.
>
> Woman: I'm afraid, I'm afraid of war!
>
> Man: War, war, where is war? Do any of you see war? There is no war here!
>
> Woman: Look round you, there are signs everywhere: unemployment is one for example, we have about two million people that are out of work!
>
> Woman: You call that peace? Peace, when there is violence all over the world. In our society children are beaten, women are raped ...
>
> Man: Yes, I, too, am afraid of this world, this life, why do you think all these people and I wear these masks? — Because we are frightened ... We are numbed, can you wake us up?
>
> Woman: Show your fear, take your masks away, let us join up to gain strength, to be strong and powerful ...
>
> Man: Against violence which makes us speechless, against the mendacity of politics which makes our will submissive and obedient and clouds our brain.

Man and Woman: Remove your masks, join together. We will win against fear, we will triumph over fear. Awake! It's time to live!

The piece ends with the poem *Say no!* by Wolfgang Borchert, recited by the whole group.

3. Evaluation

The students performed the play three times in public. The following evaluation refers to the first performance in one of the main shopping areas in Berlin. This was particularly impressive. The students wrote in their report:

> We planned to perform the play in the Wilmersdorfer Strasse. It was very cold on the day. Our feet were cold, our hands freezing and our bodies were shivering — not only from the cold (cf. Arbeitsgruppe Friedenspädagogik, 1982, p. 176).

> On our way to the place of performance we distributed leaflets in order to draw attention to the action. This was supported by the wearing of masks, a way of showing the stereotype presented in the play. Even at this point there were some alarming reactions from pedestrians: 'Go to the East', 'leave us alone', 'Concentration camps should be built for you'.

The experience of public performance made the group self-confident and gave it a sense of solidarity; members of the group felt they had become a part of the peace movement by turning into an affirmation group. Students demonstrated a willingness to act, political courage and the ability to transfer the knowledge acquired in the course.

Project 4: visit to concentration camp memorials

1. Responsibility to deal with our history

More than fifty years after the liberation of the concentration camps, respect for the victims dictates that the events of the Third Reich should not be seen as historic, and therefore to be put aside. Within the framework of teacher training, we see our duty in the sense of Eli Wiesel's statement:

> the younger generation should be made responsible — not for the past, but for how it deals with it, what it does with the memories, which are part of its inheritance.

For this reason, we have visited concentration camp memorials with students in connection with seminars dedicated to the pedagogical problems of Holocaust Education. Below we discuss a project which encompasses a visit to Auschwitz/ Oswiecim in Poland, which we visited in 1985 and 1995 within the framework of one-week excursions.

We want to emphasise the special features of the project, because the act of visiting a concentration camp memorial with students in a teacher-training programme involves experiential and project-oriented learning. For example, the project participants were permitted to use the Auschwitz Memorial Archives to research the fate of an individual victim, and in this way to get to know the person by his or her name rather than a number. This is an activity which has repeatedly helped school classes to come to grips with the genocide which was bureaucratically planned by the Nazis.

2. Understanding the Holocaust

The holistic nature of project learning, the encompassing of head, heart and hand, has proven to be particularly productive for visits to concentration camp memorials. However, one danger must be kept in mind: the authenticity of the concentration camp venue can be jeopardised if historic experience is confused with prepared memories: 'The authenticity implies ... the presentation of historic reality, although, like all memory processes, it is a creation' (Schmoll, 1994:18). The expansive memorial site is not a concentration camp; its history is simply reconstructed at the historic location, through the presentation of pictures, artefacts and text, and in particular, in the way these are presented. In other words, much too often the elements of National Socialism are left out of the overall impression, leaving the viewer with an impression created by the exhibit, which might seem to be the reality, but which threatens to restrict the interpretation or understanding. For this reason, memorial sites need some explanation. We as teachers saw this element as one of our most important functions in the preparation and performance of the project. Auschwitz allows us to confront directly our own history. The tour through the memorial, which also led the students past children's toys, past baby and children's clothes, and past suitcases which contain the names of children, was a reminder that the arbitrary violence by the Nazis gave no consideration to even the smallest people, children.

In such situations, many students left the guided tour and tried to hide from each other their tears and feelings of speechlessness. One of the student reports, presented after the visit to Auschwitz, reads:

> Children's bags, orphans. I begin to understand the full dimension of the catastrophe. Nobody ever told me the things I am learning from these artefacts. The systematic annihilation of a people, no, many peoples. Why? They died so senselessly ... Tears are a sign of the weak, and weakness means death. I could not even cry at Auschwitz; I forbade myself; I didn't want to show a sign of weakness. Then the others would also become weak. What good would come from another group of crying Germans? It is difficult for me to accept the incomprehensible, but it is important to realise that there are places and occurrences where people have lost their humanity. Places which show me what people are capable of doing, which steal my illusion that some

magical power could somehow turn history to the good ... What does it mean to mourn? It has nothing to do with looking away from certain places, piles of hair, or children's shoes. I don't have the right to look away. If I feel sick, I run away. Mourning means: for me to take a look, and to accept Auschwitz (Rathenow and Weber, 1986: 34- 35).

Participants on both visits were moved by the question: what does Auschwitz have to do with me? The reflections of the 1985 participants and the project outcomes have been published as: *Auschwitz — mehr als ein Ort in Polen* (Auschwitz — more than a location in Poland) (Rathenow and Weber, 1986).

Through the encounter with the biographies of real-life people and their fate in the brutal reality of a concentration camp, the students were able to acquire an empathy, which is an important step toward making a moral judgement. It became clear to us that each generation has to come to grips with its own spirit and morality, behaviour and viewpoints, and it would be wrong for the teacher to tell the students what to do. In the spirit of Adorno, we made an effort to ensure that both the content and the arrangement of the project would help nurture the 'strength to reflect, to make up one's own mind, and to refuse to go along'. In this context, Adorno demands that people should not 'try to avoid confrontation with the horror'. He warns of the danger that Auschwitz could be repeated if the horror is something 'people refuse to accept, and if someone is rejected for just talking about it, as if he ... was guilty, and not the perpetrators' (Adorno, 1967: 115).

3. Résumé

During all of our visits to former concentration camps, it was very clear we would have to release ourselves from the traditional teachers' role of the all-knowing director. Due to the moving impressions which accompany the tour, we too were just as affected as our students, and our role evolved from that of teacher, to companion and partner, experiencing the learning process along with our students. A historical-political learning project allows students in a teacher training programme, who in their school careers had few opportunities for ex-periential learning, to engage in their own field research at a historic location. This enables them to make connections with current political-social problems such as anti-semitism, xenophobia and racism.

Projects are characterised by multi-disciplinary learning. Independent of the usual fields of scientific disciplines, they take on topics, the study of which requires knowledge of approaches used in a number of disciplines. In the case of the excursion to Auschwitz, it was necessary to convey more than simply the historic facts, which were provided during the preparatory seminars through lec-tures by historians and in discussions with witnesses to the events and survivors of the Holocaust. It was also important to relate the situation to current political and social developments, which in the case of the most recent excursion in 1995, was influenced by the series of 50th anniversary commemorations. Here we were influenced by Adorno's (1967) approach, and motivated by the conviction that those elements of technical, social and political development, which led to the creation of Auschwitz, need to be identified. Furthermore, we, today, need to encourage elements which might have prevented such an event. There is much truth in the statement made by Adorno in a radio report (1966) that civilisation itself creates uncivilised situations, and his fear that the process of creating civilisation also creates barbarism.

Holocaust Education has the duty to do more than to commemorate the victims and to present the motives and the strategy for violence of the perpetrators. It also needs to reveal the effects of the Western European policies of exclusion and cultural dominance, without denying the uniqueness of Auschwitz (Todorov, 1982). This could be seen in the National Socialist policy of rejecting people who were seen to be different, and must be seen as part of the objectivising and classifying tendency in the European Enlightenment, which found its most extreme and distorted expression at Auschwitz.

Baumann (1992) noted that the Holocaust was by no means the result of irrational power, but rather encompassed bureaucratic routine and industrial perfection: the special Reichsbahn train schedules, the development of Zyklon B, the construction of crematoriums are all part of a mosaic of devilish efficiency, which in other contexts has been described as German industriousness. The German bureaucracy performed magnificently in the service of the annihilation apparatus.

Technology and the natural science disciplines proved to be the corner-stone of university education in the service of the dictatorship, which stems from the innocent use of morally neutral science. A belief in the objectivity of technology seems to have made people particularly vulnerable to ideology. For scientists, moral hesitation and social responsibility were (and still are) less important than scientific and technical advance. As educators our mission must be to ensure that the moral and social dimensions of any question are always considered.

References

Adorno, T. W. (1967) Erziehung nach Auschwitz, in H.-J. Heydorn et al. (Eds) *Zum Bildungsbegriff der Gegenwart. Frankfurt: Diesterweg,* pp.lll-123.

Arbeitsgruppe Friedenspädagogik am FB 22 der TU Berlin (Ed) (1982) In *Zukunft nur noch friedliche Lehrer?* Vorbereitung, Durchführung und Auswertung eines friedenspa- dagogischen Projekts in der Lehrerbildung. Berlin: Technische Universität Berlin

Baumann, Z. (1992) *Dialektik der Ordnung. Die Moderne und der Holocaust.* Hamburg: Europische Verlagsanstalt.

Galtung, J. (1975) *Strukturelle Gewalt. Beiträge zur Friedens-und Konfliktforschung.* Reinbek: Rowohlt.

Hicks, D. and Steiner, M. (Eds) (1989) *Making Global Connections: A World Studies Workbook.* Edinburgh and New York: Oliver and Boyd.

Krappmann, L. (1971) *Soziologische Dimensionen der Identität.* Stuttgart: Klett.

Loewer, H.-D. (1984) Hochschulen — eine Institution, in der Frieden geschaffen wird? in P. Heitkämper (Ed) *Neue Akzente in der Friedenspädagogik.* Weinheim: Beltz, pp. 113-123.

Niklas, H. (1982) Friedensforschung und Friedenserziehung in der Bundesrepublik Deutschland, in N. H. Weber (Ed) *Frieden.* Berlin: Colloquium, pp. 11-22.

Pike, G. and Selby, D. (Eds) (1988) *Global Teacher, Global Learner.* London: Hodder and Stoughton.

Rathenow, H.-F. and Weber, N. H. (Eds) (1988) Der Workshop — Eine Methode zur Friedenserziehung in der Lehrerbildung. Berlin. Technische Universität Berlin.

Rathenow, H.-F. (1993) Global Education — Ein ganzheitlicher Beitrag zur politischen Bildung in reformpädagogischer Tradition, in U. Richter and H.-F. Rathenow (Eds) *Politische Bildung im Wandel.* Opladen: Leske und Budrich, pp. 61-82.

Rogers, Carl R. (1983) *Freedom to Learn for the 80s.* Columbus, Ohio: Charles E. Merrill

Schmoll, F. (1994) Authentizität und Überlieferung. Fragen des Holocaust- Gedenkens in der Denkmalskultur und in Steven Spielbergs 'Schindlers Liste', *Puzzle* (3)3, pp. 15-18.

Todorov, T. (1982) *Die Eroberung Amerikas. Das Problem des Anderen.* Frankfurt/M.: Suhrkamp.

Valk, L. (1984) Problem-oriented Learning in the Study of International Relations, Gandhi *Marg,* 6(4-5), pp. 367-379.

Wolff, R. (Ed) (1984) *Piscator, Erwin: Das ABC des Theaters.* Berlin: Nishen.

Wulf, C. (1992) Education for Peace. *Peace, Environment and Education* 3(2), pp. 3-10.

Chapter 8

Urban Protest, Citizenship and Human Rights:
curriculum responses to local issues

Audrey Osler

Introduction

This chapter explores the concepts of human rights and citizenship, drawing on a locally-focused study. While international legal instruments provide a framework for understanding human rights, and teaching about human rights arguably should have international agreements and covenants as a point of reference (Council of Europe, 1985), it is of course within local contexts that individuals struggle to claim these rights and develop a deeper understanding of what it means to be a citizen.

In September 1985 there was an uprising in Handsworth, Birmingham which received international media attention and led to many debates about development priorities within the city. While each community has its unique features and history, it is clear that many of the concerns expressed by the people of Handsworth in 1985 are also shared by many other people in communities across Europe today, including those of 'race' and gender inequalities, differing identities, housing, employment, and crime. These are issues which often attract the attention of the media, and form the basis of political campaigns, both local and national. They may also all be properly seen as human rights and citizenship issues.

The tenth anniversary of the Handsworth uprising provides an opportunity to reflect on a number of these debates, to set them within their wider European and global contexts, and to look forward ten years. This chapter describes a curriculum development and research project co-ordinated by the author, set up in partnership between the Birmingham Development Education Centre (DEC) and the School of Education at the University of Birmingham to explore human rights, citizenship and development in the local community. One aim of the project was to produce a teachers' handbook which might be used locally in secondary schools and further education (FE) colleges to encourage a greater understanding of human rights and citizenship, but which would also include material which might act as a stimulus for teachers and students wishing to explore similar issues in their own communities.

This chapter examines first the press reporting of the Handsworth uprising of 1985, highlights images of the area and other inner-city communities which were conveyed through such reporting, and considers the media-led portrayal of a community. The chapter then describes the project structure and participants and the processes of combining a curriculum development project with a university course. It explores the participating teachers' developing understandings of human rights and citizenship, and the design and production of the curriculum materials. It concludes by considering the potential of a locally-focused study to contribute to education for human rights and citizenship at local, national, European and global levels.

The 1985 Handsworth uprising

On 10 September 1985 Birmingham residents awoke to radio and television reports that parts of the Handsworth district of the city had been devastated by a violent mob which had looted shops and set fire to buildings. That evening they were able to watch film footage of then Home Secretary, Douglas Hurd, being chased by a group of youths when he arrived in the area to inspect the damage. The images and words of the media had tremendous impact as they were beamed across the world, yet many of the people of Birmingham and of Handsworth itself had difficulty in relating these images to the city and district they knew. In fact the area of the city which suffered serious damage on the night of 9 September would be more accurately defined as Lozells, but Handsworth was the district most closely associated in the public imagination with the problems and images which the media wished to convey, and so newspapers, radio and television dubbed the events of 9-10 September 1985 the Handsworth riots.

On 11 September four national newspapers, the *Daily Express, The Mirror, The Star* and *The Sun*, each gave a full front page coverage of Handsworth; all carried the same photograph of a young black man carrying a lighted petrol bomb. The headlines and stories were as follows:

England, 1985: Handsworth ablaze again after night of horror

He walks with a chilling swagger, a petrol bomb flaming in his hand and hate

74

burning in his heart. This is the ugly, menacing face of Handsworth, England, on September 10, 1985. A day when riot and arson flared again after a night of terror. A night when racial violence boiled over into an orgy of fire, looting and murder (*Daily Express*).

War on the streets

This was the terrifying face of Front Line Britain yesterday. A black youth strides coolly down the riot-torn streets of Handsworth clutching a lighted petrol bomb in his hand. In a nearby street a lone policeman shelters behind his riot shield as a car blazes fiercely before him. It was the second day of war in the streets of Britain's Second City which has left two brothers dead in a burned-out post office, two others missing, and at least 45 shops petrol-bombed and looted (*The Mirror*).

Torch of hate: crisis cities on alert as rioters rampage again.
Fear stalks city

This was the menacing face of riot torn Handsworth yesterday. A youth brandishes a petrol bomb as he strides down the street. Police came under siege once again as mobs rampaged through the run-down area. Cars were turned over and set alight and police vans were stoned. And fears were growing last night that Handsworth's torch of hate could spread to other parts of Britain (*The Star*).

Hate of a black bomber *by Ian Hepburn, who was attacked by the mob*

A black thug stalks a Birmingham street with hate in his eyes and a petrol bomb in his hand. The prowling maniac was one of the West Indian hoodlums who brought new race terror to the city's riot-torn Handsworth district yesterday. And as darkness fell over the smoke-blackened ruins of a stunned community, fears of more mayhem loomed. Sullen gangs of coloured youths roamed the area watched warily by squads of weary police. Hundreds of other officers stood by in riot gear in case of trouble. At least two innocent Asians have died and 45 shops have been burnt out and looted (*The Sun*).

The press coverage of the uprising presented images of war, mayhem and destruction, and emphasised the emotions of hatred and fear. The image of a lone black youth, representing the 'gangs' of rioters, was used to embody these negative emotions. It was variously the police, the 'stunned community' and 'innocent Asians' who were presented as the victims of the 'racial' violence. There was no indication that any one other than from the black community was involved in the arson and looting, which appears from these accounts to have happened spontaneously, without any direct or indirect cause. Only one newspaper, the *Daily Express*, offers any explanation for the 'savagery' in its front page story, an explanation which it implicitly challenges: 'Labour and Alliance leaders predictably blamed Government policy and inner city deprivation. Handsworth's unemployment is running at 50 per cent'.

Much of the press coverage of the Handsworth uprising of 1985 was shallow and sensationalist. It provoked racial prejudice and reinforced stereotypical images of Handsworth and other inner-city districts, which were presented as equally vulnerable to mob violence. Many of those living and working in the inner-cities found it difficult to recognise the places they knew from the images presented.

It was anticipated at the outset of the *Handsworth Ten Years On* project that the press might well respond to the tenth anniversary of the uprising by featuring Handsworth today. While it was difficult to predict what images of Handsworth they might chose to promote in 1995, it is clear from the press reporting of 1985 that teachers and their students might value materials which encouraged informed debate on local human rights and citizenship issues and on local development priorities. The next section describes the context in which the project materials were developed.

Project structure and participants

DEC is an educational charity which has an established tradition of working with teacher groups to explore ways of introducing development perspectives into the curriculum. The *Handsworth 10 Years On* project resembled a number of other DEC projects which have sought to combine professional development opportunities for project members with the production of curriculum materials. Although the general aims of professional development and materials development were clearly stated from the outset, the precise use of these materials was to be agreed by the teacher group, so that project members might focus on those issues which they judged to be of greatest significance and contribute to the design of materials which they considered would be of greatest value to their colleagues.

The project was designed in three main phases over three terms:

1. Autumn term 1994: research and data collection by project coordinator; modification and preparation of university module.

2. Spring term 1995: participation in university module; development and trial of materials with students in schools and colleges.

3. Summer Term 1995: collation of curriculum materials by project co-ordinator; writing of teachers' handbook.

An advice group was also established consisting of local teachers and headteachers, an education adviser, a community worker, a journalist and an academic. This group included not only people with a range of professional skills but also those with a close understanding of the Handsworth communities. The group met at the beginning of the project to discuss its broad aims and focus, during the second phase to advise on the development of the materials, and in the third phase to consider effective dissemination of the project outcomes through the curriculum materials and associated teacher workshops. The project coordinator was also supported at each stage by the director of DEC with whom regular meetings were held to assess progress and develop plans.

Publicity was prepared some six months in advance and applications invited; most importantly each applicant was required to make a brief written statement outlining the reasons for wishing to participate. All applicants were offered an interview at DEC and those who were offered a place were also required to apply separately to the university in order to register for a university-based module entitled *Human Rights Education, Citizenship and the Environment*. This module lasts for 10 weeks and includes 30 hours of classes. DEC paid the module fee for those who had no other sponsor.

As well as being an opportunity for curriculum development, the project, like many other DEC projects, was also designed as a means of personal and professional development for participants. The university module would provide project members with a framework in which they might set their research and curriculum development work and a means by which their involvement in the project might be formally accredited. Students attending the module are expected to complete an assignment, which represents 100 hours of study. It was planned that curriculum materials produced by the project teachers might form the basis of their university assignment. Successful completion of this assignment entitles registered students to receive a credit towards a university qualification at first degree, advanced certificate or master's level.

The project team consisted of the coordinator, who is a lecturer at the university, and seven local teachers and lecturers, working in Birmingham or neighbouring local education authorities. Half the project members had a close association with the Handsworth district, and were living and/or working in the area. It is interesting to note that all applicants to the project were women. Those who were selected represented a broad range of experience: two of the participants had been educated abroad in Jamaica and Uganda; two were of African Caribbean and one of Asian descent. One was a history teacher working in a boys' school; four were curriculum support teachers working in language and curriculum development across a range of subjects and schools; one was a lecturer in a further education college teaching social sciences and business administration, and another an adult education worker teaching a range of courses including women's studies and courses for women returning to work after a career break. Most were thus in relatively privileged positions as teachers in the sense that they were able to negotiate their timetables and fit their teaching commitments around a half-day attendance at the university.

In addition to their participation in the module, project members attended four additional evening meetings: a preparation meeting at the beginning of phase two; a second meeting towards the end of phase two to plan and co-ordinate their classroom work; a third meeting during phase three to share the results of this classroom work; and a final meeting to comment on a draft of the teachers' handbook. The project thus demanded a personal commitment from each of the participants.

Combining a curriculum development project with a university course

DEC has a long record of working in partnership with other organisations. The *Handsworth Ten Years On* project was innovative in that it was the first DEC project which sought to integrate university teaching and learning and find a means of accrediting the professional development of the project members. The coordinator had a long established working relationship with DEC which facilitated the process of partnership and the integration of the university module into the project structure.

Teachers working closely over a number of months on a curriculum project often develop a strong rapport and group identity; indeed high levels of cooperation and group commitment are likely to be critical to the successful achievement of project aims. Nevertheless, this project group was required to work alongside a broader group of students following the university module and it was important that they were able to integrate with the wider group. Any conflict of interests was largely alleviated by the sensitivity of project members, and by the readiness of other students to recognise the potential of exploring human rights and citizenship issues through a study of their own localities.

The other students included experienced educators from Germany, Hong Kong and Tanzania as well as Britain, and those working in a wide range of educational contexts, including primary schools, church and community work, and women's education. It is clear that the project was able to benefit from the international perspectives of such a group; students were ready to learn from each other, to challenge preconceptions and, in sessions where we considered human rights and citizenship in the local community, were able to draw on personal experience across four continents.

Given that project members were not the only students following the university course, it was important to ensure that they were not viewed as elite, able to claim more of the tutors' time or to have a disproportionate influence on the course agenda. Since the precise content of the course was open to negotiation within the student group, it was also important that the shared agenda of project members did not override the interests of other group members. These issues were raised at the beginning of the course and other students reacted positively to the locally-focused project, expecting it to enhance their studies. One way in which the module was developed to meet the needs of the project was by introducing a session spent doing field work in the Winson Green district of Birmingham and considering how the local environment might affect human rights; this enabled all students to develop some practical skills and provided overseas students with a unique opportunity of enhancing their understanding of the city.

In an evaluation of the university course non-project members were asked whether the project had had any impact on their participation or learning either positively or negatively. All acknowledged some benefit, although some found it difficult to identify its precise effects:

> It is difficult to assess its influence since the project has not taken off as such, but as part of the course it has been positive (Birmingham primary teacher).

> The links between human rights, citizenship and environmental education were made clear to me through the Handsworth project. A local study in either town or in rural areas is especially relevant, people can identify problems or areas which need attention and take action, for example, in dealing with problems of pollution (Tanzanian health educator).

Although those who were not members of the project were able to recognise its beneficial effect on the module, the project members had differing reactions to the module and the extent to which it had prepared them for classroom work. While some were confident that it had provided them with a useful framework for work with their own students, others were less certain about the relationship between the module and the project:

> The module has been useful in laying a sound foundation of general information and questions which I hope will prepare me for the work ahead (History teacher).

> I would have found it very difficult to continue with the project without doing the course. It is still *quite* difficult (English teacher).

> I feel it's given me some insight into preparing diverse teaching materials on human rights — but not totally prepared me for the continuing process of the project (FE lecturer).

> Links between the module and the Handsworth project have not always been clear — a couple of sessions were useful in developing work with adults. I would have liked an opportunity to have discussed some of this a bit more (Adult education worker).

It would seem that the dual project aims of providing professional development opportunities and encouraging curriculum development leading to the publication of materials are in tension. A similar observation was made by McFarlane (1994) who examines a project which also attempted to combine professional development and curriculum development and which included a study visit to East Africa:

> The most effective material which came out of the project was developed when the teachers were able to translate what they had learned ... into effective classroom practice. Difficulties arose when the two failed to connect, for example when teachers built on their previous classroom practice without making reference to what they had learnt in East Africa, or when they translated an over-simplified understanding, for example about colonial history, or interdependence, into classroom practice (McFarlane, 1994: 230).

Nevertheless, the project teachers' comments on the relationship between the university module and their need to develop curriculum materials need to be set in context. They were made during phase two of the project, when participants had not yet attempted to apply their learning. The uncertainties which some express would seem to reflect their continuing engagement with complex issues; it would seem important for project members to remember that their work is to a large extent experimental. Total certainty and confidence about the application of their ideas in the classroom would not necessarily be desirable and might indicate over-simplification.

Teachers' developing understanding of human rights and citizenship

The university module *Human Rights Education, Citizenship and the Environment* is open to teachers and others in related professions who are studying for a range of post-experience qualifications in the School of Education, although most of the students who take the course are working for a master's degree. Some students are specialising in human rights and equality in education and will follow complementary courses focusing on 'race', ethnicity and gender, while others may be specialising in education management, curriculum studies, special education, or simply following a broad general programme. Some students are studying full-time while others, like the members of the *Handsworth Ten Years On* project team, are part-time. The course therefore has to meet the needs of a broad range of students with varying backgrounds and experience from many countries. While the programme is continually reviewed and modified, the broad outline followed by the students in the *Handsworth Ten Years On* project was fairly representative of the module:

- introduction to human rights concepts
- key international human rights legal instruments
- children's rights

- teaching for human rights and citizenship
- the human rights school
- developing policies to counter bullying and promote equality
- human rights and environmental education
- human rights and citizenship in the local context
- field work: human rights and the local environment
- human rights and political education.

Since the 1980s most schools in England will have given some attention to the issue of 'equal opportunities' in education although the emphasis has varied considerably between institutions; some have focused more or less exclusively on gender equality, while others have also given consideration to issues of 'race'. Similarly, the issue of special needs has been viewed in many institutions as an equal opportunities issue, and some schools have given particular attention to the integration of students with disabilities.

Despite this apparent growing awareness and the development of policies on equal opportunities, a considerable body of research evidence (for example, Wright, 1987; 1992; Mirza, 1992; Siraj-Blatchford, 1991; Troyna and Hatcher, 1992; Osler, 1994a) documents the nature and degree of racism that black students experience both in British schools and in initial teacher education. An Equal Opportunities Commission formal investigation into teacher education found that while 'on paper the prospects for good equal opportunities practice in both curriculum content and the organisation and management of the institutions looked quite good' and institutions acknowledged the importance of equal opportunities and expressed a commitment to gender equality, the general attitude was one of 'benign apathy towards equal opportunities'. The approach of the majority of institutions was 'reactive and incoherent' and many were unable to provide any evidence to substantiate their claims that they were carrying out programmes of work (EOC, 1989).

Even where schools and initial teacher education institutions are implementing equal opportunities programmes teachers are unlikely to be aware of the international human rights conventions which might support much of their work. They may therefore be vulnerable to accusations of political bias. Indeed, there have been frequent attacks on anti-racism in education from the political right which has characterised it at one level as a distraction from the acquisition of basic skills, and at another level as a dangerous tendency which will not only undermine 'standards' but also threaten British values and British culture (O'Keefe, 1986).

The teachers who took part in this project were all engaged in human rights education, but had not previously perceived their work in these terms; indeed four of the seven were in posts which were funded specifically to meet the needs of students from ethnic minorities. Nevertheless, most were active in organisations concerned with human rights: one was a member of Amnesty International and a number reported past or present membership of a range of organisations including a local Community Relations Council, Traidcraft, Friends of the Earth, Anti-Apartheid, and a cycling pressure group. Their broad range of interests reflected a commitment to issues of justice and equality both locally and internationally and an awareness of environmental concerns and the need for sustainable development.

Project members were invited to outline what they had learnt about human rights during the course of the module. Their responses suggest that the concept of human rights education was itself new. A number stressed that the module had given them a new familiarity with major international human right instruments which had implications for their work as teachers:

> I hadn't really thought about human rights before. What I chiefly feel that I've learnt is that most of my work is linked to human rights in one way or another and also aspects of my life outside work, for example, bringing up my children (English teacher).

> This module has helped me to understand the meaning of human rights. It has also taught me about the different ideas and teaching materials which could be used for introducing the topic area (FE lecturer).

> I had heard of human rights, but now I'm aware of the prescriptive ones, for example, children's rights (Curriculum support teacher).

> I'm now aware of the UN and other declarations of human rights. I've got information on classroom strategies. There's been a strong emphasis on children's rights in the module (Adult education worker).

> I've learnt: what is a right? How are they applied? What problems exist? It's increased my awareness of the importance of education and of the right to education, these two things cannot be separated (History teacher).

Project participants were invited to indicate what impact, if any, participation in the module would have on their teaching. The responses reflect a concern with content and concepts, with styles of teaching and teacher-student relationships, and with broader whole-school issues:

> I'll be more aware of people's rights in the classroom, and will try and implement them as much as possible in my future teaching styles (FE lecturer).

> The module, and in particular the assignment, is going to have a big impact on my teaching as I am re-writing the English department's policies and curriculum to incorporate a human rights perspective (English teacher).

I'll apply human rights concepts to anti-racist teaching in Personal and Social Education and in the Humanities department (Curriculum support teacher).

It will be useful to explore local issues in relation to 'development' and 'human rights'. I work with adults who wish to enter youth, community, and social work and it may be possible to explore some of their concerns with reference to these concepts and some of the material we've received (Adult education worker).

In Personal, Social and Moral Education I'll put some of the issues-based topics into a context of human rights, what they are, and how they can be realised. There is also scope in geography, in history and in developing teaching styles, but this needs more thought (Curriculum support teacher).

I've increased my awareness of rights and their relevance to the teaching of history. I now see the responsibility I have for including human rights in my lessons. The module has also helped me to focus on rights when planning lessons and discussing issues in Personal, Social and Moral Education. A greater understanding of concepts and language should help me to minimise insensitive comments or throw away comments. I hope to pass on my increased awareness (History teacher).

The next section highlights the issues that the teachers chose to emphasise when designing curriculum materials which raise questions of human rights and citizenship in the context the *Handsworth Ten Years On* project.

Design and production of curriculum materials

A primary aim of the project was to produce a teachers' handbook, *Learning to Participate* (Osler, 1996), which would be of use to others interested in teaching for human rights and citizenship, drawing on their own local contexts. Curriculum materials produced for the handbook were tested by the participating teachers and collaborating colleagues. It was anticipated that local and possibly national media attention might again focus on Handsworth in 1995 and the project aimed to provide materials for teachers which would allow them to make an informed response to local human rights, citizenship and development issues and avoid the hazards of a media-led debate.

It was recognised in the early stages of the project that project members would be working within a tight schedule if materials were to be ready for September 1995 to mark the tenth anniversary of the 1985 uprising. As a result the project coordinator collated the classroom activities and wrote the teachers' handbook, rather than the complex process of encouraging each group member to take responsibility for a section of the text.

Discussion with the advice group and among project members led to a draft outline for the book (see Figure 1). This was intended as a framework and was open to amendment and adaptation. During the early stages of the module it was agreed that the UN Convention on the Rights of the Child might be a useful starting point for teachers considering human rights and citizenship in the local context and might give the materials coherence. This instrument was selected because teachers and schools have an obligation to make its contents known, and because the Convention's focus on the citizenship rights of children and young people give it immediate relevance to students in secondary schools and FE colleges. It was felt that the Convention would provide teachers and their students with a set of values against which they could examine barriers to human rights and citizenship, and explore the potential of education to challenge inequality and injustice.

The teachers identified four articles from the UN Convention on the Rights of the Child which they believed should be given special emphasis: article 13, freedom of expression; article 17, access to appropriate information; article 28, right to education; and article 29, aims of education. Overall they intended that the materials would make a small contribution to achieving article 42, making the rights and provisions of the Convention widely known to adults and children. Since formal education is likely to be the main means through which the Convention on the Rights of the Child and other human rights legislation can become known to communities (Osler, 1994b; Osler and Starkey, 1994), it is essential that teachers become familiar with such international legislation and that it is included in teacher education courses.

Project teachers discussed articles 13 and 17 and used them as a starting point for selecting teaching methods that would best serve their needs and encourage the development of appropriate skills for understanding human rights and citizenship. An unofficial summary of these articles states:

Article 13: freedom of expression
The child's right to obtain and make known information, and to express his or her views, unless this would violate the rights of others.

Article 17: access to appropriate information
The role of the media in disseminating information to children that is consistent with moral well-being and knowledge and understanding among peoples, and respects the child's cultural background. The state is to take measures to encourage this and to protect children from harmful materials (UN Centre for Human Rights/UNICEF, 1990).

The project teachers noted much of the press reporting of the 1985 Handsworth uprising to be in contravention of the spirit of article 17. They considered it important that students be equipped to look critically at media reports, to learn to

Figure 1: Draft outline for teachers' handbook: Learning to Participate

Human rights, citizenship and development issues in the local community

1 INTRODUCTION

local development issues: why study Handsworth?
— local development issues
— tendency of development education to study distant places
— where might local development issues fit into the curriculum?

human rights and citizenship: what are human rights/ citizenship rights?
— why are they a useful framework for looking at issues of development and justice in the local community?

2 BARRIERS TO HUMAN RIGHTS AND CITIZENSHIP

poverty and unemployment
housing and homelessness
racism
gender inequality
crime, drugs, policing issues

3 CHALLENGING INEQUALITY AND INJUSTICE

Handsworth 1985 uprising: what happened? why did it happen? (alternative perspectives) could it happen again?
education for equality: can education help? is it a method of social control? education as a right
community organisations

4 CHANGE

alternative futures
claiming human rights/citizenship rights

5 UN CONVENTION ON THE RIGHTS OF THE CHILD

recognise bias in reporting, and to identify when such reporting may be in violation of the human rights and citizenship rights of individuals or groups. In preparing students to develop such skills they would also be supporting article 13; without adequate skills or judgement and means of expression students will be in a weak position to claim their rights or those of others.

The project team originally selected five broad areas through which they might explore human rights issues. One of these, as an example, is policing and the protection of rights. The terminology used to describe the events which took place in Handsworth in September 1985 may have influenced reactions to the events themselves. Materials developed by the project team and tried in schools included worksheets which examined these words:

incidents	rebellion	disturbances
disorders	events	attacks
riots	eruptions	troubles
uprising		

Students are asked to classify these words into those which are neutral; those which put the blame on the people and those which suggest the people were justified. They then examine the text of the title song of the album *Handsworth Revolution* produced by the Birmingham reggae band *Steel Pulse* seven years before the events of 1985. The picture on the record sleeve and the words are analysed for the impressions they give of Birmingham and the human rights issues which are raised. Students assess the kind of action that *Steel Pulse* was advocating at that time.

Other material argues the case for and against the use of new riot equipment for the police. Students identify these arguments, as presented in quotations, and then consider the human rights implications of the use of such things as baton rounds (plastic bullets). Other sources available to students include extracts of interviews with local people from the Silverman report (1986), an inquiry into the Handsworth disturbances, material on police harassment, community policing, the ethnic make-up of the police force, and racism in the criminal justice system. In all the above material students are encouraged to look at the issues in terms of human rights and to consider the rights and duties of citizenship. Students are also given extracts from the Chief Constable's report (West Midlands Police, 1985) which suggested that criminal activity and drugs were the causes of the Handsworth disturbances and further extracts from the Silverman report (1986) and the West Midlands County Council Report (Bhavnani et al., 1986) which dispute this. They are invited to examine the evidence, find reasons for the differences in points of view and consider which they find easier to believe and why. Additional activities encourage students to interview residents and police about the situation in relation to crime in their own communities today and discover whether there is any concurrence of opinion between community members and those engaged in policing.

It can be seen that many of these activities are designed to encourage a critical examination of the issues today as well as in the past. Teachers and students using the materials should be able to find current newspaper articles and television reports which highlight parallel current concerns. One worry that some teachers may have is that the material they are using may be seen to be controversial or political in nature. Nevertheless if they use the UN Convention on the Rights of the Child and other relevant human rights instruments as the basis of this work students can use these internationally agreed basic standards as a measure against which they can make judgements. The Council of Europe Recommendation on Teaching and Learning about Human Rights in Schools acknowledges the political dimension of such work and stresses the importance of using inter- national human rights legislation in this way:

> Human rights inevitably involve the domain of politics. Teaching about human rights should, therefore, always have international agreements and covenants as a point of reference, and teachers should take care to avoid imposing their personal convictions on their pupils and involving them in ideological struggles (Council of Europe, 1985).

We have so far considered barriers to human rights and citizenship as identified by the project team. The materials in the project also sought to look creatively at how individuals and groups might challenge injustice and inequality and bring about change in society. One means identified is through education, yet students are rarely, if ever, encouraged to look critically at the processes of schooling or at their own education. As Davies reminds us, it would be naive to assume that this is no more than some historical oversight. Reviewing the situation inter- nationally she observes:

> Exposure to one's rights, and skills in challenging discrimination are not in the forefront of reasons for increased government expenditure on education. ... It is difficult to reconcile the screening function of schooling with an acceptance of universal rights (Davies, 1994).

Materials which invite young people to examine critically their own education are very rare and so the teachers' handbook devotes a section to education as a right and as a means for challenging inequality and injustice. The UN Committee on the Rights of the Child, in its first audit of children's rights in Britain, drew attention to a number of violations of the UN Convention in British education policy and practice; it urged particularly that children should be given the means to participate in the running of their schools (*The Guardian*, 28 January 1994). If this participation is to allow children to share in decision-making and to initiate developments, then students will need to look critically at the aims of education.

A section of the handbook provides some starting points for teachers and students interested in examining education as a right. It provides material on some of the current debates in education, including the question of 'standards', school exclusions, and education for equality.

Conclusion

There are considerable opportunities for developing an understanding of human rights and citizenship in the local context, and for exploring the means by which individuals and communities can claim these rights. The 1985 Handsworth uprising, with its international media coverage, provides a useful starting point for such a study since many of the concerns expressed by the people of Handsworth in 1985 and today are shared by others in communities across Europe.

While not all uprisings and riots are given the level of media coverage that Handsworth received in 1985, such events continue to occur in a variety of European urban contexts. Whether they are explained in terms of unemployment, poverty, racial inequality, policing policies, community tensions, a divergence in values between young people and their elders, or even the indiscipline of the young, they raise important questions about participation, citizenship and human rights. Various forms of urban protest across Europe cause us to focus on the experiences of young people, their place in the community and the opportunities for real participation which are open to them.

The curriculum materials which have been produced for the *Handsworth Ten Years On* project reveal the teachers' perspectives. They have identified poverty and housing as key areas in exploring barriers to human rights and citizenship and have also highlighted policing, protection and rights. With these they seek to combat racism and gender inequality.

The project set out to find ways of enabling students not only to identify barriers to human rights and citizenship but also to explore ways of claiming rights. In this respect a local study has considerable potential, since there are real opportunities not only to equip students with the skills they need to claim their rights but also to enable them to make changes. Education alone cannot adequately address the underlying causes of urban protest yet an education which fails to address the concerns of urban youth is unlikely to support them in becoming participative citizens able to contribute to the development of the local community.

By choosing to use the UN Convention on the Rights of the Child as an overarching framework, and the right to education which explores human rights, the *Handsworth Ten Years On* project has identified a theme which might be developed internationally. The universality of these rights means that students might examine them through case studies drawn from a variety of contexts and cultures. While it is not mere chance that schooling has traditionally neglected

88

rights and skills to challenge discrimination, the Convention on the Rights of the Child provides teachers and students with a powerful force for change. This Convention, the most widely signed piece of international human rights legislation to date, offers a strong basis for teachers wishing to explore citizenship rights with their students, making explicit as it does the participatory and citizenship rights of children and young people.

References

Bhavnani, R., Coke, J., Gilroy, P., Hall, S., Ouseley, H. and Vaz, K. (1986) *A Different Reality*. West Midlands County Council.

Council of Europe (1985) *Recommendation No. R (85) 7 of the Committee of Ministers to Member States on Teaching and Learning about Human Rights in Schools*. Strasbourg: Council of Europe.

Davies, L. (1994) Focusing on equal rights in teacher education, *Educational Review*, 46, 2, pp.109-120.

Equal Opportunities Commission (1989) *Formal Investigation Report on Initial Teacher Training in England and Wales*. Manchester: EOC.

McFarlane, C. (1994) What is the value of a study visit for in-service education? in: A. Osler (Ed) *Development Education: global perspectives in the curriculum*. London: Cassell.

Mirza, H. (1993) *Young, Female and Black*. London: Routledge.

O'Keefe, D. (1986) (Ed) *The Wayward Curriculum: a cause for parents' concern*. London: Social Affairs Unit.

Osler, A. (1994a) Education for democracy and equality: the experiences, values and attitudes of ethnic minority student teachers, *European Journal of Intercultural Studies*, 5, 1, pp. 23-37.

Osler, A. (1994b) UN Convention on the Rights of the Child, *Educational Review*, 46, 2, pp. 141-150.

Osler, A. (1996) *Learning to Participate: human rights, citizenship and development in the local community*. Birmingham: Development Education Centre.

Osler, A. and Starkey, H. (1994) Fundamental issues in teacher education for human rights: a European perspective, *Journal of Moral Education*, 23, 3, pp.349-359.

Silverman, J. (1986) *Independent Inquiry into the Handsworth Disturbances September 1985*. Birmingham: Birmingham City Council.

Siraj-Blatchford, I. (1991) A study of black students' perceptions of racism in initial teacher education, *British Educational Research Journal*, 17, 1, pp. 35-50.

Troyna, B. and Hatcher, R. (1992) *Racism in Children's Lives*. London: Routledge.

United Nations Centre for Human Rights/ UNICEF (1990) *Convention on the Rights of the Child: briefing kit*. Geneva: UN Centre for Human Rights/ UNICEF.

West Midlands Police (1985) *Handsworth / Lozells September 1985*. Birmingham: West Midlands Police.

Wright, C. (1987) Black students — white teachers, in: B. Troyna (Ed) *Racial Inequality in Education*. London: Tavistock.

Wright, C. (1992) Early education: multicultural primary school classrooms, in: D. Gill, B. Mayor and M. Blair (Eds) *Racism in Education: structures and strategies*. London: Sage.

Chapter 9

Geography and Multicultural Education: using students' own experiences of migration

Carmen Gonzalo and Maria Villanueva

Introduction: from emigration to immigration in Southern Europe

Countries world-wide have been affected by migratory movements, internal and external, from the periphery to the centre. The fact that the world is multicultural is frequently overlooked although the history of humanity is the history of inter-culturality. Evidence has shown this history to be one of conflict. Europe, above all, is and will irreversibly be, multicultural. This affects all aspects of life, forcing the integration of communities of very different origins.

Since the late 1950s, international migration has made a major contribution to the changing economic and social geographical structure of Europe. Work-seeking migrants were a significant element of the economic growth of many countries in the 1960s. Immigrants from Spain, Portugal and Greece have, for many years, been a major source of legal and illegal workers in several countries. They provided cheap labour thus increasing profits. But at the same time, these countries' economies were heavily reliant on their emigrant remittances. The labour-demand countries came to seek their supplies in an ever-widening arc: Yugoslavia, Turkey, North Africa. The immigrants and their descendants have not only altered the face of many European cities but of the European populations themselves. Foreigners have compensated for the decline in local population because of their higher fertility rates.

The crisis of the 1970s led to a fundamental reshaping of European labour migration patterns. On the one hand, the economic restructuring modified the character of internal migration. 'Guest workers' were concentrated in industries which were most affected by closure and redundancies, leaving many migrants trapped in old inner city industrial regions without the opportunity of employment. King (1994) argues that the growth of high level services, the expansion of the informal economy and the 'casualisation' of whole sectors of employment has caused a division in immigrant labour and a polarisation between highly-skilled well educated migrants and less skilled and poorly educated migrants. The latter, often illegal, and concentrated in the informal economy rather than in factories, are drawn predominantly from poorer countries.

On the other hand, since the 1960s most southern European countries have become countries of immigration. People from the Third World, where more than a half of humanity lives in poverty, are moving in search of employment and opportunity. Mediterranean countries are now coming to terms with a wave of immigration mainly from the Maghreb but also from Africa south of the Sahara, Latin America, and more recently, from Eastern Europe. Furthermore, it seems inevitable that international migration will remain an essential element responding to and affecting Western European labour markets and societies.

In 1990 the total number of legal non-Spanish residents in Spain was 407,671, according to the Ministry of Social Affairs.

The breakdown by region of origin was as follows:

Europe	60%	Africa	7%
Americas	20%	others	5%
Asia and Oceania	8%		

The Ministry of Social Affairs estimated the number of illegal immigrants to be between 90,000 and 130,000. The estimates from non-governmental organisations are higher, ranging between 170,000 and 294,000. In 1991 a further 103,675 residence permits were issued, to migrants who had been on waiting lists for a number of years. Just under 39% of these were to migrants from Morocco.

As a result, the cultural and ethnic mixture of the school population, especially in large urban centres, has brought 'the world inside the classroom'. Teachers must be trained not only to cope with groups of students where cultural and linguistic heterogeneity is the rule, but also to adjust themselves to the concept of multiculturality. Only if teachers are equipped with the necessary conceptual instruments and with values of tolerance and dialogue will they be able to offer children a climate in which these issues can be approached with objectivity. The education of teachers is, without any doubt, a key issue in the development of education for a multicultural society.

Investigations carried out in 1982 in a large number of European countries by the British subcommittee of the Geographical Union on Geographical Education about the significance of multicultural issues in the educational systems and the role of geography in meeting these, showed little interest or even recognition of the topic. This was certainly the case in Spain at the time. Multiculturality is a relatively new issue in school and in the ambit of initial teacher training. We must acknowledge, though, that today multiculturality is given variable emphasis in different teacher training institutions and that various lines of research are being followed.

As teacher trainers and geographers we are engaged in research on how best to give our students the conceptual instruments to understand their society, putting emphasis on the values and attitudes they need in order to be made aware of their own and other people's attitudes and values. Our aim is make them feel that they are citizens of a cross-cultural society, of a Europe which must be open to the rest of the world, committed to an international new order based on equality and solidarity.

A research project at the Universitat Autònoma of Barcelona: methodology

We carried out the research with 156 students who were following a 40 hour compulsory course on the Geography of Europe for future primary teachers. Students study current migratory movements in Europe and the encounter of different cultures through qualitative research into the migratory experiences of their own families. We started with the assumption that the majority of the students would have migratory experience within their recent family histories.

Our aim was first, to emphasise the attitudes and values in learning geography by involving the students in the subject, and second, to introduce and test a relatively new method in geographical education: oral history. We consider this, not as a new kind of history, but as a part of the qualitative research methodologies now being used in historical, sociological and anthropological research. The legitimacy of qualitative techniques is far from universal in geography departments but they are increasingly recognised by geographers as a legitimate means of under- standing social phenomena (Pile, 1993).

Oral history has proved itself to have a pedagogical function; it provides data for understanding diversity, it makes it easier to appreciate the values of others and it introduces new qualitative elements of analysis and encourages the removal of prejudice. Some authors consider oral history ideal for teaching students to value other peoples and their way of life. Furthermore, if oral history is, as in the case of our students, their own history, it can become a particularly effective approach to personal involvement in study. As the aphorism says *Tell me, I forget; Show me, I remember; Involve me, I understand.*

The students' backgrounds

Our Faculty of Education is located in the Metropolitan area of Barcelona, an area which during the 1960s and 1970s underwent the most intense process of industrialisation in Catalonia and the whole of Spain. Today it covers an area of 30 kilometres radius from the city centre forming an urban conurbation of 4 million people. The city of Barcelona, with 1.1 million inhabitants in 1955, reached 1.74 million in 1970. The metropolitan area grew from 1.9 million inhabitants to 3.6 million during the same period. This enormous increase was partly the consequence of a rural exodus within the Catalonian region but even more, a migration from the less developed areas in Spain. There was, in fact an internal migratory movement towards the industrial areas in Spain and external migration to the rest of Europe.

Barcelona and its surrounding area received in only fifteen years, a large number of people mainly from the rural southern regions of Spain. These people brought with them their own cultures, social structures and values. They left rural villages and found themselves not only in an industrial urban environment, often in slums or dilapidated areas, and later in suburban 'ghettos' of high population density, but also immersed in a significantly different culture with a language they barely understood.

This intense migratory movement has been one of the most significant events in our contemporary social history. The process of the integration of immigrants has deeply marked present Catalan society, especially its relations with Spanish regions of emigration.

Spain, like other European states, as a result of its long and complex history, houses a variety of cultures and different languages. Catalonia, an autonomous region in the north-east of Spain, has a strong cultural personality and its own language, Catalan, which is spoken as the first language although every one can also speak Spanish.

For individuals, migration within Spain may involve a personal experience similar to migrating abroad. On the other hand, more than 3 million Spanish people migrated in the same decade, providing cheap labour to the most indus- trialised countries: France, Belgium, Switzerland, Netherlands and Germany.

In order to confirm our hypothesis about the students' family background, we asked them to complete a form stating their place of birth and that of their parents and grandparents. They were also asked to state whether, in their extended circle of relatives and friends, they have returnees who could tell them about that experience. The results of this inquiry confirm our hypothesis. While 87 per cent of the students were born in Catalonia (84 per cent in the province of Barcelona), only 43 per cent of their parents and 34 per cent of their grandparents are of Catalan origin. This means that 66 per cent of the students' grandparents were immigrants mainly from Andalusia. Data referring to the second question showed less clear-cut results. Although 80 per cent of the students were linked in some way with people who had emigrated to Europe or Latin America, the links were of different kinds.

The majority of our students are descendants of people who left home in search of opportunities for themselves and their families. Therefore their homes and neighbourhoods and families may still contain memories of their regions of origin, of the integration process in Catalonia, and of the years of external migration. The students' first hand experience of life history research could be used to increase their understanding of migratory phenomena in the past . The aim is that they will also learn to approach, in a positive way, recent migratory movements which brought to Europe and now to Spain, people from countries with ethnic and cultural differences.

Exploring past histories of internal and external migration

Working in groups of four, students had to choose two people to interview: first, a relative who had come to Catalonia from another region of the state, and secondly, an acquaintance who had spent time working outside Spain. Interviews were open and unstructured. Thus the interviewee could talk about and explain their own memories spontaneously. We agreed that in order to have common elements for comparison, all should be asked to talk about the following common aspects of their experience:

- causes of migration
- personal feelings on leaving their homeland and first impressions on arrival
- housing and employment difficulties
- cultural differences and adaption to the new society
- present feelings about the whole experience and the future

Students should listen and record carefully, selecting relevant elements relating to the objectives of the work. We made clear that we were not looking for objective data. The purpose was not to explore family roots, although this might engage some students at a personal level. We wanted to gather spontaneous feelings, allowing us to connect with subjacent values and at the same time get students thinking about the complex process of migration from an unusual perspective in academic work: that of the affective sphere.

We obtained 39 interviews with internal migrants and 39 with people who had emigrated from Spain. In the case of the internal migrants, 24 of the 39 were women. A few women had followed their husbands to Barcelona, but the majority came looking for employment, as did all the men. All of them were following in the steps of friends and relatives who had left, usually from the same village, for Catalonia. We can find some common elements in their memories:

very long journeys on old and slow trains, full of people like themselves, or in illegal bus services obliged to travel only at night; an arrival in a well lit city that did not resemble the world they had left behind.

Women found work as domestic servants or in textile factories, men on building sites or in factories. They give the impression that jobs were plentiful and that it did not take long to find one or to move to a better one. Almost all of the migrants shared their first home with people who had helped bring them. Housing conditions were often very overcrowded, with one or two room flats for eight, sometimes ten people. In some cases they lived in barracks. None of the migrants found it difficult to adapt to the Catalan culture. Some learned the language, many did not, because the people could understand them, and besides, nearly 90% of them lived in areas occupied by immigrants like themselves. Their children and grandchildren have learned Catalan. It was seen as a positive step to enable them to integrate more fully into society and give access to better jobs. The family language though, is still Spanish. It is only since the death of Franco that Catalan has become the first language in schools.

Most of those interviewed visit to their home villages regularly, but only two are thinking of returning when they retire. 99% now consider Catalonia as their home and, above all, the home of their children and grandchildren.

Of the 39 interviewees who had left the country, 28 were men and 11 women. Although it was quite common for women to travel with their husbands or to follow them later, these women were selected for interview because they themselves had led the migration. Countries of destination were as follows: Germany 17, France 6, Switzerland 7, Netherlands 3, United Kingdom 2, Argentina 2 and Colombia and Brazil 1.

The main difference between the people who had gone to Latin America and those who chose Europe was that the former were qualified workers sent by their employers to an American branch of the company or professionals wanting to start a new life there. Those who migrated to Europe worked largely as unskilled factory workers. All of these migrated with the intention of saving money in the shortest possible time and returning to Spain.

Those who led the migration viewed the process as a positive experience. However, they also commented on the fact that it was much harder for the family, especially the wife if she remained at home. In some cases they returned early. They lived well. They worked very hard but salaries were higher than in Spain and they were able to save and send home part of their wages. Nevertheless, they had to make sacrifices. Language was one of the main problems; learning a new language was essential to secure better working and social prospects. They recognised cultural differences and feelings of solitude as one of the main problems that they tried to mitigate by being in close contact with the Spanish community. On the other hand, they appreciated certain differences in the way of life: a more liberal life style, especially in the case of women, and the openness of the family structure. Of course, all of this was when Spain was a closed country under a dictatorship and seen in the context of the 1960s; the Catholic church was strongly embedded in society, especially in the rural areas from which most of immigrants came.

They appreciated the politeness of people and the social advantages of good public services. They did not feel they had been discriminated against or suffered from xenophobic treatment. According to some of them, this was because after them came other immigrants who were said to be 'bad workers' or 'untidy people'. It can be noticed in some interviews how they assumed their role and the need to behave properly, not only to receive fair treatment but also to show that Spaniards could behave and work properly. Some of them described how ashamed they felt when another Spaniard behaved in an incorrect manner.

Studying the present

Using their family experiences the students are in a position to reflect on the new protagonists in similar situations: different people with the same intention of leaving their homeland in search of a better life for themselves and their families.

Spain, traditionally a labour export country, has since the 1970s been experiencing net immigration. A number of factors have contributed to the turn around of the trend. The growth of unemployment following the 1974 oil crisis gave birth to restrictive policies in Europe and in the USA. The main external factors were: measures to support migrants' return to their countries of origin and to restrict migration; political and economical difficulties in some Latin American and African former Spanish colonies; the growing crisis in Africa and, since the end of the 1980s, refugee and migration movements from Central and Eastern Europe.

The process of political democratisation in Spain since 1975, the integration in the European Union and the end of the rural exodus, are some of the internal causes. Africa being so close to Spain, just 14 kilometres at the nearest point, and the permeability of the frontiers, has caused all countries bordering on the northern Mediterranean, especially Spain, to be confronted with large numbers of immigrants from North Africa, with illegal immigration rising to considerable proportions.

Spain became a country of immigration in the context of the fuel crisis of the 1970s. This period was a turning point in popular perceptions: 'guest workers' became 'foreigners'. However, the proportion of immigrants is still smaller than in most European countries. However the increasing number of immigrants in schools and their concentration in certain urban areas, has been accompanied by xenophobia as has been witnessed elsewhere in Europe. Immigrants in Spain have been vulnerable to sporadic outbreaks of racial violence.

Each group of our students had to interview one of these recent immigrants. Our first finding was that many of the students confessed to not having had direct contact with what could be considered a typical immigrant. Nonetheless, all groups managed to find someone who agreed to be interviewed. Their selection was a very representative sample of the current trend of migration into Spain. Of the 39 interviewees, 24 came from Africa (15 from Maghreb countries), nine from Latin America, one from the Philippines and five from Eastern Europe. Although they shared some common characteristics, in other respects they were very different and they have been divided into two groups.

Of the first group, those coming from Latin America and Eastern Europe, half are women who, in most cases, came with their families. Either they or their husbands are of Spanish origin. In the case of two of the women from Eastern Europe (Ukraine) they met and married Spanish men in Germany and have ended their migratory process in Barcelona. The most complex example of migration was the case of a woman from Kazakstan who married a Cuban man of Spanish origin, who had gone to Cuba as a university student. Due to recent outbreaks of anti-Russian behaviour, the couple were forced to leave the country. In all cases, due to the personal links with Spain, their problems are more of an economic rather than social nature. Women work mainly in the tourist sector and most of the men have unskilled jobs.

The experience of the women who came alone is quite different. They migrated to Spain because of difficult economic circumstances, leaving their families behind while saving money to feed them. The most effective way of doing this is working as a domestic servant, thus having a place to live. Their personal circumstances are very hard and they look forward to going back, although they consider leaving Spain very difficult. All the others think of their position as permanent.

The students found the histories of the African people most interesting. Only five were women and in most cases they had divorced before coming, two of them migrating with their children. Of the men, more than 60% were unmarried, two had married here and two had been able to bring their families. In most cases, it was not easy to persuade them to talk freely, and most of them asked to remain anonymous. In 30% of the cases they are in an illegal situation. Extreme poverty and total lack of opportunity in their own countries forced them into what they see as an irreversible situation. A few of them expect to go back because they feel they belong in Africa. Two are political migrants.

Their journeys were real adventures. Some coming from countries south of the Sahara tell about having used all kinds of methods of transport: car, train, plane and of course, foot. In a few cases they had crossed the Gibraltar Straits in fishing boats after having paid enormous amounts of money and been frightened of being caught by the Spanish coast police. Some tell of how they used to watch Spanish TV, and Europe was seen as a dream; but that dream was shattered for many of them, very quickly. The majority work in agricultural jobs, on building sites or as street sellers. To have a permanent job, a decent home and a legal citizenship is their obsession.

They try to keep their own cultural and religious traditions alive, even in certain cases traditions restricting women's rights. Some of the women dare to say they consider these unjust and appreciate the freedom and liberty they have found in Spain.

Although none of the interviewees have been direct victims of xenophobic conflict, they all say that they have friends who have. Most feel that they are not seen as equal. The ones who feel more integrated are those living in rural areas with more or less permanent jobs in agriculture. In urban areas they are in a far more unofficial and marginal situation and they try to live close together, one problem being that there are far more men than women.

Conclusions: the students' findings

After sharing and discussing the migration histories in several workshops, students were asked to draw conclusions, attempting to move away from personal feelings and experiences towards global conclusions on the most important aspects of migration, those affecting individual values and attitudes and those in the socio- economic sphere.

First, the process of emigration always implies a personal disruption and leaves people facing problems of solitude, having been uprooted and with a sense of being marginalised and vulnerable. Such feelings are as important as material considerations.

The process of integration and assimilation to the values of a new society seems to be a process full of contradictions. It is seen as necessary for economic and social reasons but it brings personal conflicts. It is common, especially with children, to find feelings of belonging nowhere. It is frequently felt that in the search for material gain, valuable features of more traditional societies, such as solidarity, are lost.

The stories given by women tend to be richer in feeling and detail. Perhaps the women live the whole process in a more holistic way and it becomes imprinted upon their minds. This is particularly evident in older people talking about past experiences. They also consider the experiences emancipatory. The process of migration is seen as more difficult in most cases for women than men; nevertheless they develop confidence and freedom, and tend to show more progressive attitudes when adapting to the new culture. It is worth noting that when women stay at home to raise their family, they have greater problems integrating. An evident difference between past and present histories is that in the 1950s and 1960s, migrants found, in general, what they expected in terms of employment, salaries and the economic fulfilment of their needs. Today, life is much more difficult and disillusions greater because of the globalisation of television images of material-ism, contrasting with a world that for them takes the form of unemployment, marginalisation and often, xenophobia from which they see no escape.

Reflections on the process

This project provided a very rich experience. First, we have learned that students did not have themselves to be migrants in order to understand the migratory processes. It seemed on occasion as if our students felt distanced from their family histories yet we recognise that many may have found it difficult to relate painful family experiences in the classroom. Despite this we have realised that hearing first-hand accounts of migration is the most effective way to involve students. Their learning is both affective and conceptual.

Secondly, the students have learned that the causes of the migratory processes are quite similar across time and that to understand them, they need to know how world systems work. The problems that immigrants have to face depend partly on ethnic and cultural differences but mainly on the socio-economic situation that makes them more or less welcome. This global perspective enables us to analyse the right to equal opportunities for all and to consider the role of the school system.

We believe that although the school must be an instrument to convey attitudes of respect, solidarity and justice to avoid or soften conflicts, it should not consider itself to be solely responsible for doing so. Teachers can help to create individual attitudes but the causes of problems are not individual but structural; their solutions are not in the hands of the teacher alone.

To educate in human rights needs something more that 'convinced' teachers, trained in the methods of such teaching. Multicultural education and human rights education need to develop citizenship and political literacy; they demand procedural knowledge as well as an understanding of basic concepts; a know-ledge of how political and economical systems work. We consider political and economic literacy to be prerequisites for teacher training students which will pro-vide them with the conceptual framework to understand the world in which they live.

Geography has an important contribution to make in explaining many of the issues and decisions that affect our society, and for this reason it should be conspicuous in human rights teaching. It has the advantage of being inter-disciplinary, and having global relevance. The teaching of geography must be combined with developing the tools to understand and have control of their lives and places. Geographical understanding can be a powerful resource for people making decisions in the world but how useful this teaching is will depend on the issues we choose to study. Knowledge, reflection and action must necessarily be linked and combined in various ways.

Issues of social reality should be the concern of geographical studies. Geography should be used to develop pupils' critical awareness of existing social structures and their ability to transform society. It can provide a practical and theoretical understanding of work and economy, a critical grasp of the social relations under which they take place and a view of the political process as a whole. A geographical education which develops students who will be active in society should aim at building confidence and skills in using political judgement.

We agree with Huckle that:

> human geography can contribute in significant ways to personal and social education.... In helping young people to recognise the structural forces which shape their world and to consider identification with agents working for change, it can be a powerful agent for promoting democracy. Geography should play a significant role in creating more fulfilled and happy individuals in a fairer and less troubled world (Huckle, 1983).

References

Botey, J (1994) Els conflictes de classe, els d'identiutat i les actituds *Interaula,* 21-22 pp. 3-6. Barcelona.

Cox, B. (1986) Reflections on geography teaching for a Better World, in: J. Fien and R. Gerber (Eds) *Teaching geography for a Better World.* Brisbane: AGTA.

DCIDOB(1991) La immigració *Quaderns CIDOB!* Barcelona pp.

Fassman, A. H. and Münz, R. (1992) Patterns and trends of international migrations in Western Europe, *Population and Development Review.* (18) 3 pp

Huckle, J. (1983) *Geographical education: Reflection and action.* Oxford Oxford University Press.

Huckle, J.(1987) What sort of geography for what sort of school curriculum ? *AREA,* (19) 3.

Johnston, R, J. (ed.) (1993) *The challenge for geography.* Oxford: Blackwell.

King, R. (1994) Migration and the single market for labour, in: M. Blacksell, M. and A.M. Williams, *The European Challenge.* Oxford: Blackwell

Pile, S. (1992) Oral history and teaching qualitative methods, *Journal of Geography in Higher Education,* 16, 2, pp.135-143

Chapter 10

Intercultural Education Through Foreign Language Learning: a human rights approach

Hugh Starkey

Introduction

The acquisition of a foreign language is a powerful element of intercultural education. Learning a language is also learning another culture on its own terms. Monolingual teachers are handicapped in multilingual Europe. Indeed, if there is one area of the curriculum that ought to be central to global education it is languages. If there is one set of skills that all global citizens ought to possess it is to communicate in languages other than their own. In order to empathise with other people it is useful to look at how their language encapsulates and interprets the world.

French as a foreign language is one possible main subject in a four-year (B.Ed) degree course leading to qualified teacher status at Westminster College, Oxford, in England. The course is a language and culture course with aspirations to encourage a global perspective. Students are encouraged to explore human rights issues for themselves. It prepares for and benefits from student mobility within the European funded ERASMUS exchange programme. Can such a course be effective in preparing future teachers to be supportive of the fundamental European values of 'liberty, democracy and respect for human rights'? (European Communities-Council, 1992)

A French language and culture course for future primary school teachers

It is still rare for primary school teachers to have experience of teaching or learning a foreign language as a component of their training. Even in cases, such as Spain, where 'foreign languages and its didactics' is a part of the core curriculum for initial teacher education, the time devoted to it — 40 hours out of 440 university-based hours and 320 hours in school — is not sufficient to ensure that it is perceived by the students as a priority (Sander, 1994: 362).

In Britain a substantial programme of teaching French in primary schools existed in the late sixties and early seventies. The programme was not able to cover all schools, however, and it was considered expensive. Once the political hurdle of British entry into the European Community had been passed, the UK Government and Local Educational Authorities, having other concerns such as the expansion of secondary education and the evolution of a comprehensive school system, used the excuse of an ambivalent research report to cut funding and this scheme withered away almost entirely (Burstall, 1974).

The demise of the scheme reduced the need for the training of foreign language specialists for the primary school. Westminster College, Oxford, was one of only three institutions of teacher training in England providing specialist training in a foreign language for primary school teachers. This particular Bachelor of Education course, which leads to qualified teacher status after four years full time study, is unique in that students concentrate for two years almost exclusively on subject study (French) followed by two years intensive introduction to pedagogy and the teaching profession including blocks of school experience.

The course has evolved over more than ten years, though its current form dates from 1987. It was designed by a team of three university teachers all of whom had previously taught in schools. The subject study element of the course is a full-time two-year, four-semester, programme with about ten hours a week of formal courses in French (360 hours a year). The student spends the third semester as an exchange student at a university in France or French-speaking Belgium and the entire programme of the first year is designed to prepare students for this experience of living and studying abroad. The fourth semester is able to build on knowledge and language skills acquired during the exchange. The course is based on the immersion principle, so that all teaching is conducted in French and all assignments written or presented in French.

This two year element of the course aims to enable students to:

- Achieve a high level of communicative competence in French, sufficient for them to be able to operate at university level in France. They should be able to converse fluently, understand speech including radio and television, read for information and enjoyment and write accurately; all this in a variety of language styles

- Develop their self-confidence, their ability to work alone and with others and their skills of enquiry and research. Travel, residence and work abroad are key elements in this process

- Understand and empathise with the traditions, culture, procedures and civilisation of France and the French-speaking world

- Develop sensitive intercultural skills appropriate to life in a pluralistic and multicultural Europe

- Be informed about modern and contemporary France and its place in Europe and the world. Students should encounter a variety of per-spectives and learn to use a number of frames of reference (historical, sociological, political, semiological etc) to analyse French society and its cultural and media products

- Enjoy their encounter with literary, cultural and media products and ac-quire the skills of synthesis and analysis necessary for a critical understanding and appreciation of them.

The course is presented in three components: language, popular culture and civilisation. The language courses include grammar, translation, creative writ-ing, conversation and comprehension of the spoken language. They aim primarily to enhance students' communication skills, but they also provide opportunities for introducing content of relevance to the rest of the course. For example, second year students work on videos of a case-study of the French judi-cial system and the current situation in Algeria. In both years students translate texts concerning current social issues such as racism, housing and welfare benefits.

The popular culture course covers television, films, songs and graphic novels as well as examples of recent and contemporary literature, poetry and theatre. Popular culture implies elements of the culture of the twentieth century that provide shared meanings for ordinary people. This could be described as a demo-cratic view of culture, as opposed to a notional high culture. This range of cultural references is likely to be important in helping students to understand everyday conversation and television. It is also a recognition of the contribution of French academics such as Barthes to ways of studying and analysing contemporary cul-tural products. Students learn to use some of the tools of, for instance, semiology and psycho-analysis. The learning is, where possible, active. In particular the television course includes making programmes as well as analysing them. An understanding of production of media products is fundamental to making critical judgements about the media. This is a very important part of learning for a demo-cratic society.

Further work on the media is undertaken in the *civilisation* part of the course. In both the first and the second year there is an emphasis on understanding the news as conveyed on television and in the press. Access to French television through a satellite link has enabled this course to become more and more up to the minute. A substantial part of the second year course covers French daily newspapers.

The other part of the civilisation course is a seventy-two-hour historical survey course taking human rights as the linking concept. French historians such as Winock (1988) see French history since the 1789 Revolution as a struggle between two cultures, one wedded to the universal values of human rights and the other nationalistic and hierarchical. Reflecting this analysis, the first term of the course is spent studying the Revolution and the values inherited from the first French constitutions. The Declaration of the Rights of Man and of the Citizen of 1789 is studied in detail and the opportunity is then taken to learn about human rights texts of the twentieth century, their origins and status.

Students are required to undertake a major piece of research during their first semester. They present their findings, in French, to their tutors and the other students and they are assessed for their standard of presentation, including use of visual aids, rapport with the audience and spontaneity of speech. They are free to develop any topic they have touched on in their course, but they are required to make specific reference to human rights. Presentations have included history of the press, slavery in the French colonies, AIDS, the Occupation, the political far right, women's rights. Students soon realise that the human rights perspective is not a constraint, as any topic has a human rights angle when they start to think about it. As one student put it:

> Human rights can be linked to any subject which involves people, so the main difficulty we had was deciding which subject to choose.

The course focuses on historical moments when the conflict between those favouring human rights and those favouring order at any price became acute. The Dreyfus Affair of 1894-1906, the First World War, the Popular Front of 1936, the Occupation and the Resistance, decolonisation and the Algerian war, the Constitution of the Fifth Republic, May 1968 and the Mitterrand years are all studied and illustrated with newsreel footage or reconstructions and the study of authentic documents of the time.

The first semester of the second year of the course is spent at a partner university in France. Students follow courses from those on general offer at their host university and they undertake a major research project in which they investigate some aspect of social, civil or political life in the city where they are staying. Many students take the opportunity to interview civic leaders and explore issues in their host community such as: provision of public facilities; access for people with disabilities; waste re-cycling; policing; schools; local experience of the Nazi occupation; public transport; local pressure groups.

The final semester of this part of the course is spent in Oxford and students pick up the three strands of their course. At this stage they take African literature in French, television, film and a course on current affairs, with particular emphasis on the press.

Although developed independently, the content and aims of the course coincide closely with those proposed by Byram in his seminal model for what he calls 'language-and-culture' which covers the same semantic field as the German notion of *Landeskunde* and French *civilisation*. For instance he includes in his definition the following elements, which are present in our course:

> learners need to engage actively with alternative interpretations of the world, meeting phenomena which express some of the shared meanings of the foreign culture and which they can compare and contrast with their own.

> learners need to have access to and analyse the complex values and meanings of a national culture and other cultures existing within national and state boundaries, some of which are manifest in cultural institutions and artefacts — for example, literature, film, history, political parties, social welfare, education — others being ephemeral and in the process of becoming part of a shared reality (Byram, 1993:50).

In his view, learning about language-and-culture should develop intercultural competence with the following outcomes:

> lack of ethnocentrism, cognitive flexibility, behavioural flexibility, cultural knowledge, interpersonal sensitivity, communication skills.

He maintains:

> foreign language and culture learning has the potential to develop those characteristics. It is thus feasible to see language and culture learning as a significant — perhaps the significant locus for education for international citizenship (Byram 1993:180).

He is rightly aware of the dangers of imposing a particular national or even xenophobic perspective on this selection and proposes that: 'it is the perceptions of insiders about their culture which frame the selection and the perspective from which content is presented' (Byram, 1993:52). Our decision to choose popular as opposed to high culture as a focus for the course reflects our agreement with this principle.

Students and their reactions to the human rights element

Women make up both the majority of primary school teachers in Britain and the majority of those studying languages. It is not surprising that the great majority of students taking this course are women. The College, in common with most British universities, has a low proportion of local students. It receives students from all over Britain, and the French course attracts some native French speakers, in 1994/95 from France, Belgium and Djibouti. Of forty students in the two years of the course, 90 per cent are women, 15 per cent 'mature' students (over 25 years old), 5 per cent from an ethnic minority.

A survey of students' interests, conducted at the end of the academic year in 1995, revealed that a majority contribute money occasionally to an overseas aid charity and half have been actively involved with youth work. 40 per cent have raised funds for a cause. 30 per cent are active members of a church or religious organisation and slightly more of a sports club. None of them is in membership of a pressure group or political party. All participate in elections for students' union officials as well as local and national elections. These future teachers are active and sociable, but not engaged in political issues. They bring to the course very little understanding of politics at any level.

In some respects a human rights discourse is very French. Few of the students have any previous knowledge of the topics covered and they usually bring only the vaguest notion of what the term 'human rights' means. The very strong emphasis on rights in this course might consequently be resented as an unwelcome imposition. Written comments by students at the end of their first semester show this not to be the case.

The students were pleased to have had the opportunity to study human rights and clearly saw the implications for their future as school teachers:

> I think it is very important to teach that everyone is equal in the classroom. I had never seen the principles written down on paper before.

> My knowledge and understanding has been widely extended through this course. I am very pleased to have had the opportunity to learn about human rights. I believe it is important and useful for future teachers to understand what basic rights each human being should be given in order for them to highlight how various problems around the world violate these rights.

> I think we as future teachers need to be aware and pass on the values of human rights. It has been interesting to link the various topics covered to the wider issue of human rights.

In fact the course caused some of them to wonder about the adequacy of their own school education:

l feel it is essential that children are taught about human rights and I feel that the British education system fails badly in this respect. The French are far more aware than the British.

It made me think that British children and students are being disadvantaged by not being given this information sooner.

At this stage, six months into their first year at university, the students seemed to be developing a global perspective based on human rights:

More people throughout Europe and even world-wide should automatically be taught about human rights so fewer people are exploited as more are made aware of their rights and (it is) then more difficult for them to be ignored.

Most of the current news items seem to refer to some form of human rights violation e.g. Chechnia.

Occasionally I notice human rights issues on the news e.g. invasion of privacy and also there have been recent reports of slavery in Britain.

Students' perceptions of the impact of the course

A questionnaire was administered to all students on the course in May 1995. The intention was to explore which aspects of the course had made a major impression on them and whether the course had helped to change their perception of Britain and Europe and their place in the world. Students had either virtually completed their first year, which includes a week's field work in Paris, or were about to reach the end of their fourth semester, their third semester having been spent at a French university.

Students were asked to list three topics they particularly remembered having covered as part of their language work. The most common responses for year 1 were: the political system, elections, education and various social issues. Other students mentioned: rights, Algeria, the Revolution, alcohol, L'abbé Pierre, Paris, other regions and immigration. Second-year students were more aware of the distinction between language courses and the other elements. They almost unanimously cited the French judicial system, which they had studied through accounts of a famous murder case, including a video focusing on irregularities by judicial officials and journalists and other programmes filmed inside magistrates courts. They had found these interesting.

A second question attempted to assess students' understanding of French 'culture'. They were asked to: 'give some examples of what for you are significant aspects of French culture'. First-year students were clearly very impressed with Paris and many of them mentioned buildings, impressionist paintings and cafés. Their view of French culture is very much influenced by their course. They quote singer/ songwriters they had studied: Piaf, Brel, Trenet, Renaud. In literature and culture they mentioned Sartre and Simone Signoret, and graphic fiction. In politics they choose De Gaulle and 'socialism'. Second year students had recently been reminded of Sartre in their translation class and he was mentioned by many of them. Their course includes cinema, and Jean Gabin was frequently cited. Impressionism, literature including French African writing, and gastronomy completed the list.

These responses are not surprising, given the content of the course. They do raise the question of how to represent French culture in a short course. All materials used are authentic, but the emphasis given to these aspects rather than others may be challenged from a variety of political and ideological perspectives. Perhaps it is more significant to ask whether these choices challenge the students' ideas of what constitutes culture.

The third aspect explored by the questionnaire was: 'To what extent has your perception of Britain and what it means to be British changed as a result of the course? Can you give an example?' This question gave students an opportunity to reflect on questions of identity. A substantial percentage of first-year students claimed there had been no change. Of those who did report a change in perception, in almost every case the course appears to have reinforced the students' sense of identity. They mention their patriotism and their pride in their country, as if by choosing to study French they might be perceived as rather disloyal. The following quotations give the flavour of the responses:

> Perhaps it has made me feel more proud to be British yet at the same time through learning various things of the French way of life I have begun to believe in certain aspects that maybe the French have a better way than the British.

> It has made me very aware of how little I know about other European countries, their culture and history. I am proud to be British, but have begun to feel a little 'cut off' from the events in other countries, particularly in understanding the events and the people involved.

> The course has made me think more about the structures and history of Britain and has made me consider why being British is so important. This has come from the study of French politics.

> I think that meeting students from France and comparing different ways of life has mostly changed my perception of Britain.

Interestingly the perceptions of year two students who have lived abroad, are almost identical. These findings confirm those of Coleman (cited by Santinelli, 1994), who concluded from a survey of twelve British universities that after residence abroad students look more favourably on Britain. The Oxford students, too, stress how this experience has reinforced their sense of pride and identity.

I took great pride in presenting Britain to the children in the schools in Belgium. Our presentation was very well received.

I have changed in that I now appreciate many aspects of Britain much more. I am proud to be British.

I didn't realise how different the British are as a nation to the French. I think I prefer the British way of life.

In a few cases there was a clear expression of having acquired a perspective and a wider context.

I feel now that Britain has a part to play in Europe, we are part of a bigger picture.

Undoubtedly the course does cause the students to reflect on their own culture and identity and for some it reinforces their understanding and appreciation of their own culture, whilst others are able to adopt a more critical stance:

Less importance is placed on popular culture in Britain, more on its heritage, preserving the old. Generally Britons are proud of being British, but I think it is more those who have not experienced other cultures.

The fourth question asked students to: 'comment on the extent to which the course has helped you to feel and see yourself as a citizen of Europe'. This is a difficult question for British students, whose thinking is usually influenced by the political controversy surrounding membership of the European Union, as these responses illustrate:

If anything I feel less European as a result of the course because it has made me consider who the other Europeans are. And it has made me realise how much everyone else gains from being European but Britain always loses out.

I don't know if I ever do feel a citizen of Europe as to me Britain will always be an island independent of Europe. For example, when we visited France I still felt as though I was going abroad and not simply to another country in Europe.

However other answers do indicate some movement in attitude:

Definitely felt more European when considering human rights.

Of course with the knowledge of another language and culture, one can have a larger insight into the rest of Europe and the world and feel more included and aware of events.

Being in France and being able to communicate with people made me feel more European rather than an outsider having to speak English

It has made me more aware that I am not only British but also European because we are studying another country and it is apparent that the English and the French are united with other countries as Europeans.

Some second-year students remain resolutely hostile:

I do not see myself as a citizen of Europe. Living in France for a term has shown me that I am very much English or British.

Most, however, acknowledge the influence of the course on their attitudes:

I had never considered myself European until I came here. Now my view has changed and I do feel part of a wider community.

Having learnt a lot about France..and through having stayed in Strasbourg..I feel I know enough to consider myself a European citizen.

I have a better understanding of France in general, so I feel slightly more European.

The questionnaire also attempted to elicit perceptions of the extent to which students have been enabled to see themselves as citizens of the world. The notion of citizenship is also problematic for them. As one first- year bluntly stated:

there has been nothing in this course to make me think about my citizenship either in Europe or in the world.

This was echoed by a second-year:

it hasn't really made me feel any more a citizen of the world than I felt before. I'd rather feel like a citizen of the world than of Europe though.

A number of the first-year students acknowledge the influence of the course, in particular the fact that it has introduced them to politics.

The study of the French colonies has provided a world vision.

Learning about other countries, their history and culture helps to make you realise how things have got to being today due to history not just of our country but due to the world in general.

The political aspect of the course has made me realise the part each citizen plays within the world.

It has made me feel slightly more a citizen of the world with the study of human rights.

Finally the questionnaire asked students: 'What do you feel is the most significant thing you have gained from the course so far?' By far the most common responses were the developing of confidence and increased awareness of diversity. A number of comments suggest that for many students the course is in fact fulfilling its aims:

> An (opportunity) to meet people of different cultures, religion and nationality through exchange programmes... realising how people in another country see world-wide problems.

> That we in Britain are part of a wider community and that we always have to be conscious that what we do here will have repercussions elsewhere.

Given that the majority of students on this course are British and therefore come from a tradition where political education at school level scarcely exists, where there is a strong national tradition of cultural superiority that manifests itself in a xenophobic popular press and where there is no formal constitution or tradition of human rights discourse, the responses of the students may be considered encouraging. These teachers will be self-confident and be able to situate themselves and their work in a European and global context.

The many expressions of patriotism and pride initially surprised and shocked me, but closer analysis shows that these expressions were not at the expense of empathy, and appreciation of other cultures. Rather they are a reaffirmation of a sense of personal identity which may in fact in some senses be a prerequisite for a more open attitude to others. The students voluntarily acknowledge the positive features of their own culture and background. They do not want this identity to be submerged and the course certainly does not intend students to lose their identity. On the contrary, students are given the opportunity to consider adding other identities to those they came to college with. As well as a national identity and their other religious and cultural affiliations, they are starting to see themselves as part of a continental and world society with which they can interact for their own benefit and for the benefit of the wider community.

If the course succeeds in its own terms, do students achieve Byram's goals of: lack of ethnocentrism, cognitive flexibility, behavioural flexibility, cultural knowledge, interpersonal sensitivity, communication skills?

The evidence suggests that if students do not achieve a lack of ethnocentrism, they are at least more aware of the values and attitudes they bring to their encounter with other cultures. They certainly gain cultural knowledge and improved communication skills. Some of them, particularly during their stay abroad, acquire behavioural flexibility. Any course of higher education is likely to encourage cognitive flexibility and this one certainly challenges the students in their thinking. The students engage in a considerable amount of groupwork during their course. To that extent there is inevitably an increase in interpersonal sensitivity. I conclude that these are worthwhile achievements which come about through the structuring of this course.

Discussion

In recent years the priority for linguists has been how to teach languages effectively, rather than with the content of the teaching. On the other hand, some of those concerned with promoting in schools the common European values of social justice, democracy and respect for human rights and the rule of law have largely neglected the teaching of languages as a vehicle for these concerns. In a review chapter highlighting the work of the Council of Europe in teacher education, Newman devotes two paragraphs to modern languages, immediately followed by a section on human rights, equal opportunities and intercultural education', with no suggestion that the two might be linked (Newman, 1994:11).

Baumgratz (1985), makes a useful distinction between two tendencies in international and cross-cultural communication: the *utilitarian or instrumental tendency* focusing for instance on trade or tourism and the *human rights tendency* where respect for human rights and for human dignity are the basis for communication. The former tendency is illustrated by the Council of Europe's programme of language teaching which started from important linguistic research on defining threshold levels of competence (Van Ek and Trim, 1991) and moved to an endorsement of the notion of communicative competence as the aim of language learning (Shiels, 1991). The assumptions in this programme, which has been very influential in Britain, were initially more to do with tourism and trade than with intercultural understanding.

The human rights tendency has attracted increasing interest in recent years and it is through developing this strand that an important contribution can be made to citizenship education. Amongst others, Doyé argues that:

> There exists today a widespread consensus concerning the justification of the demand that foreign language teaching should not just be limited to competence in understanding and using other languages, but that, in addition or closely linked to this, foreign language teaching should include know- ledge about the culture from which the language arises, and attitudes towards members of the culture (Doyé, 1993).

The 1985 Recommendation of the Committee of Ministers of Education of the Council of Europe on 'Teaching and learning about human rights in schools' suggests that future teachers should: 'have the chance of studying or working in a foreign country or a different environment', whilst not explicitly suggesting that learning a foreign language would be a helpful preparation for such a study period (Starkey, 1991:259).

The 'Kiev Declaration' of the 1987 UNESCO LINGUAPAX seminar which brought together the major world federations of language teachers to discuss 'The Content and Methods of Teaching Foreign Languages and Literature for

Peace and International Understanding' goes considerably further in recommending that language teachers should:

- be aware of their responsibility in furthering international understanding through their teaching

- increase language teaching effectiveness so as to enhance mutual respect, peaceful coexistence and co-operation amongst nations

- exploit extra-curricular activities to develop international understanding

- lay the basis for international co-operation through classroom co-operation using language teaching responsive to students' interests and needs (Cates, 1990)

Foreign languages and citizenship education: common objectives and approaches

Doyé identifies three dimensions to language and culture education where it becomes political education; namely the cognitive, evaluative and conative:

> These lead to the acquisition of concepts and knowledge (cognitive), the clarification of values and the transmission of a capacity for political judgement (evaluative) and the teaching of the capacity and will to become politically engaged (conative/action orientation) (Byram, 1993:178).

Whilst these dimensions are present on the course, our interpretation of the term 'conative' does not go as far as Doyé's. Action orientation is one thing, the will to political engagement is another. The course provides many opportunities for acting on knowledge and values, including presenting them to others and indeed living them out during the period of residence abroad. However, students on our course fail to become 'politically engaged' but this is a higher education course and if the students become politically aware, they can become politically engaged.

To this extent the course is not one of political education so much as citizenship education along the model proposed by Lynch. His framework is summarised as follows:

> Three *levels* of personal consciousness and social participation: *local, national, international*

> Four *domains* *social, cultural, environmental, economic*

> Three *objectives* *cognitive, affective, conative*

> Two international *dimensions* *human rights, social responsibilities*

> Professionals should be able to enhance their professional practice at *systemic, institutional and individual* levels (Lynch, 1994:2,3).

All of these elements can be mapped onto the course. The experience over the two years provides a grounding in the human rights values that enable people to approach others with respect for their dignity and the equality of their rights. It introduces students to political structures and discourse as well as to the underlying principles of democracy. In studying a foreign culture in its dynamic form and in its complexity students receive a basis for intercultural under- stand- ing which they have an opportunity to test during their period of residence abroad. Their communication skills and self-confidence improve. As with any course, its impact will vary depending, amongst other things, on the experiences and values students bring to the course. As some make clear, they find it difficult to add a European identity to their other identities — particularly their national identity. All, however, recognise the value of studying human rights. As teachers they will at least be able to develop their own and their pupils' understanding of 'liberty, democracy and respect for human rights'.

References

Baumgratz, G. (1985) 'Transnational and cross-cultural communication as negotiation of meaning' in Sixt, D. *Comprehension as negotiation of meaning*. Munich: Goethe Institut.

Beernaert, Y., Van Dijk, H., and Sander, T. (1993) *The European dimension in teacher education*. Brussels ATEE.

Burstall, C. (1974) *Primary French in the Balance*. Slough: NFER

Byram, M. (1989) *Cultural Studies in Foreign Language Education*. Clevedon: Multilingual Matters.

Byram, M. and Morgan, C.(1994), *Teaching-and-Learning Language and Culture*. Clevedon: Multilingual matters.

Cates, K. (1990) 'Teaching for a better world', in *The Language Teacher,* Vol 14:5 May 1990 Kyoto: JALT

Doyé, P. (1993) 'Neurere Konzepte der Fremdsprachenerziehung' in Byram, M. *Germany: its representation in textbooks*. Frankfurt aM: Diesterweg.

European Communities — Council (1992) *Treaty on European Union*. Luxembourg: Office for Official Publications of the European Communities

Lynch, J. (1992) *Education for citizenship in a multicultural society,*. London: Cassell.

Newman, S. (1994) 'The Council of Europe and Teacher Education', in Galton, M. and Moon, B. *Handbook of teacher training in Europe*. London: Fulton

Sander, T. (1994) *Current changes and challenges in European teacher education*. Brussels: ATEE.

Santinelli, P. (1994) 'Travel narrows the mind', Times Higher Education Supplement (1141) 16 September.

Shiels, J. (1991), *Communication in the modern languages classroom*. Strasbourg: Council of Europe.

Starkey, H. (1988) 'Foreign languages and global education' in Pike, G. and Selby, D. *Global teacher, global learner*. London: Hodder and Stoughton.

Starkey, H. (1991), The Challenge of Human Rights Education. London: Cassell.

Van Ek, J.A. and Trim, J.L.M. (1991) *Threshold level 1990*. Strasbourg: Council of Europe.

Winock, M. (1988) *La fièvre hexagonale*. Paris: Seuil.

Chapter 11

Developing Citizenship Education Programmes in Latvia

Nick Clough, Ian Menter and Jane Tarr

Introduction

Latvia declared its independence from the Soviet Union officially on 4 May 1990 and consolidated this status following demonstrations in Riga during January and August 1991. A degree of economic autonomy had been sanctioned since 1989 as in Lithuania and Estonia (Lieven, 1994), but the final achievement of the status of an independent republic marked the beginning of formidable challenges in the political, economic, social and cultural spheres. Of central concern has been the development of an education system in which students:

> will be prepared for life in a democratic society and will be able actively to provide the progress and development of their society (Education Act, June 1991).

The challenges to democracy have been distinctive in Latvia and include a continuing presence by the Russian army (officially until August 1994), the residence of significant populations of ethnic Russians (30 per cent of the population) (Apgads 'Jana seta', 1995), and the various effects of 50 years of continuous occupation by the Soviet regime which has bequeathed a damaged, damaging and ineffective industrial infrastructure, dependent on raw materials of which many are no longer available. Moreover, long historical experience of Soviet propaganda and ideology have left many sceptical and cautious about involvement in the political sphere and anxious about the slender majority status (57 per cent) of ethnic Latvians within the new republic (Apgads 'Jana seta', 1995).

Such is the broad context within which a European Union TEMPUS programme was established to support activity in Higher Education Establishments providing teacher education in Latvia. The programme is coordinated through the Danish teacher training college, Danmarks Laererhojskole, in Odense with support from the Faculty of Education, University of the West of England, Bristol (UWE). The focus of the work is the 'Updating of Teacher Training and Educational Debate in Latvia' to complement the ongoing constitutional reforms following independence. These include changes in citizenship law and language law as well as modifications of education law. The 3 year programme supports the development of educational management procedures, pedagogy and aspects of the curriculum within a democratic framework. The curriculum work relates to a cluster of themes, including mother tongue teaching, environmental studies, civics / history, and English teaching.

The purpose of this chapter is to present a reflective account of the work of the civics/history subject group with which we have been working. Before offering our account however, we need to say something about the significance of the attachment of the adjective 'reflective'. We understand it to mean a process in which we experience the dynamic relationship between self, society and the processes of teaching and learning. The term is commonplace now in the western educational world, even if it is not universally endorsed. But we have found that it has taken on even greater significance in this work. There are three major reasons for this. First, the context in which the work has been progressing has been changing incredibly fast. At both national and local level, institutional restructuring, the redeployment of individual professionals and the enactment of new laws on citizenship and trade are just a few examples of the transformations which have been going on. Second, as we shall see in what follows there is a major question about the nature of citizenship in Latvia. At one level this is a legal question, but at another everyday level, the question of what it is to be Latvian has no simple answer. Third, the three of us, coming from political positions which include elements of socialism and of non-absolutism, have sometimes found contradictions between our desire to respect locally determined goals and our opposition to the wholesale acceptance of a free market ideology. The fast expansion of market economies has begun to bring about a form of societal integration through monetary systems, but as Habermas states:

> this *system integration* competes with another form of integration running through the consciousness of those involved, that is *social integration* through values, norms and processes of reaching understanding. As a consequence the relation between capitalism and democracy is fraught with tension (Habermas 1994: 28).

It may be noted that one underlying intention of TEMPUS funding from the European Union is to bring about economic harmonisation between Western Europe and the countries of Central and Eastern Europe.

We have learnt a great deal from the experience of working in Latvia We have had continuously to develop our own thinking throughout the programme. We hope therefore that this account can be read as an attempt to make sense of a situation in which our perceptions and understandings are continuing to change.

The civics/history group

Our working group within the TEMPUS project is known as the civics/history subject group. It consists of lecturers from six higher education institutions as well as officials of the Ministry of Education and members of non-governmental organisations (NGOs). The team from UWE is made up of the three of us from the Faculty of Education, together with two colleagues, one from the Law Faculty, the other an historian. The work of this project team was coordinated through a key staff member at the University of Latvia.

Teacher training in Latvia has been undergoing rapid restructuring during the last few years. Currently all teachers are trained within the Higher Education sector, although there is still a variety of institutions ranging from Teacher Training Institutes through Pedagogical Higher Schools and a Teacher Training Academy to the Pedagogical Faculty of the University of Latvia. The programme of study lasts at least four years and has a subject specialism component which is greater for secondary than for elementary schools. Students spend about 7-11 weeks undertaking school experience. The curriculum consists mainly of subject study, with elements of didactics and some psychology but little else that could be described as education studies. However, the subjects studied frequently include philosophy and related disciplines. It is within these elements that students are introduced to political and sociological concepts. Thus, even though 'civics' or citizenship education has little or no status in schools or in the teacher training curriculum as such, some of the key concepts are made accessible to students. During Soviet times all curricula included a form of civics education and so the idea of such a subject is still readily accepted so long as the content is very different from what was previously experienced.

A central issue facing the group, is the tension between the need to disseminate information about democratic frameworks (in Latvia and abroad) and the need to develop an appropriate pedagogy.

Agreement was reached about the overall aims of the civics / history subject group during the first of three sessions in the academic year of 1994/95. These comprised intentions to:

• start from the current practices of teachers to extend and develop work in the field of citizenship;

- promote a collaborative approach within teacher training institutions involving faculties of law, political science and philosophy as appropriate, as well as pedagogical faculties;

- encourage the development of teaching and learning materials for use by students of education, by lecturers in the teacher training institutions;

- establish a network of ongoing communication within and between the institutions involved and, where possible, with other groups in Europe;

- establish an evaluation process for the learning materials and the developing programme.

Establishing a communication network for the group itself was a challenge. To facilitate communication between the six higher education institutions we set up regular consultations by the UWE project team in each institution, complemented by a series of associated conferences held in a central venue in Riga. During one academic year (1994/95) three sessions (each comprising consultations and a conference) were organised.

The wide range of subject disciplines required some clarification of the conceptual base of the discussions and developments. Of central concern was the interpretaton of the terms citizenship, rights and responsibilities in a developing democracy and expanding free market economy. The ideas which we introduced sought to emphasise the significance of the political, social, cultural and economic spheres in educational debate (drawing on sources such as Lynch, 1992). The interaction between these spheres in the case of the Republic of Latvia is particularly complex.

A changing context for citizenship in Latvia

The national identity of Latvia has a long history and was formed under conditions which have rarely been static. The history of people in this region is one of interaction with each other and with their neighbours in a way which is certainly characteristic of other parts of mainland Europe (Hiden and Salmon, 1991). Latvia as a nation state emerged in independent form in 1918 as both Russian and German empires crumbled. There were then some twenty years of independent existence before the notorious deal between Molotov and von Ribbentrop in 1939.

For the next fifty years Latvia was a dependent nation (Misiunas and Taagepera, 1993). There was a brief but devastating period of German Nazi occupation during the second world war. Thousands of Jews were murdered and this formerly significant part of the Latvian population was reduced to a fraction of its earlier size. Following the war, along with its two Baltic neighbours, Latvia became a republic within the USSR. It thus became a part of a major economic system enforced by a regime whose oppressive policies inflicted widespread fear and suffering which will be remembered through generations to come.

During the years of Soviet occupation the demography of Latvia changed quite dramatically. The economic and military strategic importance of the Baltic nations and particularly Latvia with its ports at Liepaja and Riga, meant that there was a large influx of Russian peoples. The development of heavy industry was notable during this period, with raw materials being imported from other Soviet republics for processing and manufacturing within Latvia. Labour was available (and if it was not it could be imported) and the coastal location facilitated export of the products.

By 1989 the Russian speaking population, which included people of various ethnic origins, had reached around 44 per cent. The detailed ethnic composition at various points over the last century is given in Table 1. The Russian speakers were concentrated in the towns and cities. In Riga the proportion of Russian speakers was more than 60 per cent and it reached 87 per cent in the border city of Daugavpils.

Table 1: Ethnic composition of Latvian population by percentage						
	1897	1920	1939	1959	1979	1989
Latvians	68.3	74.4	75.5	62.0	53.7	52
Russians	12	10.2	10.6	26.6	32.8	34
Germans	6.2	3.8	3.2	0.1	0.1	0.1
Jews			4.8	1.8	1.1	0.9
Poles			2.5	2.9	2.5	2.3
Ukrainians/ Byelorussians			1.4	4.3	7.2	8.0
Lithuanians			1.2	1.5	1.5	1.3
(Source: Lieven, 1994: 433)						

There is evidence that ethnicity was not a bar to involvement in the struggle for independence from the Soviet Union. Early protest and resistance was focused on ecological matters (e.g. a proposed hydroelectric scheme at Plavinas) which were affecting all citizens (Misiunas and Taagepera, 1993). In the elections of 1990 over two-thirds of candidates elected to the Latvian Supreme Soviet were supporters of Latvian independence. This large majority indicated that a considerable number of the pro-independence voters were non-Latvian (Lieven, 1994).

The continued presence of the Russian army after independence was, however, a significant cause of tension. Withdrawal of Russian troops was not finally achieved until the summer of 1994 and not without considerable internal and external pressure. The main reason given from Moscow for the delay was that the Russian minority needed protection in a new liberal context where nationalism was on the increase. The effects of the eventual withdrawal were themselves not entirely positive as there is a residue of environmental pollution (for example in the naval base at Liepaja and in other nuclear military installations) and a continuing suspicion that some key military personnel are still present together with others who are in the employ of Moscow's military factions. Such is the difficult backcloth against which discussions about the rights of the Russian minorities in Latvia are being held.

Such a confusion of internal and foreign policy has been common during the processes of decolonisation in other parts of the world. In Latvia the fear of 'Sovietisation' has been replaced by the fear of a form of 'Russification'. The effect has been to hamper Latvian attempts to resolve fundamental citizenship issues and to leave the government open to criticism from those in the West who arguably have their own political agenda to pursue, for example, the expansion of the free market economy in Latvia. After a recent visit, George Soros, the billionaire financier and benefactor of Eastern and Central Europe, has also been critical of the treatment of the Russian minority in Latvia, who are only eligible for full citizenship rights if they can prove continuous residence since before 1940. Russians are also denied some employment rights (for example, non-citizens cannot become police officers or firefighters or lawyers or prosecutors nor can they own drugstores) and the naturalisation process for prospective citizens involves language, history and loyalty tests (Freibergs, 1995). The Language Law has determined that Latvian is now the official national language and although separate schools continue to exist for Russian and Latvian children, the Russian language (as a medium of instruction) is being expunged from higher education.

The advent of the free market is visible on the streets of Riga where advertisements carry the top brand names of Western markets. Simultaneoulsy unofficial liberal market activities have brought large profits to some working in protection rackets while the opening of borders has facilitated links with western criminal associations (Lieven, 1994). All this commercial activity has been accompanied by rising levels of prostitution (Parsla, 1995).

The inability of the government to impose controls on such 'liberal' market activity has resulted in a loss of revenue and an exacerbation of the difficulty of funding public services like health and education (Vitkovskis, 1994). One teacher training establishment has proposed that trainees are first provided with qualifications in the use of the English language and computer skills so that they can supplement their poor level of pay as teachers with a second employment.

The pressures on the low paid are increasing with the rising costs of housing and fuel.

The cultural sphere in Latvia itself reflects some of the changes and contradictions described above. There is a long tradition and acceptance of different Baltic groups within Latvia, as exemplified in the Monument to Freedom in Riga (erected in 1935) in which three stars representing the regions of Latvia are being held aloft, supreme and secure. Outside of Riga our own experience has been within the Latgale region (Daugavpils and Rezekne) where a separate language (Latgalian) is often spoken as a first language and in Kurzeme, where an original cultural group, the Livs, are currently in danger of losing theirs. During occupation song festivals continued to be a significant expression of cultural identity but political independence has given a new energy to cultural activity. Some of this activity is linked to new expressions of spirituality following the suppression of the years of occupation. Lutheran, Catholic and Russian Orthodox churches are being reclaimed as places of worship, having served recently as performance spaces and even boxing arenas. Jewish community organisations are also in evidence, for example in Daugavpils. There is also a re-discovery of ancient traditional Latvian spiritual culture (Beitnere, 1994). Involvement in the free market and wider access to European and American media culture is, however, impacting on these cultural trends.

Developing perspectives on civics and citizenship education in teacher education

Such political, economic and cultural changes have raised many questions for the work of the civics/history group. We have seen how the redefining of what it is to be Latvian, in legal, social and cultural terms has been a continuous process during the recent period.

During the first conference in Riga we interviewed members of the group and used a questionnaire with them to establish their views on citizenship and citizenship education in Latvia. We made use of the three categories of citizenship identified by T.H. Marshall (1950) modelled on the legal classification of basic rights: the civil, political and social.

A majority of the returns indicated that it was political elements of citizenship which were currently giving rise to greatest concern in Latvia. Civil citizenship was also of concern to some. One respondent wrote:

> Unfortunately the question about Latvian citizenship has not been completely solved and this circumstance outshines all the rest.

We asked about how particular features of the education system, bilingual schools, separate schools for Russian and Latvian speakers or selection into higher education would in their opinion contribute to citizenship education in Latvia. Their responses indicated that, at this time, ways of achieving an integrated and united society were not being sought nor was schooling seen as an integrative force, but rather as a force for helping to establish distinct ethnic identities.

When asked about the balance between rights and duties (respon- sibilities), the majority of respondents argued for equal attention to both. However those that held a different view argued that duties were more important because of the need to form a firm and stable foundation for the newly independent nation. Written comments included:

> It is the period of development of a post-socialist country and it needs wide and stable activity of people in daily life;

Another question during the first session of the programme was about the work related to civics/history in teacher education which was already in place. We heard reports not only from historians but also from sociologists, philosophers, geographers, biologists and sports educators and it was clear that the description 'civics / history subject group' was not sufficiently inclusive. For this reason we began to call the group the 'Civics Subject Group' and described the focus of the work as 'Citizenship Education in Teacher Education'.

It was recognised that there was opportunity for different perspectives to be developed on citizenship education in teacher education from these different subject specialisms. The historians, free of the controls of the Soviet system, were able to promote awareness of democratic systems and threats to these in different times and places. A particular challenge was the lack of information and textbooks about the country's history. This had placed pressure upon teachers to research and develop their own materials about the history of Latvia.

Sociologists were already contributing to the work through a research programme on the relationship between pupils and their teachers and in particular about the changing expectations of pupils of their schooling in the new democracy. Philosophers were able to offer students assistance in developing critical awareness of citizenship issues. It was anticipated that courses on the history of philosophy and thought might emphasise the limitations of absolutist approaches. This was seen as relevant to the experience of a pluralist society emerging from totalitarianism. Geographers were excited by the new freedom to explore human geography and anticipated that local studies could provide information about environmental issues which citizens of the future need to understand. The work of biologists was seen as being relevant to such work. They had developed an Environmental Education Centre in the Latgale region. Sports educators were emerging from a context in which the emphasis had been on the excellence of performance (for example in preparation for Olympic Games) and were moving to include a new focus on sports for all. This was raising questions about ability and disability.

The historians in the group expressed a strong interest in establishing contacts with historians in the UK to overcome their isolation from information about other cultures, their historical development and their legal systems. Our historian colleague from UWE presented a historical perspective on citizenship and nationality describing experiences in France, the United States of America, the Italian Republic under Mazzini, the Hungarian Republic under Kossuth and the Independent State of Croatia under Pavelic. These accounts raised issues about the relationship between nationality and the state and about language policy, ethnicity and citizenship. This session was complemented by a legal perspective presented by a law lecturer from UWE. He offered an analysis of the current situation in the United Kingdom where citizenship can be acquired through birth or legal adoption, descent, registration or naturalisation. The group valued such access to wider historical and European perspectives on the development and application of citizenship.

As themes emerged in discussion, we described the relevance of the issue to education in the UK and asked the group to compare it with Latvia. There were often linguistic challenges to this process and it was clear that new words were being formulated as equivalent to such terms as: sustainability, assimilation, pluralism and commitment.

One specific aim was to encourage discussion of current reality in Latvia but also to consider a vision of the kind of society and education system they would like. Seminar topics included:

- Frameworks within teacher education;
- Professional competence in relation to citizenship education (Clough and Holden, forthcoming);
- Gender, rights and society;
- Culture, identity, religion and human rights: which way forward in education?
- Children with learning difficulties: a question of educational entitlement;
- Environments, markets and sustainability; what futures from education?

The session on 'Gender, rights and society' provides an interesting example of the work of the group. The complexity of this issue in Latvia had been noted by the UWE team on their first visit (Clough and Menter, 1995). Further discussion emerged because one member of the group described her experience of a conference on the position of women in Latvia and distributed a report put together for the United Nations Fourth Conference on Women (Parsla, 1995).

The UWE team had earlier noticed a general tentativeness within the group in raising questions about human rights because of the complexity surrounding the rights of the Russian minority group. The conference report raised profound questions about the rights of women which we amplified in the seminar session by providing information about the position of women in the UK. A group of participants connected strongly with the issues and worked together to produce the account presented overleaf.

GENDER, RIGHTS AND SOCIETY

Problems: a description of the problems in Latvia

- equality exists *de jure* and not *de facto*
- women are employed in less well paid jobs (teachers and doctors etc.) though they often have a higher level of education
- traditional division of duties and responsibilities leaves men as chiefs and women as deputies; the upbringing of children is not democratic

Background: an account of the background and causes of the problems / challenges in Latvia

- there is a tradition that Latvian women are good organisers of the home
- the ideology of socialism distorted understanding of equality issues as it did not encourage women to think for themselves
- a decrease in the role of the family has left greater responsibilities for women
- the low pay for women's work has created poverty for women
- women have been passive and inert

Values: a vision of the ideal situation which would exist in the absence of the problems in Latvia

- more participation by women in decision making at all levels
- the achievement of real freedom of choice for women between being a worker or carer in the house / family
- the achievement of a fair division of duties (with support from the state)
- improvement and modernisation of conditions at home and accessibility of services

Action: a set of behaviours whose purpose is to remove, solve and manage the problems in Latvia

- democratisation of public opinion in equality questions

- activisation of non-governmental organisations to support the cause of women

- the stimulation of every citizen's activity and the encouragement real actions and of the formulation and defence of opinions

- involvement in the international women's movement, exchange of information and acquiring of skills

- the stimulation of every citizen's activity and the encouragement of real actions and the formulation and defence of opinions

- involvement in the international women's movement, exchange of information and acquiring of skills.

Towards a pedagogy for democratic citizenship

The example above of the work of the civics/history subject group displays a discourse which reflects changes in the political, economic, social and cultural spheres and which is possibly capable of stimulating further shifts in thought and action. This is the process of reflective pedagogy to which we have already referred, which involves experiencing the dynamic relationship between self, society and the processes of teaching and learning. Schon (1987) describes this process as 'reflection-in-action' which is a good description of our own attempts to make sense of familiar issues within the new and different context of Latvia The professional attributes which are required in this kind of activity have been described by John Dewey (as cited by Pollard and Tann, 1993) as open-mindedness, wholeheartedness and responsibility. We saw evidence of these qualities in the positions that were developed within the civics subject group. For example a statement made by another discussion group included these recommendations for citizenship education:

> We should aim to promote tolerance and acceptance of otherness (eg national, religious), overcome the experience of isolation, create a context within which many different cultures can flourish and create a spiritually educated society.

They added these significant points:

- It is important that young Latvian children continue to be able to communicate in Russian as this is a first language for many in Latvia.

- Latvian folklore plays an important role in bringing people together. On its own it does not encourage critical thinking.

An important feature of the sessions during 1994/1995 were the regular opportunities for members of the group to report on activities related to citizenship education. Through sharing experiences across such a range of subjects it was possible to compile a broad picture of the development of citizenship education practice in universities and schools.

Examples of activities in schools

- The standard course 'Man, Nature and Society' is being modified in a school in Valka, on the Estonian border, to take account of the plural nature of the community in that city (part Estonian, part Latvian).

- The Center for the Advancement of Democracy (a non- governmental organisation based in Riga) has developed materials for use in upper and middle secondary schools. The materials for middle secondary will be introduced to all schools in the Autumn. These materials have been tested already and there have been reports made of particular lessons, including an activity about 'a day without laws', about 'different approaches to setting the state budget' and about 'possible and preferable futures for the school'.

- Materials for younger pupils have been developed (Es Pasaule) and are now available for use in schools. A series for middle primary aged children is being prepared.

- Many schools have introduced a school council in which pupils' interests are represented by elected pupils.

Examples of activities in universities

- Research into the attitudes towards and of the Russian minority community during the 1920s/1930s.

- Research on civics education programmes devised during the first Latvian Republic in the 1920s/30s. This indicates a greater emphasis on responsibilities and duties of citizens to the state at the expense of issues of rights and social justice.

- The development of a critical course about the Soviet system in the Russian language for Russians.

- Continuing research into the history of the Latgalian people.

- The development of a course on human rights in Latvia to be included in the Bachelor's Degree programme for Political Science.

- The inclusion of the theme of 'freedom' by a philosopher in her inservice work with teachers.

- The development of an inter-disciplinary 'Curriculum for Civics' which will be taught next academic year in higher education institutions in Riga.

- The independent study by a group of students of a certificated course called 'The Peoples of the Baltic Project'.

- Research into the attitudes of students in conflict resolution situations.

- The beginning of an exploration of citizenship issues through the visual arts, music and literature.

- The use of the facilities of the Sports Academy by children with disabilities.

Criteria for evaluating citizenship education programmes

A conclusion to be drawn from the Latvian case study is that citizenship education can best be understood from inter- disciplinary enquiry which is rooted in the everyday experience of society. The issues which are raised are pertinent for universities providing teacher training in other European states though the precise applications will be different in each case. In Britain the challenge is to prepare teachers for professional work in a plural society that is in part a product of inter-class struggle and a colonial past. As in Latvia this training process also involves critical consideration of power relations, rights and responsibilities.

We feel that criteria for judging the success of a citizenship education programme in Latvia or indeed any democratic context should include reference to the values of freedom and security, inclusivity and solidarity which have their roots in *The Declaration of the Rights of Man and of Citizens by the National Assembly of France* (1789) summarised in the values 'liberté', 'égalité and 'fraternité'. However, we feel that freedom and security need to be linked because of the complexity of the term freedom in the context of Latvia particularly within a new liberal market economy. We note that article 4 of the Declaration, reaffirmed as article 29.2 of the Universal Declaration of Human Rights, states:

> Liberty consists in the power of doing whatever does not injure another. The exercise of the natural rights of man has no other limits than those which are necessary to secure to every other man the free exercise of the same rights; such limits may be determined only by law.

Whereas in eighteenth century France the people and nation were considered one entity, Latvia is still composed of Latvians, Russians, Lithuanians and Poles with no agreement on national principles and priorities. The law may be used in an oppressive way and the interests of minorities need protection, hence our insistence on security. Freedom and security can be promoted through intra-group or intra-national activity. The work of the Latgale Research Centre in Daugavpils Pedagogical University or the celebration of literary or arts achievements affirm cultural / group identity without posing a threat to other groups.

We also prefer 'inclusivity' to the term equality which, in the context of Latvia, is a contentious issue. Under article 7 of the Universal Declaration of Human Rights:

> All are equal before the law and are entitled without any discrimination to equal protection of the law.

Although this may be an aim for the democratic government of the Republic of Latvia, it has not yet been achieved for all residents, for example in the case of differentiated employment rights for non-citizen Russians. A citizenship education programme based on 'inclusivity' might at least help to promote inter-group communication. Recognition within the civics subject group of the need for all children to be taught to speak the main languages in the Republic of Latvia (Latvian and Russian) and that our materials should be translated into minority languages have both been expressions of this value.

The third value, 'solidarity', is preferred to the term fraternité, which implies that a 'family' already exists, whereas in Latvia the challenge is one in which different groups must strive together to rebuild society. The links being established between NGOs in Latvia and with other NGOs in the UK and the contacts formed between students in *The Peoples of the Baltic* project have been examples of activity to promote solidarity. The term solidarity also involves building links with other democratic groups, including citizenship educators in other countries. In this respect the term describes the kind of networking that we have been encouraging during the work of the civics subject group.

The purpose of this discussion is to emphasise that terms like liberty, equality and fraternity are necessarily relative to the political, economic, social and cultural context. Like the associated concepts of rights and responsibilities they should be subject to continual debate and research, particularly within those universities which have responsibility for training professionals for work in a democracy.

During our work in Latvia we tried to develop our own understanding of democratic concepts through 'reflection-in-action'. We were cautious in drawing conclusions from our research as teachers because we were aware of:

> the dangers of ethnocentric bias in interpretation of findings combined with the difficulties of establishing cultural and contextual sensitivity where world views and languages used may differ markedly (Crossley and Broadfoot, 1992:107).

Whilst aware of our own inevitable subjectivity, we conclude that the 'open-mindedness', 'responsibility' and 'whole-heartedness' required of reflective practitioners in inter-cultural settings needs to be accompanied by a firm commitment to human rights perspectives in schools, higher education institutions and society. It is only these perspectives that can transcend and thereby unite in a common humanity the potentially divisive influences of language, culture and nation.

Acknowledgements

Many people have been involved in the work reported in this chapter and we are grateful to them all. In particular, the contributions of Lolita Spruge (University of Latvia), Ed Cape and Geoff Swain (UWE, Bristol) have been invaluable.

References

Apgads 'Jana seta' (1995) *Latvija — Nacionalais sastavs (National structure)*. Riga: Jana seta

Beitnere, D. (1994) 'Traditions and modern trends in Latvian spiritual culture', in *Latvia: Baltic State*. Riga.

Clough, N. and Holden C., (1996) Professional competence for the global teacher, in: M. Steiner *Developing the Global Teacher: theory and practice in teacher education*. Stoke-on-Trent: Trentham.

Clough, N. and Menter, I. (1995) 'Towards a philosophy and pedagogy for democratic citizenship' in Tschoumy J.A. (ed) *'Le choc de la democratie'*. ATEE, Lyon.

Crossley, M. and Broadfoot, P. (1992) 'Comparative and international research in education, *British Educational Research Journal*, 18, 2.

National Assembly of France (1789) *Declaration of the Rights of Man and of Citizens.*

Hiden, J. and Salmon, P. (1991) *The Baltic Nations and Europe*. London: Longman.

Freibergs, K. (1995) 'Soros criticises treatment of Russians by Estonia and Latvia',. Baltic Observer, 27 April.

Habermas J (1994) 'Citizenship and National Identity' in van Steenburgen, B. (ed.) *The Condition of Citizenship*. London: Sage Publications.

Lieven, A. (1994) *The Baltic Revolution* (Second edition). London: Yale University.

Lynch, J. (1992) *Education for Citizenship in a Multicultural Society*. London: Cassell.

Marshall T. H. (1950) *Social Class and Citizenship. Cambridge: University Press.*

Misiunas, R. and Taagepera, R. (1993) *The Baltic States — Years of Dependence 1940-1990* (Second edition). London: Hurst.

Parsla E. (1995) *National Report on the Situation of Women*. Riga: The Latvian National Preparatory Committee for the UN Fourth Conference on Women.

Pollard, A. and Tann, S. (1993) *Reflective Teaching in the Primary School* (Second edition). London: Cassell.

Schon, D. (1987) *Educating the Reflective Practitioner*. San Francisco: Jossey-Bass.

Starkey, H. (1991) *The Challenge of Human Rights Education*. London: Cassell.

Vitkovskis R, (1994) 'Economics — the front door and the back yard in Latvia' in *Latvia: Baltic State*: Riga.

PART 3

Children, Citizenship and the School Curriculum

Chapter 12

Children's Understanding of War and International Politics

Jean-Pierre Branchereau

Introduction

The Gulf War, an event heavily covered by the media, created questioning and anxiety in the minds of children as they tried to understand it. A single television channel, CNN, was the source of the news that was broadcast around the world. Because of this controlled globalisation of information (Ferro, 1991), we know that our children, although from different countries, saw the same images used to build a basic geo-political awareness of the Gulf War, with the help of other media, parents, friends and school.

Teachers of history, geography and civics were given a golden opportunity to study how children learn about events by this war. How do children understand war? What information stays in their minds? What knowledge of war do they build up? What images did they construct of the Gulf War?

The aim of this chapter is not therefore to attempt a psycho-social study of how children learn about events but, rather, a pedagogic evaluation of their understanding of events, which they glean by and large from the news.

The research tool used was a questionnaire distributed in two schools in Nantes (one in the town centre, the Villa-Maria school, the other on the outskirts, the La Géraudière school) and two likewise in Montreal and Heidelberg and one in Oxford.

Because it had to be chosen under the pressure of events, our sample was not scientifically selected. It is made up as follows:

France:	56 pupils	(30% of the sample)
Quebec:	56 pupils	(30%)
Germany:	50 pupils	(26%)
United Kingdom:	27 pupils	(15%)
Boys:	99	(53%)
Girls:	90	(47%)

Number from each age group:

8 year olds	5
9	25
10	69
11	36
12	28

(NB Some children did not give their age. Hereafter references to the data will use the following abbreviations: F = France, UK = United Kingdom, Q = Quebec, D = Germany, B = boy, G = girl. Thus FG9 indicates a nine year old French girl.)

The questionnaire was distributed simultaneously to all schools at the end of the Gulf War and colleagues from the various countries were asked to let the pupils respond without attempting to influence their replies. The responses were subsequently analysed using a computer program. This made it possible to take key variables into account and also to consider the way children felt that they had acquired their knowledge. It proved difficult to take socio-professional categories into account, due to the reluctance of certain teachers to ask their pupils to fill in the box marked: 'professions of parents'. One young Quebec pupil replied: 'I'm not allowed to say'.

Children's levels of understanding

The children were asked to give the causes of the war. A large majority of them answered this first question. Indeed, the crossings out show that it was a question they took very seriously. Only some of the nine year olds had difficulty answering and replied 'I don't know'. The same applied to a teacher's son who is 'not allowed to watch war'.

The consistency of the replies of the overwhelming majority of the children is striking. The causes of war are distributed around four axes as follows.

1. Oil

Oil is mentioned as the general cause of the war without further explanation. There is an awareness that the region has oil reserves and it is assumed that the war has something to do with these reserves. Oil is often linked with 'money'.

The war took place because of 'oil and money' (FB9), or because of 'the price of oil' (QB10).

2. Kuwait was invaded for its oil

Answers in this second category establish a link between oil and the invasion of Kuwait. Iraq or Saddam Hussein in person are generally blamed for the war:

He wanted the oil to make himself rich (DG10)

Saddam Hussein and his army invaded Kuwait to get some of the oil money (QB10)

Saddam Hussein invaded Kuwait for money and oil (UKG)

The oil problem is sometimes understood in a more developed way. A young French boy points out that we 'need oil'. Two Quebec pupils stress that 'the USA didn't like that'. Three young Germans give more specific answers:

Bush and Hussein both wanted the oil (DG10)

Bush wanted the oil at any price (DG10)

One day Iraq stopped supplying the USA with oil and then the USA attacked Iraq and took the part with most oil: Kuwait and Iraq (DB10)

Because Saddam Hussein had all the oil and Bush had none and Bush wanted some (DB10)

It is of course quite hard to interpret the fairly anti-American interpretation voiced by some young Germans. The television version must have been the subject of some comment in the family or at school.

In any case, generally speaking, 30 per cent of the pupils from the four countries believe that oil had something to do with the war.

3. Saddam Hussein is personally responsible for the war

A third category of reply blames Saddam Hussein in person and, more specifically, his thirst for conquest, even his greed. He is a usurper. He wanted to be 'king or president of Iraq' (FB10). He is also described as a '*Diktator*'. Adjectives used to describe him are 'jealous', 'envious', 'uncaring' (UK). 'He wanted it all': this phrase occurs in many questionnaires.

4. More highly developed geo-political explanations

At the basic level of this category of response, pupils viewed the issue, as we saw, as the invasion of one country by another. 30 per cent of questionnaires mention the invasion of Kuwait by Iraq as the cause of the war, The terms which recur most often are 'invade' (27 per cent of the questionnaires), 'take', 'seize' (*s'emparer de*) in Quebec, 'occupy' (*besetzen*) in Germany. The terms 'take back' or 'retake' in seven questionnaires from Quebec imply that the Iraqi operation had some legitimacy. We must assume that the issue had been brought up at school, especially considering that two other questionnaires from the same class refer to the '18th province'.

More sophisticated replies bring the interplay of alliances into the picture:

Saddam Hussein invaded Kuwait and so other counties came to liberate it by force. (Saddam lost). There was an ultimatum that they would liberate it by force (FB10)

The Iraqi president was jealous of Kuwait which is a rich oil-producing country. Iraq invaded it but the Americans, the French and the English, and the UN gave an ultimatum. On the 17th, the army intervened (FB9)

Because Saddam Hussein wanted to conquer a town but the people did not wish to leave it. So Saddam Hussein decided to kill them. But in the town, there was a group of people who belonged to G. Bush (QGl1)

Finally, at an even more complex level, eight Quebec questionnaires (twelve year olds) refer directly to the access to the sea that Iraq might be seeking:

Iraq was producing oil but could not export it because it had no access to the ocean. Kuwait was near the water so Iraq was ready to devastate everything to be near the ocean (QB11)

At the end of this consideration of the causes of the war, we can conclude that the pupils were substantially informed, giving broadly similar responses which clustered around four main axes, but with very different levels of complexity. What we must now ask is how the pupils' knowledge came to be formed.

Television is the main source of information

The survey does not allow us to analyse with any precision the contribution of the different media to the formation of the geo-political awareness of the pupils. It does however give us an idea of how the pupils themselves felt that they had learned about the Gulf War. The replies were distributed as follows (percentages):

	not at all	a little	a lot
Radio	23	60	17
Newspapers	40	40	20
Television	3	19	78
Parents	23	51	26
Friends	40	55	5
School	36	49	15

(NB Only five pupils said that they never watched television.)

It is therefore from television above all that children felt they obtained their view of events (one child from Quebec even added a column headed 'an enormous amount' feeling that 'a lot' was not strong enough to convey the influence of television). In this case, television means CNN's pictures as filtered by the military information services, above all those of the Americans.

Television is followed by radio and then the press. Television's dominance is is not surprising in the case of nine to twelve year olds. Only 15 per cent of the pupils felt that the war was something that they had studied seriously. School thus surrenders the geo-political education of children to the media, above all television. What, we must then ask ourselves, are the specific features of a geo-political awareness that children build from the small screen?
The questionnaire included the following questions:

- Name the countries where the fighting took place.

- Name the countries which played an important role.

- Name the people who played an important role.

Pupils had an apparently clear awareness of the locations involved

369 replies (82 per cent of the total) are correct as opposed to 78 (18 per cent) which are wrong. This means in fact that the children know the names of the countries where the fighting took place: 89 per cent mention Iraq, 73 per cent Kuwait, 33 per cent Saudi Arabia and 24 per cent Israel, undoubtedly because it was the target of Iraqi missiles. 13 per cent mention Iran, 4 per cent (above all immigrants aware of the Kurdish problem) mention Turkey. The pupils do mention the names of countries, but it is by no means certain that they are able to locate them. As one of them said: 'we know what is going on but we don't know where' (FB11). However, some sketch maps do provide a more or less correct lay-out of the theatre of operations.

The children have a good knowledge of the countries involved in the intervention

When asked about which countries played an important role in the Gulf conflict, 77 per cent of the pupils named the USA, 40 per cent France and 32 per cent the United Kingdom. Too much importance should not be attached to the order in this case due to the uneven sample. The main point is that overall there are 358 correct answers (77 per cent of the responses) as opposed to 105 wrong ones (23 per cent of the responses)

Individual personalities are prominent in the children's vision of international relations

93 per cent of the answers to the question about the most important personalities involved are correct. The results are, in rank order (percentage of pupils mentioning):

Bush	73
Mitterrand	12
Schwarzkopf	11
Major	8
Tarak Aziz	6
Gorbachev	5
Perez de Cuellar	4

The USA is thus correctly perceived by our young Europeans as being the main actor in the intervention in the Gulf. Bearing in mind the make-up of our sample, the order of the remaining personalities is not particularly important. We can however note the prominence of a general with a high media profile and a name that would probably stick in the mind. Perez de Cuellar's audience rating certainly reflects that of the UN in the international community.

The children have an impressive knowledge of the military hardware

The children's arsenal is assembled by 734 responses which is by far the largest number of answers. They are also perhaps the least badly spelt. On average there are three to four weapons per child.

While some children can only name one weapon and others limit themselves to general replies ('planes', 'tanks'), others can list a dozen by their 'technical' name or by that of their manufacturer.

- Scud missiles, Patriot anti-missile missiles, Mirages, F-18s, F-19s, tanks, M-16 (QB11)

- Scud missiles, Patriots, Tomahawks, F-18 fighters, B-52s, gas-masks (QB12)

- Stealth bombers, Jaguar fighters, tanks, Scuds, missiles, Tornadoes, F-15s (UKB)

- Rockets, missiles, Tomahawks, Awacs, F-16s, F-15s, F-117s, Jaguars, Scud missiles (FB9)

- F-117s, F-111s, Scud missiles, Cobra helicopters, Desert Fox, B-52s, Tomahawks, Mirage 2000s, Tornadoes, Republican Guard (FB8)

The social group does not seem to be a determining factor in this case. All social categories assemble impressive groups of weapons. On the other hand, there is a noticeable difference between girls and boys: the boys know a lot more weapons and are more often able to give their 'technical' name.

Number of replies:

	Girls	Boys
aeroplanes	15	35
named types of aeroplanes	15	93
missiles	20	25
named types of missile	31	88
tanks	46	50
chemical bombs	35	25

Interestingly, the helicopter is only mentioned once as a fighting machine. It only appears on one drawing and even then as a means of medical evacuation. Nor do naval forces play a visible role for the children.

Overall, it might seem that the information reproduced by the children is quite substantial. It is however built upon a few simple, indeed simplistic ideas, crystallising around the names of a few people and of some military hardware. Schools played very little role in developing this information in the examples studied. The influence of social factors is hard to discern even if in two specific groups (working class children and children of teachers) we can identify differences to do with where the children locate the events; the teachers' children are more precise. On the whole, however, the responses are fairly homogenous. We will now turn to the influence of nationality which we will look at from the perspective of comparative pedagogy.

National perceptions of the Gulf War

The nationality of the pupils does not seem to be a major factor in replies to questions about the causes of the war or the location of events. It is a factor in questions to do with:

- important personalities
- countries involved in the war
- military hardware

The children put the 'important personalities' from their own country in perspective

The children were asked to name the most important personality. Scores obtained were as follows:

Oxford	Heidelberg	Nantes	Montreal
Bush: 18	S. Hussein: 45	S. Hussein: 38	S. Hussein: 53
Major: 18	Bush: 33	Bush: 34	Bush: 52
S. Hussein: 16	Schwarzkopf: 8	Mitterrand: 21	Schwarzkopf: 7
Tarak Aziz: 4	Kohl: 3	Gorbachev: 2	Tarak Aziz: 7
Schwarzkopf: 3	P. de Cuellar: 2	Major: 2	Gorbachev: 5
Gorbachev: 2	Mitterrand: 1	Schwarzkopf: 2	P. de Cuellar: 5

Two people thus dominate: Bush, the righter of wrongs, and Saddam, the villain of the piece. Political leaders come next in those countries most clearly engaged in the conflict: the United Kingdom and France. General Schwarzkopf, the man in charge of battlefield strategy, figures large in Heidelberg and Quebec. There follows a group of people of lesser importance in the eyes of the children. Perez de Cuellar scores badly due to the low-profile of the UN, faced with an assertion of American power. Gorbachev's score is hit by the absence of his country from international media coverage of events. It might appear surprising that English children should forget Mitterrand while the French omit Major, but the war is really American and Europe only provides supporting troops under their national flags.

The primary role of the USA

The pupils were asked to name the most important country involved in the war. Their replies to this question produce the following ranking:

Heidelberg	Nantes	Montreal	Oxford
USA	France	USA	USA
Iraq	USA	The Allies	UK
France	UK	France	Kuweit
UK	Saudi Arabia	UK	Iraq
Germany	Germany	Iraq	Saudi Arabia
Kuweit	Iraq	Saudi Arabia	France

The primary role of the United States is thus confirmed, except in the case of the French children, but even then, there was only a difference of one between the scores of the two countries. It should be pointed out that many troops from the Nantes region left for the war and that this may have influenced the ranking produced by replies from that area.

The children know their own country's weapons

Replies to the question about weapons vary noticeably from one country to the next:

	Oxford		Heidelberg		Montreal		Nantes	
	Boys	Girls	Boys	Girls	Boys	Girls	Boys	Girls
Planes	3	2	20	0	3	4	6	6
Named planes	21	0	3	0	31	7	36	9
Missiles	1	2	6	3	7	8	8	3
Named missiles	17	6	14	3	28	17	24	9
Tanks	6	8	22	15	5	10	15	13
Machine guns	0	1	15	6	1	8	8	9
Chemical bombs	1	1	15	15	2	12	2	1

The results are hard to interpret. The most one dare do is to venture some observations.

The traditional image of the soldier is of a man with a rifle, a machine gun and a grenade. This image seems to be more evident among young Germans and perhaps more among girls, of whatever nationality.

The French and German children in our sample may have a more classic image of war (involving tanks).

There is a contrast between these classic images of war and other perhaps more contemporary images.

The Heidelberg youngsters mentioned 'chemical bombs' more often than the others, but they were also more sensitive to the position of Israel which found itself threatened by those weapons.

Boys remember the names of missiles and aeroplanes better, perhaps more so in France and in the United Kingdom. Can we make a link between this knowledge of military technology and the fact that these countries export planes and missiles? Are children in these countries already familiar with certain weapons from the news or from games? Such questions cannot be answered but they do lead us on to the issue of children's representations of the Gulf War.

Towards an analysis of children's representations of the Gulf War

The aim of the final set of questions was to find a way into the children's representations of the Gulf War. The children were given the freedom to describe briefly in their own words or draw 'the scene which had stayed the longest in their memory'. The 74 drawings vary widely in size, ranging from vignettes to a full page.

Because of the difficulty of analysing children's drawings, and of deciding what weight to attach to 'sensorial' and 'rational' elements, and also because the simple fact of drawing supposes a reconstruction we simply used the computer programme to enumerate the elements which made up the drawings: desert, town, aeroplane, soldiers, civilians, houses.

Some themes do however recur in many of the 74 drawings or the texts. These include:

The environment

The burning oil wells, the polluted sea and air, sometimes a bird (which we later learned, in the French case at least, was taken from archive footage shot in Brittany).

Exploding Kuwaiti oil wells (FB9)

Burning oil wells (FB11)

When the oil flowed into the Gulf (QBll)

When a bird got both feet stuck in the oil and couldn't fly anymore (FG10)

When Saddam poured oil into the Gulf (QB10)

The sea black with oil (QGll)

When they had some oil wells set alight (QG10)

In Iraq, all the houses have been knocked down, the air is black because the oil wells are on fire (QG12)

I felt that it was a serious matter that we weren't allowed to have pictures except for a few cormorants covered in oil which already gave a miserable impression. It means that it was all worse than that. (DG10)

Six drawings out of 74 show burning oil wells and blackened air ...

Death and suffering: generally seen affecting the allies

When the Iraqis fire missiles at civilians, that's when you discover the horror of war (FG9)

It was when Saddam fired a Scud at Tel Aviv, there was a lot of wounded and some deaths (FG10)

When Saddam captured some enemy soldiers and wanted to use them as a human shield' (QGll)

When the war was over and television showed thousands of dead bodies (QGll)

The American soldiers who were taken prisoner (QG12)

The suffering of the men and the fear they felt for a friend who was threatened with death in Iraq (DG10)

sometimes but very rarely seen affecting the Iraqis

> When a wounded Iraqi got captured by a Frenchman (FGll)
>
> Thousands dead or mistreated (QB10)

torture

> The scene when they show prisoners who have been tortured (FG9)
>
> When they showed the torture chambers on television (FB8)
>
> The death of a a fourteen year old boy. Two Iraqis scooped out his eyes with a small spoon and cut off his arms and legs with a chain-saw (FB10)

Only ten drawings out of 74 show victims of the war, which might lead us to believe that the image of a victimless war was echoed somewhat by the children.

civilians: they are bombarded

> It was striking to see an unexploded rocket which had come to earth with only a few dents. The night was brightly lit up (DB10)
>
> The bombs were very bad in my opinion (DG10)
>
> The beginning of the war when there were several air raids on Iraq (UKB12)
>
> The first bomb which fell on Baghdad (QG12)
>
> The explosion of a Scud missile in Tel Aviv (QB10)
>
> Bang smash crash (UKB)

children are sometimes hit

> When there were little children and parents lying dead outside a building (FG10)
>
> Killing babies in children's homes (QGll)
>
> When children were wounded or killed (QB11)
>
> When Saddam had young Kuwaiti children attacked in different ways (QG12)
>
> When I saw parents crying on television because Saddam killed their children (OG11)

Feelings towards the soldiers: admiration, pity, reproach

> The soldiers were very brave going to Irak to fight without thinking about their own lives (DG10)
>
> The American soldiers who were prisoners of war (QG12)
>
> When the soldiers were surrendering in their thousands to the Canadian and American armies (QB12)
>
> When they were killing each other with their weapons and they were destroying everything with their bombs (QBll)

The ruined houses and towns

> When a missile fell on an occupied building (QB12)
>
> When I saw all the houses in ruins (FG9)
>
> When houses were destroyed and half-dead people were pulled out from under the debris' (QG12) 'Iraqi soldiers plundering Kuwaiti houses (FB8)

Eight drawings out of 74 show towns (sometimes with an oriental skyline).

Highly 'effective' planes and missiles: the destruction of ground-based military hardware (above all tanks and trucks)

> Dead men, wrecked tanks and buildings (FG9)
>
> overturned tanks, blown up planes, wreckage (UKB)
>
> Overturned trucks at the roadside (UKB)

The performance of the hardware impresses some pupils

In a French jet' (QBll); words accompanying a drawing based on a television picture showing the details of a French plane.

It is above all the drawings which show this fascination with technology: 45 drawings out of 75 depict military hardware and a number of pictures attempt to convey its accuracy and efficiency.

Chemical weapons worry some of the pupils

> The combat planes, the gas alerts, when Saddam is praying (DB10) When they launched missiles with poison gas (QG10)

Sometimes they are hooked by the eye-catching image of an isolated event

> The photo of a guard in Iraq, he was from Canada and it was evening time (QB12)
>
> A car was crossing a bridge and a bomb fell behind it (QB12)
>
> When Iraqi soldiers were surrendering to American photographers (QB12)
>
> Soldiers surrendering to a journalist (UKB)

The above are scattered observations. It would seem however that different representations of the war overlap.

They oscillate between hyper-realistic representations and a kind of epic inflation, produced by children's imaginations which run ahead of the images. The picture received by the adults is generally of a 'clean, surgical war', without victims. Our aim was to test the hypothesis that this vision had likewise been accepted by the children.

The hypothesis seems to be confirmed by the drawings which generally show a technological war (45 drawings out of 75) with few victims. A different story is told by the written accounts which often emphasise the suffering of soldiers and civilians. Such a vision seems however to have been quite rarely included in the television coverage. We certainly did not see the images of thousands of dead bodies described by some of the children, much less some others they produced which would have been worthy of a horror film. The news coverage certainly failed to undermine certain pre-existing visions of war.

Conclusion

It is thus television, or rather one particular television network, which was the pupils' principal source of information about a subject which school does not generally tackle. Children used this information to establish explanations of events. They primarily held on to the names of political personalities and of military hardware, with some variation between girls and boys and between nationalities.

It would be wrong to trivialise this geo-political awareness acquired through television. We could even hope that school might help children to recontextualise it, to structure it, and to enrich it. Teachers have of course been working on the press for years, but younger children hardly read the newspapers, except perhaps a few aimed specifically at a child readership. They prefer to watch television.

Would it not be profitable to help teachers to make use of the images viewed by their pupils? This help could take various forms: for example, written or audio-visual teaching materials. These materials could not of course be produced at a national level but could instead be developed by colleagues of different European nationalities. Such an approach would doubtless prove a very fruitful way to gain an understanding of other much more complex conflicts, such as the war currently tearing apart what used to be Yugoslavia.

Acknowledgements

Thanks to Hugh Starkey, and to Dr Gerhard Treutlein at the Pedagogische Hochschule, Heidelberg and colleagues at Laval University in Quebec. Our thanks too to the colleagues who made the translation and distribution of the questionnaires possible: D. Breteau, R. Debois, H. Copin, A. Gaquère, M. Steiner. Thanks to my colleague Georges Gayrard for the computer program.

Reference

Ferro, M. (1991) *L'information en uniforme: propagande. désinformation, censure et manipulation*, Paris: Ramsay.

Chapter 13

Education for European Citizenship and the Teaching and Learning of History

Ian Davies

Introduction

The importance of a good historical education to improve students' citizenship capabilities has long been asserted (Laslett 1956; Heater 1974; Davies 1986) and recent English National Curriculum History documentation declares that 'History is a priceless preparation for citizenship' (DES, 1990, p.2). We are now citizens of Europe (Lodge, 1993) and should educate our young people accordingly.

And yet education for European citizenship has been neglected. Despite the growing concern with courses on European history for adolescents (e.g. CIDREE, 1993; Rogers, 1993), and the many examples of attempts to heighten awareness of Europe (Central Bureau, 1991 and 1993), there may still be a need to concentrate more directly on education for European citizenship (Heater, 1992; Oliver and Heater, 1994). Recent valuable work by the Council of Europe (Council of Europe, 1986; Hawkey, 1995), projects which focus on particular aspects of teaching European History (Austin, 1992), and new organisations which aim to allow teachers from different European countries to work on common issues (e.g. Euroclio) still have not encouraged pupils in History classrooms to develop explicitly the knowledge, skills and dispositions of European citizens. There is a need to question the real extent of the commitment to education for European citizenship in the National Curriculum in England and Wales which gives little prominence to European matters, insists that History itself is not compulsory beyond the age of 14, and does not include at any Key Stage a proper commitment to work which allows for rights and responsibilities to be addressed directly.

This, of course, implies that there should be some sort of clear understanding of how education for European citizenship can be characterised and achieved through History teaching. But, as there are many different conceptions of the nature of political learning (Davies 1994a), and very many different styles and purposes proposed for teaching History across Europe (e.g. Rust 1993; van der Leeuw-Roord 1994), this is not straightforward. There is, in short, only political rhetoric — and no real evidence — for the potential of History to educate for European citizenship.

A project to promote education for European citizenship through History teaching

A recent research and development project in England was devised which attempted both to promote education for European citizenship, and by so doing, explore further its meaning.

The initial attempt to characterise education for European citizenship, which was used to explain to teachers who intended to become involved in the project, focused on the importance of the practices of the civil, political and social rights and responsibilities of individuals, groups and nations within the EU, and within other conceptions of Europe. It raised controversial questions in a variety of contexts, and it aimed to illuminate relevant concepts and established and alternative societal frameworks.

The project described here is framed within pupils' capacities to hold multiple citizenships. It aimed to allow people to develop critical understanding and potential for action — for Europe.

The project team hoped pupils would:

- develop enquiring, analytical minds and so become more capable of making reasoned judgements

- go beyond *thinking* about, and for, Europe and begin to explore the potential for action.

- develop a futures perspective which builds on a practical and theoretical study of the recent and contemporary Europe.

- explore the nature of tolerance, prejudice and discrimination in Europe to strengthen constructive toleration.

The above four points would, it was hoped, develop into a more sophisticated understanding. Thus the project gave an initial outline of what education for European citizenship might be, but its main aims were to focus on two key questions:

> What are the essential elements of education for European citizenship that might be taught in secondary schools?

> and

> To what extent do the project materials support education for European citizenship?

The aims were ambitious and, unsurprisingly, were not all achieved. Nevertheless, some important positive work was undertaken which suggests that this area is in further need of investigation.

Methodology of the European History and citizenship project

Five schools took part in the project. All schools were based in the north of England. Heads of History departments in those schools were already known to be interested in the development of courses for European citizenship. Involvement in the project was voluntary. Three of the schools were for pupils aged 11-18; the remaining two schools were for pupils aged 11-16. The project materials were tried out with pupils aged 14.

In phase one of the three phase project, questionnaire data were gathered from pupils in four of the five participating schools. A number of experts and teachers were interviewed. The interviews in this first phase were influenced by four issues which seemed to be important at the start of the project. The nature of Europe, the type of history which was to be deemed relevant, the most appropriate pedagogy, and the form of citizenship that was to influence practice were explored. (For a fuller consideration of the reasoning behind the selection of those issues see Davies (1994b)).

Analysis of data from phase one led directly to the second phase in which a member of the project team, who is a serving Head of a History Department in a secondary comprehensive school, produced classroom materials. Those materials provided approximately three to four weeks of work in History lessons.

The third phase involved testing those materials and collecting data from teachers and pupils. One visit to each project school took place to observe a lesson and to interview the teacher whose work had been seen. Samples of work which were broadly representative of the sort that a class was producing were requested from teachers. This allowed for an insight into the levels of ability that were represented and the level of achievement that had occurred during the project (although, of course, any causal links could not be established in such a short project). Pupils supplied written feedback in the form of a reply to a letter in which they were asked to make comments in key areas, but were also encouraged to raise other relevant issues.

Three meetings of the project team took place during the course of the project. The project team consisted of myself and the five Heads of History who were involved in the project (including the author of the materials).

The nature of the materials written to support education for European citizenship

It was felt that it was vital to have a contemporary focus which allowed pupils to explore a range of social, political and economic issues. Constitutional history was to be used only insofar as it helped illuminate key points. A broad European focus was preferred rather than exclusive attention to the European Union, although the latter would have a significant profile within the unit of work. The teaching and learning methods to be employed would reflect a very carefully structured project style with pupils writing less than is the norm and having opportunities to become involved in debate and small group work as well as watching videos.

The materials provide a broad overview of the main political developments in European History over the last fifty years. At the same time they allow pupils to develop a deeper understanding of the economic, social and cultural forces which have shaped the lives of people on both sides of the Iron Curtain during this period. The learning activities are structured around four key questions:

* How has Europe changed since 1945?
* Why has Europe changed?
* What was life like on different sides of the Iron Curtain?
* Should the European Union be widened to include the countries of Eastern Europe?

The emphasis is on small group discussion and problem solving, though opportunities for individual written work have been built into the materials.

In Activity One pupils were asked to sequence a series of pictures and text which represent some important events in European history since 1945 (e.g. building and collapse of the Berlin Wall; the Prague Spring of 1968; the signing of the Maastricht Treaty in 1991). The purpose of Activity Two was to develop an understanding of some of the underlying causes of the events shown on the timeline. A video was used to allow for a deeper analysis of changes in Europe than was allowed for in the sequencing activity. Three questions were considered:

- Why was Europe divided after the Second World War?

- Why have some of the Western European countries moved closer together since the war?

- How have some of the countries of Eastern Europe reacted against communist rule?

In Activity Three pupils were asked to consider the advantages and disadvantages of life on either side of the Iron Curtain. Classes were split into small groups with half working on the West, and the other half on the East. Pupils were provided with source sheets which covered four aspects of life: industry and work; standard of living; welfare; and freedom and protest. A range of material was included covering different countries during the period from the early 1950s to the early 1980s. In the freedom and protest sources, however, there is a more specific emphasis on Britain and Czechoslovakia in the 1960s.

In the concluding activity, pupils were asked to use their historical knowledge to put forward a point of view on a contemporary European issue. In preparing their reports, pupils were encouraged to go beyond the information provided and use their wider knowledge of political, social, economic and cultural change in Europe since 1945. They also had to consider whether integration will be easier for some European countries than others.

Discussion

To what extent can a course in History be seen as contributing to education for European citizenship?

Throughout the duration of the project one of the central dilemmas concerned the extent to which the materials have allowed pupils to go beyond an awareness of Europe and the History of Europe, to an improvement of their citizenship capabilities. It is argued that the project described here provided an extremely useful platform from which to develop education for citizenship, but that it cannot be seen as providing a complete model.

A) The contribution made during the project to knowledge and skills for education for European citizenship

Written work submitted by pupils was often very impressive. For example, booklets were produced by one school to display groups of pupils' answers to the question: should the EU be widened? Pupils showed that they have a good grasp of international relations and are able to posit a variety of options while still being able to develop a coherent argument. In answer to a question asked at a fairly early stage in the project about whether certain events suggested that Europe has become more united since 1945, one pupil, who gave a fairly typical response, commented that:

> It all depends on what you mean by united. In some ways I would say yes, in other ways no. I would certainly say that Europe hasn't become any less united. The Cold War is virtually over but I would say there is a public cold war in Britain against many European foreign people e.g. the French, the Spanish.
>
> The Rome and Maastricht Treaties are two actions in bringing Europe closer together. We still have individual languages and currencies. The CAP (Common Agricultural Policy) is an example of Europe working closer together.
>
> The Berlin Wall coming down and the Iron Curtain being drawn has obviously brought people and countries closer also.

The above response, of course, does show a lack of understanding about many European issues. For example, the CAP would not be regarded positively by everyone. It omits key factors and there is confusion about the nature of Europe. There are too many conceptions of an integrated Europe which have not been effectively differentiated. And yet, this answer for a pupil aged 14 who has done very little formal educational work on modern Europe is impressive. It synthesises a number of issues and arguments, and creates a coherent and positive position about Europe.

The teachers are aware of approaches to teaching History which are relevant to developing education for European citizenship. The emphasis is clearly on issues about which pupils have to exercise their own judgement. The author of the materials argued that:

> it's the rights thing that I wanted to focus on, really, in terms of employment or social welfare and freedom of expression, cultural rights. I mean that's the citizenship focus really ... the broad spectrum of political, economic, social rights, and the difference between east and west.

The aim, the author argued, was to teach about citizenship as it was, is and could be experienced.

But other, less encouraging points need to be noted. Firstly, pupils who use the project materials (and of course those pupils who are not involved in such work) may not develop a proper and necessary understanding of the roles of key European institutions. Given the underpinnings of this project it would not be considered important for a detailed constitutional awareness to be established, but there is a possibility that the rights and responsibilities that are associated with European citizenship are left unclear. This may in part be due to the lack of clarity among policy makers as to the exact nature of those rights and responsibilities. And yet, the stated preference to focus on rights as experienced may have led only to the identification of areas for discussion rather than an understanding of, for example, legal rights. When one teacher was asked about whether there was a need to have such an extended historical overview the response was: 'What other substance would you have ... What's the alternative substance?' At the suggestion that the focus could be made more explicitly on rights the teacher commented that:

I don't really know what the term citizenship is led really to sort of imply.

Similarly, the decision to see Europe broadly rather than concentrating exclusively on the EU meant for some teachers that valuable work could be done on questions associated with 'nationality and internationality', but is the focal point of the Community or Union being lost in an awareness raising course? To aviod making Europeanism into a form of narrow nationalism may result in a lack of strict attention to issues of citizenship in the European Union. As Heater (1992, p.62) has argued:

citizenship is a legal-political status in its strict sense and consequently can be exercised only in the context of a polity ... And Europe must be understood in the limited sense of the Community for this purpose.

Further, history teachers work under a wide range of professional constraints. For good reasons the materials used here were 'like the GCSE stuff that we do'. It was seen as :

a good well constructed history course. It's the same skills that I wish all my lessons were as well organised as that. It's good of its kind but it is still the same kind (pause) as the sort of thing that we do in History lessons.

This may have been part of the explanation for why the materials were deemed to be so demanding. Post-war European History is traditionally not tackled in secondary schools until years 10 and 11. The materials were seen by one teacher as being 'stuffed full of concepts' and with the perceived necessity for an historical overview of the last 50 years pupils were faced with much material that was unfamiliar in a very short period. European History had not been tackled in any depth before by any of the participating schools. A point was raised by teachers in one school that at least part of the course was perceived as being of more interest to the boys. A new approach is perhaps needed for the treatment of European issues so that they can be tackled by a range of pupils. Just as, for example, the highly complex Roman Empire is now thought to be appropriate for year 7 pupils, there is some need to think carefully about demands associated with differentiation and progression in relation to European matters rather than assuming that the only acceptable way to proceed is to focus on material which may be thought of as difficult and unfamiliar. For many, Europe is assumed to be about politics; it is complex; and courses concentrate on set piece, rather negatively based questions such as 'should Britain be a part of Europe?' It need not be like this. We can characterise Europe in more valid ways.

If the work is being conceptualised and delivered in much the same way as History lessons then, while this may lead to some achievement (especially if the rhetoric about History's closeness to education for citizenship is believed), it may also mean that the aims of this project are in danger of being subsumed under other concerns. The author of the materials commented that:

> I think there's a whole range of aspects of what being a human being is that can be developed and explored through History. Citizenship is just one ... I think it [i.e. History] fulfils that really broad purpose of what it means to be a human being, but I'm not as committed to its role in developing citizenship because I think that's just one part of it.

While the project team meeting at the end of phase one concluded that the focus of the work should be human rights with material drawn from legal case histories this was not followed through. Initially teachers felt that human rights would provide good human interest material, a sense of purpose because it had to do with multicultural justice and because it had international connotations. However, this did not occur. One of the reasons for this shift from human rights to a more history based course was that the legal cases were seen as too difficult for pupils. The teachers were concerned to promote the broader aims of History education. One noted that a course based on human rights:

> would have led me too far away from the history really ... There is potential ... but it's not history really. I mean it's not building up kind of raw ideas of historical change or ... causation or ... attitudes.

B) Attitudes towards Europe by teachers and pupils

Teachers in this sample are, on the whole, very positive about the importance of education for European citizenship. They were generally not suspicious of Europe, or of European institutions. Teachers and advisers are very keen to refer to the insular nature of British people and argue that 'somehow you have to break that down'. Education for European citizenship is seen as part of a wider effort to reduce prejudice and discrimination. This form of education would not aim to establish a ring fence around Europe. One teacher reflected the views of others by saying that this form of education would aim:

> to develop an understanding in teenagers that they are part of a wider community than the local community ... Citizenship operates on a number of different levels doesn't it; it's about belonging to a community that might be a family, might be a locality, it might be a nation, it's a global community, it's Europe and Europe is kind of one element in that ... There are shared values in a pluralist society [and so] the materials need to put forward not just two sides of an argument but a many sided argument.

There was a very professional concern that History should not be used as a crude agent of socialisation and in that sense there seemed to be rich potential for the development of a form of education which was positively critical about Europe.

It is more difficult to see as clear a response from pupils, as the following data, collected during phase one of the project, show (see below).

There are a number of interesting issues raised by the above data. I wished to ask pupils about their feelings related to European citizenship and this may of course not equate properly with the wording of the question which asks essentially about identity. Further, if I have asked pupils if they would say they are European, some confusion might be encouraged. People simply do not say they are European unless, as some pupils point out, they happen to be visiting somewhere other than Europe at the time. Confusingly, pupils making this point do not opt for 'yes' or 'no' in a uniform way. There is the possibility that geographical dimensions are considered more strongly by pupils than I had imagined and so they may have been keen to declare that they were part of a geographical Europe, without recognising the political dimensions associated with citizenship. There are examples of xenophobic statements. The learning of European languages is not liked and even those who want to help Europe become a better place may only want to do so from a position of national superiority.

However, it is, of course, fair to say that the need for education of the type under discussion here would be heightened if pupils were seen to be responding in xenophobic and unthinking ways. But, more reassuringly for the purpose of this project which hopes to be able to start from a favourable position with pupils when educating them about, and for, Europe, there are many positive points. The total number of positive responses to the final four statements shown above is

	YES	NO
Would you ever say about yourself 'I'm European'?	39	45
	POSITIVE	NEGATIVE
I am interested in European History	61	25
I like learning European languages	31	55
I like (or would like) to visit European countries	82	4
I would like to help Europe become a better place	74	11
Table 1		

287; the total number of negative responses is 130. Many of the pupils' written comments show that they think Europe is important, enjoy learning about it, and seek to contribute to its improvement. While it would be wrong to present the picture as being entirely clear, it does seem reasonable to suggest that pupils will neither be bored or firmly against all aspects of European education. If it is a form of education which is regarded by teachers/advisers as being important, and if it is regarded as being genuinely significant rather than some from of crude political indoctri- nation, then attention needs to be given to the way in which it can be carried out effectively.

When pupils were asked about the impact history can have, most (68 responses from a total of 85) say that history neither makes them like or dislike the idea of being European. This is not always positively stated. There are four types of negative response here: a belief that history just does not matter 'because in history you learn things that happened a long time ago and things are different now'; a general apathy 'it doesn't really matter to me'; history does not have the power to influence them: 'because I have my own ideas'; or they have insuf- ficient knowledge to form an opinion: 'I don't know what Europe is'.

However, the final two types of response could be viewed in a very positive light. Pupils are perhaps being sophisticated in recognising that history lessons do not have the power to inculcate certain loyalties; and also if pupils are recognising that they lack knowledge this could be a good starting point. Admittedly, there is some naiveté on the part of pupils who tend to suggest that they can make up their own minds on the basis of limited knowledge, but there are also many very unambiguously phrased positive responses:

> history explains events that have happened in the past without taking sides, it is and always should be up to us to decide our ideas without any pressure any way.

This sort of answer may be naive, but it does allow us to see that education for a narrow and negative European identity is not wanted by pupils, and it may show that they are keen to have a form of education that allows them 'to decide our ideas'. Europeans should not be open to crude manipulation by those who may have party political agendas. Simply put, adolescents, if they are to become proper European citizens, *need* to be introduced explicitly or implicitly to the sort of understandings that history should be able to deliver, and so to the pitfalls of assuming that certain answers are to be accepted uncritically, or that we can always simplistically make up our own minds.

This positive interpretation can be supported. By the end of phase three of the project the overwhelming reaction from teachers and pupils was very positive. Teachers said that they had no concerns about the material being unprofes- sionally biased. Many pupils responded in terms which suggest that they feel more like potential or actual citizens of Europe:

Since the work I feel more like I belong to Europe and that I understand about it.

The materials did make me feel more European.

Maybe now when I see something about it on the television I might know what's going on instead of not having a clue.

These materials made me feel part of Europe as I didn't before and I hated the French as I didn't understand Europe properly and I thought they were just being fussey (sic).

The work on the EU will be helpful as in a few year's time I will be able to vote on the European Parliment (sic).

It is perhaps in relation to identity more than in the development of a 'corpus of knowledge and skills necessary for the exercise of the status of European citizen' (Heater 1992, p.62) that the project has been most productive. The teacher who said that History raises issues about what it means to be a human being represents a general view that this work is relevant in a particular way to education for citizenship. This is important, as the issues raised here coincide with important debates about the meaning of substantive and procedural values and about the development of individualism in Europe (Jonathan 1993; Hoelman and Ester 1994). It is clear, though, that before this can be asserted with confidence more work needs to take place on the notion of identity. The data is too superficial to support unequivocally the idea that history as practised in this project can support the development of a European identity. In particular the relationship between identity and the particular form of Europe that is being considered needs careful attention if this work is to be a coherent addition to the debate on citizenship.

Conclusion

While much valuable work can take place in History classrooms, the rhetoric associated with some National Curriculum and other documents need to be viewed cautiously. History teachers in England may be able to lay the foundations for the development of education for European citizenship, but more explicit work is needed on the links between History and citizenship education, both in relation to knowledge and skills and also for the nature of European citizenship. Satisfaction that (for some) teaching resources have become less xenophobic (e.g. Millat 1993; Tholey 1993), and a feeling that in some parts of Europe a more genuinely investigative approach to History is being developed (e.g. Lewis et al 1993) should not disguise the lack of knowledge that we have about the real power of History to contribute to the development of European citizens. Nevertheless, the conclusions from this work are generally positive. There is, at the very least, a strong case for continuing to investigate the work that can be done by History teachers in the development of education for European citizenship.

References

Austin, R. (1992) Britain, Ireland and Europe: steps to historical understanding. *Teaching History,* number 67 pp.28-31.

Central Bureau (1991) *European Awareness. Report No.1.* The Central Bureau, Seymour Mews, London.

Central Bureau (1993) *European Awareness. Report No.2.* The Central Bureau, Seymour Mews, London.

CIDREE (1993) *History and the Core Curriculum 12-16: a feasibility study for comparative research in Europe.* Report of CIDREE workshop, Madrid November 1992.

Council of Europe (1986): *Against Bias and Prejudice: the Council of Europe's work on history teaching and history textbooks.* Strasbourg, Council of Europe.

Davies, I. (1986) Political Education Through History Teaching. *Teaching Politics*, volume 15 number 1 pp.3-15

Davies, I. (1994a) Whatever Happened To Political Education? *Educational Review*, volume 46 number 1 pp.29-38

Davies, I. (1994b) Teaching and Learning the Recent European Past For the Purposes Of Developing Education for European Citizenship. *Discoveries* Number 4. Centre for History Education, Trinity and All Saints College, University of Leeds.

DES (1990): *History For Ages 5 to 16.* London, HMSO.

Hawkey, K. (1995) History Teaching and the Council of Europe. *Teaching History,* number 78 pp.17-19.

Heater, D. (1974) *History Teaching and Political Education.* London, Politics Association.

Heater, D. (1992) Education for European Citizenship. *Westminster Studies in Education.* volume 15 pp.53-67.

Hoelman, L. and Ester, P. (1994) *The Ethos of Individualism In Cross Cultural Perspective: exploring the European values data.* Paper presented at the 4th conference of International Society for the Study of European Ideas at the University of Graz, Austria.

Jonathan, R. (1993) Education, Philosophy of Education and the Fragmentation of Value. *Journal of Philosophy of Education.* volume 27 number 2 pp.171-178.

Kettle, M. (1991) A Continent With An Identity Crisis. In *Citizenship,* edited by G. Andrews London, Lawrence and Wishart.

Laslett, P. (Ed) (1956) *Philosophy, Politics and Society.* Oxford, Basil Blackwell.

Lewis, R., Newitt, M., and Sokolov, A. (1993): *Reform of History Teaching and Research in Russia.* History Education Centre, University of Exeter.

Lodge, J. (Ed) (1993) *The European Community and The Challenge of the Future.* 2nd edition. London, Pinter Publishers.

Millat, G. (1993) Britain and European Integration Through British History Schoolbooks Published Between 1961 and 1971. *European Journal of Teacher Education,* volume 16, number 2 pp.125- 136.

Oliver, D. and Heater, D. (1994) *The Foundations of Citizenship.* London, Harvester Wheatsheaf.

Reid, A. (1985) An Outsider's View of Political Education in England: Past, Present and Future. *Teaching Politics* volume 14 number 1 pp.3-19.

Rogers, P. (1993) Common Core History For Young Europeans. *European Journal of Teacher Education* volume 16 number 2 pp.113- 124.

Rust. V.D. (1993) Transformation of History Instruction in East German Schools. *Compare* volume 23, number 3, pp.205-217.

Tholey, M. (1993) *A European Dimension in the Curriculum; the quality of textbooks.* Paper presented at the Council of Europe seminar on 'Educational resources of teaching about Europe in schools' held at Donaueschingen, Germany October 1993. Enschede, National Institute for Curriculum Development.

van der Leeuw-Roord, J. (1994) A Letter from the Continent. *Times Educational Supplement* 2 December.

Chapter 14

A New Model of Moral Education for Polish Schools

Roman Dorczak

Introduction

The political breakthrough of 1989 gave an impulse for rapid changes and reforms of the educational system in which moral, human rights and civic education issues became crucial. The importance of moral education has been stressed in almost every serious discussion and in all educational law documents since 1773 when the last Polish king, Stanislaus Augustus, established the Committee of National Education, the first ministry of education in the world. Unfortunately, the concept of moral education was never openly discussed. For historical reasons, schools in Poland were always an instrument of ideological struggle and indoctrination, not only during the foreign administrations of the nineteenth century but also under the new Polish state in the interwar period, to say nothing of the 45 year-long period of communist rule when a new model of the socialist state citizen and 'socialist morality' were promoted in schools.

After 1989 the new political elites inherited this tradition and way of thinking about education. Quite quickly after the overthrow of the communist government they started to use the educational system as a means of promoting their own points of view and values, in the same way as the former regimes used to do. The need for the moral and spiritual rebirth of the nation was stressed in every official discussion about educational reform. Conservative Catholic political parties together with the Church hierarchy became influential, which resulted in the introduction of Catholic religious instruction in schools of all types as well as some major changes to the syllabus in other subjects, especially the humanities. Slogans about socialist morality were replaced with slogans of Christian (meaning Catholic) morality (Dorczak and Szyjewski, 1994). Surprisingly quickly, people in schools, especially students, started to feel that such a model of religious education and Catholic indoctrination was imposed from the outside and was inadequate for the needs of the young generation in a rapidly transforming society facing the challenges of a new European context.

Moral education in 1989-1994

There are several ways in which moral or ethical education takes place in contemporary Polish schools. First, there is the traditional way, through separate subjects. Following the introduction in 1990 of Catholic religious instruction to all types of schools, from 1993 schools had also to offer non-compulsory religious education or, optionally, courses of ethics. The 1993 Instruction says that such a course can be introduced when at least 15 students in a school opt for it. In practice only Roman Catholic religious instruction takes place in schools because there are neither trained teachers of ethics nor money to pay them, and religious minorities are too small and too dispersed to have their own religious instruction.

The Church prepares and runs courses of religious instruction without being subject to the education authorities . The Instruction states that the curricula should be '...approved by the Church authorities and sent to the Ministry of Education'. Courses of ethics, in schools, have nothing to do with real life issues. They are very theoretical and are courses in the history of philosophy rather than courses in moral education.

Moral education can also be taught through the curricula of other subjects, especially the humanities. It is important to stress the role of Polish literature in the spiritual development of young people in Poland. Moral standards conveyed by literature were assimilated by many generations of Poles (Niemczynska and Niemczynski, 1992). Curricular changes in literature and the other humanities were also strongly influenced by the Catholic Church.

Thirdly, there are, or were, civic education courses. During the communist period the curricula of such courses were full of ideologically correct communist slogans about the socialist state and ideology. They were withdrawn from schools in 1990. Numerous proposals and attempts to introduce new curricula failed for two reasons: lack of money to pay for curriculum development, and the rapid changes of government. No minister had time to decide what to teach and then implement it. In such circumstances civic education as a separate subject almost disappeared from schools.

One very important vehicle for moral education is tutorial form time. Form teachers organise the programme which can cover any problems and issues that may arise from everyday school life. The Ministry has prepared a series of books, brochures and teaching materials known as the 'form teacher's library' with suggestions on how to deal with certain problems. In practice, form teachers who are specialists in their subjects do not want to deal with problems other than the register, discipline and order in the class. Frequently they use 'form hours' as additional lessons for their own subject.

Finally, there is the approach to moral education which seems to be the most influential as regards the way students think and behave. We may call it school climate or school culture, which can be described as a set of values practised in the school and expressed in, for instance, the quality of relations between all members of the institution, teaching styles, and the knowledge and skills that are valued (Power, Higgins and Kohlberg, 1989). This implicit or hidden curriculum has been disregarded by many unsuccessful reformers of education and it deserves careful attention.

Having looked at different approaches to moral education we may try to define the main obstacles to achieving it. There is a *lack of clarity* of basic values, typical of a period of socio-political change but also a feature of government education policy and the expectations of teachers and students. Discussions about school reform are overloaded with slogans such as 'democratic education', 'moral and spiritual education', 'values', 'development of students' potential'. Unfortunately there are no real discussions or attempts to get agreed clarification of these basic concepts, the main cause being *political dogmatism* which can be described as an attitude of disregard for the rights of other points of view and ideas to exist. Such an attitude has become characteristic of Polish political life in the 1990s. Another danger, *religious fundamentalism*, comes from the Catholic Church which tries to impose its own vision of the world and use the educational system in Poland as a means of indoctrination. Last but not least, there is the idea of *commercialism* and the language of the free-market economy which, in times of economic transformation, invades people's minds and glorifies material acquisitiveness and economic success. In education it is visible in curricular changes. Subjects such as computer sciences, business studies and modern languages were not only introduced to schools but also involved giving careful attention and money to develop curricula and teaching materials. Polish schools have in fact always been knowledge and test-oriented and more concerned with subjects giving 'solid knowledge' and opening professional or academic careers than with subjects dealing with moral, spiritual or ethical issues. In such a context pupils are seen as persons to be trained to fit into the economic machine of a prospering society. This gives results in a short term perspective but does not allow children's potential to be fully developed and may finally cause serious psychological and social conflicts.

Why a new model of moral education?

It is quite understandable that in such a context there is growing awareness among educationalists of the fact that the situation requires clarification of the basic values underlying education, its aims and its role in the transition from totalitarianism to democracy. Examining the basic meaning of such words as 'education', 'morality', and 'development', and reading basic educational texts (Starkey, 1992) it becomes clear why moral education is crucial for the educational process According to the UNESCO recommendation:

> The word education implies the entire process of social life by means of which individuals and social groups learn to develop consciously within, and for the benefit of the national and international communities, the whole of their personal capacities, attitudes, aptitudes and knowledge. This process is not limited to any specific activities (UNESCO, 1974).

This broad definition of education leads us to question the traditional, knowledge-oriented style of education which is so dominant currently in Polish schools and which may limit the potential of young people. Traditional education does not allow for the all-round development of individuals, nor does it encourage them to contribute to society. However, in stressing the social nature of the educational process, more democratic teaching methods immediately raises moral issues and the issue of morality itself. Education always implies consideration of moral issues; it is about the way in which teachers treat and influence students, and also about the choice of future thoughts and styles of behaviour (Bottery, 1990). In Polish schools there were and still are forces that wish to decide this choice, to impose a traditional, conservative, cultural transmission model of education (Kohlberg and Mayer, 1972) which is no longer adequate in the rapidly changing, multicultural societies of a unifying Europe.

I have described the inadequacy of existing, traditional ways of moral education on the one hand and the importance of moral education on the other. These two observations led to the setting up of a project.

A new curriculum for moral education in Polish schools

The main assumptions underpinning the project to introduce a new curriculum for moral education were as follows:

- it should not be limited to one subject or one curricular area but must be reflected in every aspect of teaching
- it should not be limited to any specific activities
- it has to raise real life issues important to students, even if these issues are difficult and controversial

- it has to deal with different opinions, points of view and values, promote understanding of others, respect and tolerance

- it presupposes the equal rights of all involved in it

- it should involve new, active methods of teaching and learning.

The course was prepared and implemented as a part of the TEMPUS *Developing Schools for Democracy in Europe* project. It is part of a broader action plan which aims to change the whole organisation and management of several schools in Kraków to make them more democratic and transform their moral climate, teaching styles, decision-making processes and communication processes (Sayer, 1993). The course itself was developed as an individual subject, yet it can be successful only as a part of a broader integrated school curriculum with special stress on the hidden curriculum.

The main aims of the course can be best shown in three main groups:

cognitive

- to provide knowledge about different religions and denominations in doctrinal, ritual and institutional dimensions, as well as knowledge about non-religious systems of thinking

- to develop vocabulary to describe and interpret the religious and moral dimension of human life

- to develop skills of critical thinking and discussion.

social

- to develop sensitivity and respect for different world views and promote tolerance and understanding of others

- to develop attitudes of openness towards the diversity of religious ways of life and ways of life in general

- to promote issues of human rights in the local context

- to consider reasons why people hold different beliefs.

personal

- to recognise and express one's own beliefs, attitudes and values

- to develop sensitivity to moral and religious questions

- to understand one's own system of beliefs and traditions

- to provide opportunities to enter into and examine feelings which can be the source of spiritual experience.

The course consists of fifteen units designed after the careful study of students' needs. These were developed into a more detailed curriculum taking account of the local context of a particular school and the specific needs of students. The main themes of these units were:

1. Who am I?
2. The meaning of life.
3. Searching for meaning — social pathologies.
4. Searching for meaning — friendship, love, care, religion.
5. Love, sex and parenting.
6. Good and Evil.
7. Suffering.
8. The Holocaust.
9. Prejudice, Racism, Intolerance.
10. War, Pacifism.
11. Human Rights.
12. Animal Rights.
13. Spaceship Earth; Ecology.
14. Law and Order.
15. Crime and Punishment.

Active methods of teaching and learning

The issue of teaching methodology or teaching strategies appeared to be a very important issue while developing the course. Our vision of moral education, as opposed to Catholic religious instruction and ethics, requires the rejection of traditional, passive, lecture- style teaching. It implies the involvement of students in every phase of the educational process starting from designing the curriculum. This active role for students is the expression of mutual respect that should be the foundation of a new style of teacher — student relations (Piaget, 1971).

Among many other methods of active learning, the method of dilemma discussions was preferred. By setting two or more values of equal validity in opposition to one another, dilemmas give the opportunity to:

— tackle conflicts of values;
— become aware of value conflicts and reflect on one's own sense of values;
— recognise and understand a diversity of points of view;
— promote and develop understanding, tolerance and respect for others;
— learn how to resolve conflicts. Due to the fact that real life dilemmas are the best for such dilemma discussions we always use stories (dilemmas) arising out of everyday school conflicts and student life (Kuhmerker, 1986).

The course in practice

At the time of writing, the course is not yet fully operational. We have had to face many problems of an institutional and an organisational nature. The education authorities were simply not interested in our proposal, maybe because of existing education legislation or maybe because of the fact that local education authorities are afraid of the Church's response to such a proposal. We were, however, able to run our course in three schools that were involved in the TEMPUS project. The course was optional and it was offered to groups of students of 14 to 16 years old. In two cases it was put into the compulsory part of the curriculum by teachers who gave us their 'form hours'.

Looking at the two-year experience of running the course, there are positive as well as negative observations.

On the positive side we note that:

— students may reject the traditional dogmatic and theoretical religious/ethical education but can they still be sensitive to moral issues?

— they are open-minded, and enjoy raising difficult and controversial issues

— they quickly adapt to active methods of teaching and learning

— they are more critical and radical than their teachers are as far as teaching styles are concerned, but at the same time they are rational and responsible

— they are curious about alternative worldviews, as well as tolerant and respectful.

The positive features prevail when the teacher who runs such a course is competent and enthusiastic and the school provides support through its climate and organisation.

However, there is also a less encouraging perspective on our work. Unfortunately, young people are heavily influenced by commercialism and the desire to achieve good grades. Students simply do not regard as valuable subjects and issues that are not giving them the 'solid knowledge' needed to pass exams. The second issue that must be mentioned is a tendency to accept the traditional teaching style of lecturing as convenient for grasping as much knowledge as possible with minimum effort.

Conclusions

The new challenges that we as a society face need transformation of the education system, a transformation that can be achieved only when we openly and thoroughly discuss the basic values which underlie education. The area of moral education can be seen to be crucial in this process. Changes in this area are not easy because of ideological, political and economic pressures on schools and the school system. Nevertheless, they are a necessary condition for transition to democracy and success in the modern world.

References

Bottery, M. (1990) *The Morality of the School.* London: Cassell

Dorczak, R. and Szyjewski, A. (1994) The Narrow Path Between Ideology and Economy. Educational Change in Poland, *The international network of principles centers newsnotes,* (8) 1, Harvard: Harvard University INPC

Kohlberg, L. and Mayer, R (1972) Development as the Aim of Education *Harvard Educational Review,* (4), pp. 449-496.

Kuhmerker, L.(1986) *The Kohlbergs' Legacy for Helping Professions.* Birmingham, Alabama: Religious Education Press

Niemczynska, M. and Niemczynski, A.(1992) Perspectives from Past and Present on Moral and Citizenship Education in Poland, *Journal of Moral Education* (21)3, pp.225-234.

Piaget, J.(1971) *Dokad zmierza edukacja? (Where is education heading?)* Warsaw: PWN

Power, C., Higgins, A., and Kohlberg, L. (1989) *Lawrence Kohlberg's Approach to Moral Education.* New York: Columbia University Press

Sayer, J. (1993) *The training and development of teachers.* Oxford University Department of Educational Studies TEMPUS JEP-1477 DSDE Interim Consultative Document

Starkey, H.(1992) Back to Basic Values: Education for Justice and Peace in the World, *Journal of Moral Education* (21)3, pp.185-192

UNESCO (1974) Recommendation Concerning Education for International Understanding, Co-operation and Peace and Education Relating to Human Rights and Fundamental Freedoms. Paris: UNESCO

Chapter 15

Children's Rights and the Listening School:
an approach to counter bullying among primary school pupils

Sue Thorne

Under Article 19 of the UN Convention on the Rights of the Child, schools have a duty to protect the children in their charge from physical and mental violence. Children have a right to feel safe and secure at school. They have the right to be able to attend school without the fear that they will be harassed, intimidated, teased, physically attacked or bullied in any way. Unfortunately, violent behaviour in schools is still common. This chapter describes one school's attempt to involve children in creating a peaceful school environment.

The school, where I am the headteacher, is a Junior and Infant school with 212 pupils drawn from a range of social, cultural and ethnic backgrounds. In a survey carried out in May 1994 it was recorded that sixteen different languages were spoken as the first language in pupils' homes and that nineteen different countries were represented. The school has a reputation as a caring school and aims to provide a secure learning environment in which all pupils are valued as individuals.

The action research project on which this chapter is based was conducted from 1991 to 1994 in our primary school in Birmingham. We wanted to compare the pupils' perceptions of bullying. As children are the victims of bullying and also the perpetrators, we decided to find out whether our pupils perceived it to be a problem, and if so what they thought could be done to help. After all...

if we do not know the nature of children's thinking about society, it is difficult to plan appropriate learning contexts for them (Carrington and Short, 1989:59).

We found that the children held strong views about bullying. They perceived it to be a problem and wanted something done to help them. Above all they wanted facilities to enable them to talk about their problems.

At the start of the project I believed that a caring environment was provided at the school, but as the headteacher I felt that something more was needed. We started by reviewing the equal opportunities policy to ensure that the school was indeed providing an appropriate environment for all pupils. All children have a right to an equal chance to learn and reach their potential but this will not happen if some children are discriminated against in any way. We therefore decided to develop the existing policy, to look at the ethos of the school and to review the curriculum in general. Our new policy would set out the principles and practices that should be adopted to counter discriminatory behaviour such as bullying, racism and sexism. I undertook this research project as part of my Master's Degree at the University of Birmingham.

I wanted to gain a greater understanding of bullying in the school so that policy could be based on what was actually happening. We used questionnaires, interviews and observation to find out the extent of bullying, to find out children's perceptions of bullying, and to evaluate the situation. The findings of the initial survey were used to help formulate the policy which evolved over a period of two years. It developed from a statement about bullying, to a comprehensive anti-bullying policy. This was incorporated into the school's policy for encouraging positive behaviour. The policy was revised over time and issues about bullying were addressed through the curriculum.

The children's views were paramount in formulating a whole school policy, based on respect. We helped them to counter bullying behaviour by creating a 'listening' school and a 'telling' school where all children are valued and listened to, where they feel safe, and where they can play an active role in the democratic process at the school. They are encouraged to contribute fully to policy and decision-making.

Why have an anti-bullying policy?

Bullying is the most malicious and malevolent form of deviant behaviour widely practiced in our schools... (Tattum, 1989:7).

In the UK it was widely acknowledged that bullying was prevalent and persistent in schools but until the late 1980s it was ignored by the educational research community. The two-year Kidscape project, which began in 1984, found that it was one of children's major concerns and affected over one-third of pupils

(Elliott, 1991:8). In 1989 bullying in UK schools was also identified in the Elton Report on *Discipline in Schools* which stated that it was widespread but tended to be ignored by teachers. The first European Seminar on Bullying in Schools was held in Stavanger in 1987 and helped to raise awareness (Council of Europe, 1988). At that time most of the empirical data came from the Scandinavian countries.

Bullying is a complex problem and one that is difficult to define as it can take many forms. What may be considered bullying by one person may be 'just a game' to another. Bullying may be short-term or continue for years, it may be carried out by one person or by a group and the victim of bullying may also be a bully. Bullying may be physical or psychological, it may be overt aggression or subtle intimidation, or it may be verbal or even just a look. Different people in authority, for example teachers, may define it differently and put different interpretations on what they see. Racial harassment is a particularly insidious form of bullying which attacks:

> the most fundamental characteristics of a person's being — their sense of self (Tattum and Herbert, 1993:4).

Although incidents of bullying can be diverse I believe that the definition put forward by Johnson, Munn and Edwards can be applied to all forms of bullying. They state that:

> Bullying is the wilful, conscious desire to hurt or threaten or frighten someone else. To do this, the bully has to have some sort of power over the victim, a power not always recognisable to the teacher (Johnson, Munn and Edwards, 1991:3)

The important word is power and in the case of bullying the power is illegitimate. Any behaviour which involves the illegitimate use of power to hurt others is bullying.

Bullying may involve physical intimidation or threats of violence; or it may involve verbal tactics or social ostracism. All bullying may have a long-term effect on the victim leading in some cases to absenteeism, under-achievement, childhood depression or even suicide. It is for these reasons that every school should have a policy giving strategies and guidance for dealing with incidents of bullying behaviour.

For as Tattum states:

> Schools have a responsibility to create a safe and secure environment for children who are in their care so that parents may hand their children over in the confident knowledge that they will be protected from the bullies (Tattum, 1989:7).

Professor Dan Olweus at the University of Bergen began investigating incidents of bullying in the 1970s and was for many years a leader of research into bullying in schools. In 1983 the Norwegian government launched a National Campaign which was led by Olweus and was essentially an intervention programme. He found that the schools with a well developed whole school policy were the schools which had fewer incidents of bullying (Olweus, 1993).

In 1990 a UK government funded project, led by Professor Peter Smith at Sheffield University, was set up to investigate the impact of whole school policies to counter bullying in 24 Sheffield schools. The findings of this research has been circulated to all UK schools as an anti-bullying pack entitled 'Don't Suffer in Silence' (DFE, 1994). The research findings both in the UK and in Scandinavia showed that the successful schools had made bullying everyone's concern: they had a whole school policy, and dealt with it if it occurred.

Pupils' perceptions of bullying

Before introducing a policy for dealing with incidents of bullying in my school I wanted to find out more about it. I wanted to find out whether bullying was occurring or not, and if it was I needed to know more about its frequency, methods and outcomes. For as Askew said:

> Recognising the pervasive nature of bullying in schools and the damage it does to pupils is the first step towards working towards its elimination (Askew, 1989:69).

As it is the children who are directly involved and are able to give first hand information I wanted to use them to help me to gain an insight into their perceptions. I used a questionnaire, conducted interviews and used observations to find out:

- Is bullying seen as a problem?
- What do the children mean by the term bullying?
- How great is the problem?
- Where does it take place?
- What do the children think should be done to help?

Initially the survey was confined to Year 6 (aged 10 and 11) and Year 3 (aged 7 and 8), to represent the oldest and youngest junior children, and to see if there were any age-related differences in the responses. A questionnaire was used during the last two weeks of the Autumn Term 1991, to see if the children thought that bullying was a serious problem, an occasional problem or not a problem at school. It also asked if they had seen anyone being bullied, or if they themselves had been teased, upset or physically bullied during the term. It asked if there was anyone else in their class who bullied others or who had been bullied, whether they had bullied anyone, and whether they would tell a teacher if they or someone they knew was being bullied. There were further open-ended questions where the children could express their feelings about bullying, describe what they under-stood by the term 'bullying', mention where they thought that bullying happens, and what they thought should be done to help.

Before completing the questionnaire the children were told they could write exactly what they thought, that their answers would be confidential, and no one would know what individual children had written as they did not write their names on the form. They were told that the purpose of the questionnaire was to find out what they thought about bullying in school, and to help the teachers to do something about it if it was seen to be a problem. When the questionnaire was completed they were told that they could discuss bullying with me in private. The Year 6 children suggested the types of things that they would like to discuss and their suggestions were used to help compile the interview questions. The most significant and worrying finding of the questionnaire was that the majority of children surveyed (82 per cent) thought that bullying was a problem in school and approximately half of these thought that it was a serious problem.

The questionnaire responses however did not distinguish between bullying and different forms of aggression as the children were not using a commonly agreed definition but were using their own interpretation of bullying. What one person perceives as bullying may not be considered as such by another. It is not known if the reported incidents were all deliberate or not, whether intimidation was involved, or whether they were provoked, or repeated. Also it did not dis-tinguish between physical bullying and teasing as these two overlap consider-ably. For the purposes of the investigation however, the questionnaire served its purpose and confirmed that there was a problem.

In order to find out more about the children's views, interviews, whole class discussions and observations were used to gain a clearer understanding of how they felt.

The responses to the questionnaire and interviews clearly showed that the children in the school wanted something done about bullying behaviour. Analysis of the open-ended questions of the questionnaire showed that the children wanted help, they wanted someone to talk to, and to be given strategies to help them if they were being bullied. The children indicated that they wanted help in ways which ranged from statements like 'help you' to detailed sugges-tions of what they would like teachers to do. The following replies were given and they show how the majority of the children felt; they wanted to be able to talk to teachers and they wanted them to help:

• Call/tell the teachers
• Tell a teacher / friend / head / parent
• Help you / them
• Do something to help

- Stop it NOW
- Have a talk about it
- Stop the fight
- Find out why they are doing it and try to stop it
- Watch and stop it
- Try to get the child to tell you who it is
- Teachers can be more serious about it and make sure that it doesn't
  happen again.

Three children were able to express their feelings in a very articulate way and their words sum up the feelings of the majority. They wrote:

Get the pupils to tell a teacher or a parent so that the person bullying knows that someone knows what they are doing.

Have a conversation with a teacher — they should be able to sort it out.

I think that teachers should say to children who they think are being bullied, 'You can trust us and tell us anything'.

This implied that the children thought that a school policy was needed to help them and this was articulated by the child who wrote:

I think at school we should have more information to help the person tell someone about who is bullying them.

The research findings clearly showed that bullying was perceived as a problem and that the school, that is the staff and governors, needed to look at bullying, to acknowledge that it was taking place, to consider ways of intervening, and formulate a whole school anti-bullying policy.

Once again much could be learned from the pupils about what should be in the policy and how the school could help. Almost one third of the children emphasised playground supervision. One child wrote:

Teachers and dinner ladies should look more and be more alert. Have more teachers on playground duty.

Even the boy who did not think that anything could be done to help, and who wrote that it was up to the victims to stand up for themselves, was implying that the victims needed to be given strategies to help them cope.

The children's participation in policy making

It was obvious that a whole school policy was needed to help counter bullying behaviour at the school and the children's views were paramount in helping to develop this policy. It was also decided to consult with parents and a meeting, which was well attended by over a third of the children's parents, was called to discuss behaviour at school. Some of the older children took an active part at the meeting and set the scene by presenting a scenario, using drama and role play, about bullying and strategies that could be used to deal with it. The children were given responsibility for organising this themselves and wrote their own script. Their role play session was followed by discussion groups and the Year 6 pupils formed their own group and impressed everyone by the quality and depth of their thinking. The children mentioned the following points:

- If a parent is bullying a child, the child must be able to talk to a teacher about it and the teacher should contact the parent to discuss it. If it happens a lot the school should involve someone who can help.

- There are parts of the school where bullying occurs without the teacher or dinner supervisor knowing about it.

- Children must have more courage to tell a teacher — *When? Where? Why?* and *Who?*

- There should be a box where children can write about their problems. Somehow this should be confidential. Children could be involved in answering and trying to help.

After the meeting the children's contributions and the questionnaire findings were used to help formulate a whole school policy. The children wanted something done to help them, they were treated seriously and their ideas were adopted. They wanted someone to talk to, someone to listen to them and action to be taken when necessary. They no longer wanted to suffer in silence.

A 'telling school' and a 'listening school'

The lasting effect that bullying can have on a person was demonstrated when a week after a parents' meeting to discuss bullying a mother phoned to say that the Year 6 role play had stabbed at a nerve and brought back memories from her own school days. She wished that such things had been discussed openly when she was at school and that there had been people and strategies to help her. Strategies for its prevention must be an integral part of the school's aims and ethos. It was agreed that behaviour issues would be on a staff meeting agenda each term so that policies could be discussed and reviewed on a regular basis, and all new members of staff would be aware of them. It was agreed that bullying should be tackled through the curriculum and not in isolation. Every class must have the opportunity to discuss bullying, to discuss why some people become bullies and to explore strategies for dealing with bullying, to write about it and to take part in role play.

Above all it was decided that the school must become a 'telling school' and a'listening school', which would be safer and happier. Ways to encourage children to talk were needed because, as the questionnaire findings showed, only about half the children said that they would tell a teacher if they were being bullied and for the older children this figure decreased to 43 per cent. The children's reasons for not wanting to tell were invaluable when formulating the policy to encourage children to talk. They said:

• I want to sort it out myself.
• I don't want my friends to know that I can't handle it.
• I would discuss it with my parents first.
• It would depend how bad it was.

Tattum and Herbert explain this unwillingness to talk as inadequacy:

> Their feeling of self-reproach is part of the reason why they are reluctant to confide in their parents or teachers (Tattum and Herbert, 1993:10).

Children may also be reluctant to talk because they fear that there will be repercussions and that they are frightened about what the bully will do when he or she finds out that they have talked.

The children need to know that they have a right to talk and that they do not have to suffer; that they can talk about their problems; that it will help to talk; that they will not suffer more because they have talked; and that they will be given strategies to help them. They need to know that bullying is not tolerated at the school and that they have the right to be safe at school. One of the means for encouraging children to talk about problems is through the problem box which has become an established way for the children to bring attention to their problems. The issues raised are dealt with individually as they occur, and are discussed during the half-termly problem box assembly. The problems range from how to cope with friends that are being nasty, to complaints about school policies and issues about the playground, school dinners and the toilets.

The children were listened to and taken seriously, their suggestions for sanctions were used when drawing up the behaviour policy and each class agreed its own rules. The only stipulation was that the rules must be positive and fall within the framework of the agreed behaviour policy. In this way it was hoped that the pupils would have a feeling of ownership and belonging and that they would feel secure and confident enough to talk to someone if they experienced problems. A summary of the policy was circulated to all parents and they too were asked to contact the school if their children were experiencing difficulties. The attempt was to create a 'telling school' and a 'listening school', for as Frost states:

> Children should be strongly encouraged to think of 'telling' as positive behaviour, not as 'sneaking'. In this way, the bully cannot be sure of maintain-

ing a conspiracy of silence, and it becomes more difficult to single out his victim without interference from others (Frost, 1991:35).

Procedures for becoming a 'telling school' and a 'listening school' were included in our school's 'Encouraging Positive Behaviour Policy':

- A *'telling school'*: Children must be encouraged to 'tell', if they experience problems, if they have been bullied, or if they witness bullying.

- It is not wrong to 'tell' and children must know this and be encouraged to talk to teachers, parents or other adults, or to report their anxieties through the problem box if something worries them.

- Children need to feel that they can trust us and will only tell if they are confident that they will be treated seriously and fairly.

- A *'listening school'*: Children must know that we care, that we will listen and respond.

- We must investigate the situation and respond appropriately.

During a staff development day in April 1993 behaviour and discipline were discussed and the following simple rules were agreed:

ALWAYS REMEMBER TO SAY PLEASE AND THANK YOU
ALWAYS ADDRESS PEOPLE BY THEIR NAMES
HAVE RESPECT FOR PEOPLE AND PROPERTY.

These may seem simplistic but the message was to be that everyone has the right to be treated and spoken to in an appropriate manner, including the way that teachers and adults speak to children. It was agreed that the rules should apply to all people connected with the school and should be positively applied and encouraged by everyone. They were displayed around school, discussed with the children in the classroom, circulated to parents, and discussed with all members of staff and with helpers in school. At the end of the term when these rules were being discussed staff commented that it had made them modify the way that they spoke to children and that children were more polite to each other.

The policy for 'Encouraging Positive Behaviour' was written in January 1994. It was felt important to base it on tried practice before committing it to paper. It includes sections about the ethos of the school; about being a 'caring school', a 'telling school' and a 'listening school'; about ways to promote self-esteem through the curriculum; it gives guidelines about rewarding positive behaviour; and includes sections about sanctions, and about forming a partnership with parents. There is a section about dealing with bullying and aggressive behaviour. It outlines positive steps to help reduce bullying and gives guidance for working with parents. Parents are always informed in writing if their child has been deliberately hurt by or has hurt another pupil. Parents are also referred to the Scottish Council booklet for information, *Bullying and how to fight it — A guide for families* (Mellor, 1993). A checklist for monitoring and evaluating the policy and an action plan for developing the policy have been drawn up. This includes opportunities for INSET in behaviour management, courses for non-teaching staff and dinner supervisors, and consideration of ways to improve the playground environment.

In their responses to the questionnaire the children emphasised that playtime was a time when bullying took place and made many suggestions. However it was still thought that the playground environment could be enhanced and this is our next priority. To involve the children in the plans to improve the playground, each class has discussed matters with their teacher and their comments were noted. The Infant classes have drawn pictures to illustrate their suggestions for improving the playground and Year 6 has carried out an investigation about the playground. They have conducted a questionnaire to discover other children's views and have analysed their findings, drawn plans to show their suggestions for improving the playground and devised new games and tried them with other children. A landscape architect is currently working with Year 5 to help put the pupils' ideas into practice. It is also planned that a booklet about the school which will include a section on how to cope with bullying will be ready for the start of the next academic year. The booklet will be written by children at the school and circulated to every child. The aim has been to create an atmosphere where all children are valued, to listen to children and act upon their wishes in order to make the school a safe place for all pupils.

Evaluating the anti-bullying programme

In order to evaluate the success, or failure, of the school's policy the question-naire was used again in May 1994. Analysis of the data showed that although incidents of bullying had declined it was still perceived as a problem. The children had a greater understanding and awareness of bullying. Their responses included:

- Upsetting someone when there is no need.
- Making someone's life unhappy.
- When they are on their own you can deal with it but in a group it is different.
- Upsetting someone on purpose.
- Something that is said that is cruel or deeply offends you.
- Being deliberately hurt for no reason.
- To get something that you've got but they haven't.

They had been involved in discussing bullying and helped to formulate the policy for countering it. They were aware that all children have the right to feel safe. So although the incidents appeared to have declined the children knew that it still existed.

The 1991 survey indicated that the children wanted someone to talk to but only half of them said that they would definitely tell a teacher if they were being bullied, but in 1994 only four pupils said that they would not tell and two of them qualified their responses with:

> It would depend how serious it was.
>
> I would if I thought they could stop it privately and quickly.

The children repeatedly said that you must not be afraid to tell, and that you should tell parents, friends or teachers. They also indicated that they wanted more strategies to help them. This was summed up by three children who wrote:

- Teach about not to be a bully or a racist.
- We need encouragement to tell and a topic about it (bullying).
- Tell them how to cope and not to be scared to tell.
- Talk it over calmly with a teacher or a person of authority.

Thus the policy seemed to be successful but there is no room for complacency as the questionnaire responses showed there was still a problem. The anti-bullying initiatives must be ongoing and become part of school life and be everyone's concern.

I believe that by acknowledging the children's right to participate in issues that directly concern them, by giving them responsibility for identifying their problems and for suggesting strategies for helping to solve them, the children have been helped to consider the rights of others and to take shared responsibility in their future. The next step is for the school to develop the children's active participation further by setting up a system of pupil counsellors. Many countries in Europe have established such a system and it has been found that the establishment of the school as a human rights community (Walker, 1992) has helped to create a positive environment in which children feel respected and have the opportunity to shape their own surroundings.

Bullying is widespread and is an issue in many countries and I think that the process of listening to children and giving them a say in policy making is one that could be adopted successfully in a wide range of schools in a variety of different situations. Children must have their rights acknowledged, they must be listened to and taken seriously if they are to develop as caring, responsible citizens.

References

Askew, S. (1989) 'Aggressive behaviour in boys: to what extent is it institutionalised?' In Tattum,D. and Lane, D. (eds) *Bullying in Schools*. Stoke-on-Trent: Trentham Books.

Carrington, B. and Short, G. (1989) *'Race' and the Primary School: theory into Practice*. Windsor: NFER-Nelson

Council of Europe (1988) *European Teachers' Seminar on 'Bullying in Schools' 1987*. Strasbourg: Council for Cultural Co-operation.

DFE (1994) *Bullying Don't Suffer in Silence — An Anti-Bullying Pack for Schools*. London: HMSO.

Elliott, M. (1991) 'Bullies, victims, signs, solutions', In Elliott, M. (ed.) *Bullying : A Practical Guide to Coping for Schools*. Harlow: Longman.

Elton Report (1989) *Discipline in Schools*. London: HMSO

Frost, L. (1991) 'A primary school approach — what can be done about the bully?' In Elliott, M. (ed.) *Bullying: A Practical Guide to Coping for Schools*. Harlow: Longman.

Johnstone, M. Munn, P. and Edwards, L. *Action Against Bullying — Drawing from Experience*. Edinburgh: The Scottish Council for Research in Education.

Mellor, A. (1993) *Bullying and How to Fight it — A Guide for Families*. Glasgow: The Scottish Council for Research in Education

Olweus, D. (1993) *Bullying at School: What we know and what we can do*. Oxford and Cambridge, Massachusetts: Blackwell Publishers.

Tattum, D. (1989) 'Violence and Aggression in Schools', In Tattum, D. and Lane, D. (eds) (1989) *Bullying in Schools*. Stoke- on-Trent: Trentham Books.

Tattum, D. and Herbert, G. (1993) *Countering Bullying: Initiatives by Schools and Local Authorities*. Stoke-on-Trent: Trentham Books.

Walker, J. (1992) *Violence and Conflict Resolution in Schools*. Strasbourg: Council for Cultural Co-operation.

Chapter 16

Civic Education in Russia

Irina Ahmetova and Ekaterina Rachmanova

Introduction

For many years schools in the former Soviet Union were teaching a course entitled 'The Constitution and the Law'. The same course was taught at all Universities and Pedagogical Institutes. The main feature of that course was a particular interpretation of the material, namely that the basic needs of a person can be met only through the interests of the state. The same course was used throughout the entire former Soviet Union. The main teaching method was lecturing, with students required to reproduce the key ideas of the textbook. It was a system grounded on ready answers with no questions asked. In other words it was a system of training students for their future life in a totalitarian state.

After 1990 the obligatory courses were cancelled and as a result schools and institutes found themselves in a vacuum, although this lasted only for a short period. In 1992 a new Russian State Law on Education was adopted. Its Article 2 envisaged entirely new principles of Russian state policy towards education, particularly humanitarian education. State policy in the field of education is based on the following principles: the humane character of education, based on general human values, life and health, the free development of every person, the education of citizens, and freedom and pluralism in education.

The law also provided the right of schools to add their own materials and courses. This right was based on official instructions which specified the compulsory minimum content of the curriculum. This right gives the school the option of additional courses and subjects.

The content of education is one of the factors of economic and social progress and in accordance with the law it has to provide for personal choice and the means to achieve this. It also gives education a role in the development of civil society, and in strengthening and developing the rule of law. Education should contribute to the shaping of people, that is citizens who are integrated into contemporary society. Thus the new law stipulated the necessity to create new democratic and civic education.

One of the conditions of functioning of any contemporary democratic society, including Russia, is an awareness of human rights and an understanding of the mechanisms of legal protection, both on a national and an international level. This can only be achieved through carefully planned civic education. It is very difficult to define this, since citizenship is not a theoretical model but rather a practical mechanism that functions in real life. Today in schools and universities there is a broad understanding of the fact that education should be provided not only in the traditional way of learning by heart a certain number of facts, dates, laws, properties and rules. It is not enough simply to explain about rights and obligations, about the principles envisaged in different international documents, about different concepts, attitudes and ideas. The goal of education in this field is much broader: it is educating people who are aware of their human rights, freedoms, obligations and responsibilities to the society. It is also to create legal awareness both at a personal level and for society as a whole. Civic education should involve not only students and teachers but also their parents.

Today, schools in Russia are gradually coming to the realisation that the final objective of education is to create a new system of values independent of religion, culture, party or racial and ethnic particularities. The necessity of such education is indisputable, as the tragedy in Chechnia clearly demonstrated.

An analysis of civic education in Russia allows us to highlight the following new features:

- democracy in choosing curricula;
- the state, public and non-governmental organisations all involved in civic education;
- uniting teachers into public associations based not on their profession but on their personal desire to participate in the dissemination of new ideas on civic education in Russia;
- the creation of new textbooks and manuals.

We shall examine each of the above points more closely.

Democracy in choosing curricula

Civic education should begin not with the students, but with the teachers. Pedagogical Universities and institutes play an important role in this process. As mentioned above there was a special course at all the institutes: 'The Constitution and the Law'. It was held during the final graduation year and lasted one term with the total number of hours ranging from 24 to 32.

The programme of that course only a couple of years ago included studying the Soviet Law, the structure of governing bodies, and the legal status of students and teachers. The course was pragmatic and was an integral part of teacher training. At the same time pedagogical institutes and universities provided teacher training in such disciplines as history and law for secondary school teachers. In the history department legal subjects were taught for three years. The main aim was to study Soviet Law and basic ideas about the State and Law from the point of view of Marxism-Leninism. Any ideas that ran contrary to those generally accepted by the State could only be presented from a critical angle. The mere term 'human rights' was either not used at all or was deemed to have been created by a devious bourgeois ideology. Under conditions where there was a complete absence of any sources of information on human rights this was uncontroversial. We must also bear in mind that the Universal Declaration of Human Rights was only published in Russian at the end of the 1980s. The great changes that took place in the country, including the new law on education, enabled the teachers of the pedagogical institutes to change radically the subject 'The Constitution and the Law' and to consider law as a property of civilisation and culture which reflects humanitarian values, registered in international documents and also in national documents published before the revolution.

One of the authors of this article has prepared and published a new programme where, theme by theme, labour, civil and other branches of Russian law are compared with international standards and recom- mendations. New topics such as aspects of human rights, civic society, and law state were added to the programme. Also, at the beginning of the 1990s, a new course entitled 'Human Rights' was introduced at the Moscow State Pedagogical University, which is the leading pedagogical university not only in Moscow, but in the CIS, since it trains teachers for schools and teacher trainers for pedagogical universities and institutes. Originally it was introduced as an optional course, but gradually a number of faculties included it on their list of compulsory subjects. So it is studied in the history, sociology and primary school faculties. The students write course papers and take examinations on human rights.

At present teachers from the University have prepared several different programmes on human rights for senior forms of the secondary school and for the students of the pedagogical universities. They have also published theoretical and practical manuals for the students and teachers of the pedagogical universities.

At this point we must say a few words about Russian secondary education. Children spend 11 years at one school. Education is divided into three steps: primary school comprises forms one to three, secondary school lasts until the ninth form and provides basic secondary education. In principle it is possible to leave school at this point. Then forms 10 and 11 complete secondary education.

Up to the ninth form schools can decide within the framework of the school and regional instructions which subjects should be given preference. A lot of schools include in their curriculum the subject 'Civic Society Studies'. This course was designed by Ya. Sokolov and includes several modules: the Family, the Law, Economics, Psychology and so on. There is also a course designed by L. Bogolubov and A. Ivanova: 'People and Society'. This integrated course, which draws on a number of social sciences, consists of two parts: part 1 — People, Nature and Society; part 2: Personal and moral development and the Law.

In forms 10 and 11 civic education is compulsory. The state instructions allot two to three hours per week for its study. But even at this stage the school has a choice. At present the school can offer its students either 'The Foundations of Civilisation' or 'Activity in Human Life and Society' as a compulsory subject.

Involvement in civic education of the state, public and non-governmental organisations

A lot of public and non-governmental organisations have shown interest in civic education and particularly the issues of human rights. These organisations are concerned mainly with teacher training for secondary schools, teachers of institutes and anyone else interested. For example, in 1991 a non-governmental Department of Human Rights was created at Moscow State Pedagogical University. It united secondary school teachers, teachers of other pedagogical institutes and representatives of a number of public organisations. The Department has been conducting seminars on human rights for several years. First they were conducted with the support of the Council of Europe. Now the Department works on its own.

Other examples include the Russian Foundation for Promoting UNESCO which conducts seminars for Russian school teachers two or three times a year, normally during the holiday season. The International Centre for Human Rights also conducts intensive training on human rights and distributes free of charge the newspaper *Barricades*, containing material for role-playing on human rights.

A Teachers' Union to promote civic education

The measures above are not enough in themselves. That is why, not so long ago, teachers interested in civic education in Russia created a Union to promote civic education. The goal of this Union is not only to unite all the interested parties, but also to promote the ideas of civic education at all levels of state power, to create textbooks and curricula, to conduct seminars, to carry out experiments, to involve the mass media, and to create the basis for an information service for teachers. The first steps in this direction have already been made. The Russian educational telecommunication network *Russian Education Line* was set up by the *Uchitelskaya Gazeta* in June 1994. It offers its users participation in tele-conferences in different telecommunication networks and gives access to information on civic education. The Ministry of Education is planning to set up a new data base *All Education*.

This network broadens considerably the opportunities for teachers in various regions of Russia, particularly the more remote ones. The Ministry of Education has agreed to link all the in-service teacher training institutes into this network. Finally, the Union is planning to publish a weekly newspaper *Civic Education* as a supplement to the *Uchitelskaya Gazeta*.

Creation of new textbooks and teaching materials

It is very difficult for a teacher to teach effectively without a textbook. A number of textbooks on human rights have been published in Russia, all of them reflecting the desire of their authors to present the material in a new way and to teach children democratic motivation. In connection with this it is worth mentioning the teaching materials on human rights for school children particularly young learners: *The Adventures of A Small Man* and *Your Rights*. They are based on the Universal Declaration of Human Rights, but it is presented in a form accessible to children, using such characters as Pinnochio.

Civic education at school: some practical aspects

Since activity in the field of Civic Education is just starting a lot of schools are devising their own methods of teaching within the curriculum and beyond it. It is interesting therefore to look at the experience of Moscow school No 199. In 1990 the Moscow secondary school No 199 joined the UNESCO project of associated schools. This project enabled pupils to develop as individuals by participating in the work of various clubs, by attending the Vavilov Institute of General Genetics and the Mother and Child Welfare Centre, the republican library for children and various sports sections.

It is now recognised all over the world that ecological problems should be solved by united efforts. Senior pupils participate in the Russian-American project *A Person in a Big City* working on the subject *My Family's Garbage Can*. They conduct their creative work independently and maintain contact with US high school students by means of telecommunications. Work on the project was organised in stages. The first stage included an experiment in the analysis of the content of the waste bin. At all stages they systematically exchanged information with their American partners using a computer. Moreover, they had several live conferences where they could hear and see each other on the monitor. Three studies were completed: 'The Influence of Waste on People's Lives'; 'The Problem of Garbage Utilisation'; and 'The Landfill Process'.

In the course of the work the school children contacted the relevant organisations and read a great deal on the subject. Thus in the course of their work school children had a chance to try their hand at research, to brush up their English and to learn to operate a computer, etc. The School found several partner countries for the study of culture, the national heritage and historical and architectural sights. School studios and hobby groups work on interesting new projects. The literature studio took up the theme: 'The Influence of Christianity on the Development of the Individual's Spiritual World', the folklore group will look at 'General Traditions in the Folk Culture of the Peoples of the Russian North and in the Finnish Culture', the ecology club will deal with the 'Influence of Industry on Soil, Water and Air'.

Five years ago the school introduced a new subject *The State and Human Rights*, which has become very popular. At that time there was practically no information about human rights in Russia. Neither students nor their teachers knew anything about the Universal Declaration of Human Rights or the Convention on the Rights of the Child. They used the extensive experience of their foreign colleagues. The Humanities Department on Human Rights and International co-operation of the Ministry of Foreign Affairs of Russia co-ordinated this project. It was upon the recommendation of this department that the participants of the project created *The ABC of Children's Rights*, published in 1994. They also conduct lessons on subjects related to human rights.

The project has united a group of senior secondary school students headed by a young history teacher. Every student investigates a certain aspect of Human Rights, for instance, the right to education and its implementation in this country, the rights of disabled children and their protection, and freedom of expression in the arts. The students of this group correspond with a humanitarian high school in Kakmar, Sweden.

Another direction of work is the use by senior students of the results of their research to conduct classes for the elementary school students, when they act as teachers themselves. They have already elaborated six such lessons on different subjects based on human rights. The first lesson takes place annually on 10 December — International Human Rights Day. The theme of the lesson is 'What do I mean in this world?'. The aims of the lesson are as follows:

- To explain the basic notions such as human rights, the Universal Declaration of Human Rights, the Convention on the Rights of the Child, the United Nations — a house of friendly neighbours

- To demonstrate that there exist special texts that set forth human rights, and that emphasise respect for all human beings

- To demonstrate what can be done to implement human rights in every class.

The preparatory stage includes the following:

- In the classroom the students get an assignment: 'Write a letter to your foreign friend about yourself' (draw pictures). In the lesson the children draw the pictures of the world that surrounds them: their house, their family, pets, nature.

- The school psychologist helps to analyse the pictures, the character and the mood of the author.

The lesson is divided into three parts:

- What is it to be a human being in this world?
- The Universal Declaration of Human Rights regulates the relations of people in society, the state and worldwide. Historical background.
- How can we ensure that human rights are observed at school, in class and at home?

The lesson starts with the demonstration of drawings that are analysed by the senior students. The main idea here is to stress that all these drawings were made by different people. But they all have something in common. Each of them is a unique personality. Each deserves respect, though they express themselves in a different way.

There are billions of people in the world, they differ from each other. Yet each of them is unique, a creation of Nature. That is why everyone should be treated with respect. The grown-ups have waged a lot of wars. During the lesson the children are told about the terrible losses and horrors of World War Two. That is why the United Nations was created in 1948 — a house of good neighbours. Then it is explained what that organisation is and what it does, what documents it adopted — international laws, that set out the rules for the people in the world. What rights should people enjoy? What do people need for a normal life?

Not only grown-ups have rights. Children have rights too. They are set forth in the document the UN Convention on the Rights of the Child. However very few people in the world know about them and very often the rights of children are abused. This is followed by discussion on breaching the rights. The question is asked whether there are any children in the class whose rights have been breached. Did they feel upset? Then the children participate in a game, 'The tree of wishes'. On specially prepared sheets of paper that are made in the form of a leaf the children write their wishes. And then they are fixed on the tree which was drawn earlier. The wishes should be connected with children's rights. When the wish is fulfilled the child takes the leaf off the tree. The children are asked what they think should be done for their wish to come true. Then they play a game that is called, 'A secret friend'. How should we make friends? What if you have a sick or a weak person close to you? At the end they role-play a famous Russian fairy tale — 'The Magic Flower', in which a girl gives the last petal of the Magic Flower to a sick boy and he is cured. At the end the conclusions are drawn. What have we learned about human rights? Should everybody enjoy them and what is necessary for that?

Another interesting lesson teaches respect for other people's opinions. The aims of this lesson are:

- to define the notion of freedom of expressing oneself and one's opinions
- to show that there may exist different opinions on one and the same question
- to develop a sense of tolerance and respect for other people's opinions

  The structure of the lesson is in two parts:

  - a discussion on a certain topic to show how many opinions there may exist simultaneously
  - a discussion about how important it is to listen to other opinions and to treat them with respect.

For example, the children are offered the theory of the creation of the world as a starting point for discussion. They can express points of view of writers, scientists, their own, they can invent fairy tales and stories.

Thus, they are shown that there are a great many points of view on this question. Is it good or bad? What could happen if someone disagrees with another opinion? What is understood by the expression 'freedom of expression of thoughts and ideas'? How do we find ways for peaceful discussion of problems? What qualities should people possess to discuss this problem?

At the end of the lesson students discuss why it was necessary to discuss the problem. They consider new things they have learned about each other during the lesson. Then they draw their conclusions.

Conclusion

To sum up it must be pointed out that not everything happens so well. Lack of finance results in a shortage of teaching materials. Schools and institutes have insufficient international documents. But there have emerged additional problems. Sometimes school children's awareness of their human rights, and the fact that they study such textbooks as *The Adventures of a Small Person* lead to conflicts between teachers and their students and between the students and their parents. Sometimes it is difficult to conduct a lesson because the students believe that the international rules have no bearing on Russia; it has its own rules and traditions. This is a manifestation of traditional Russian nihilism and scepticism with regard to the state, the court, and the law, against a background of lingering economic difficulties. We should also point out the low level of legal awareness amongst the school administrations, teachers and parents. The analysis shows that civic education should simultaneously involve everybody: children and adults.

Chapter 17

Promoting Citizenship through International College-School Links

John Halocha

Introduction

Some of the most significant moments for trainee teachers are those spent working with children. A central question in the design of teacher education courses is how to create practical opportunities for them to use these experiences to begin to develop their understanding of key concepts. This chapter discusses a project which sets out to make the European dimension come alive for students and children; it also aims to give students first hand experience of working in democratic ways. The benefits of this approach are assessed and the insights achieved by students, pupils and the teaching staff involved are discussed. The project is called *School on Site* and takes place within the Bachelor of Education honours degree course at Westminster College, Oxford.

School on Site

School on Site is an intensive two week project linked to the main Teaching Studies course which covers the fundamental topics of classroom organisation and management, child development, curriculum subject studies and theories of learning. One unit is called *Child as a Learner* which combines theoretical perspectives and practical experience of ways in which children learn. A local school is invited to become involved with students studying this course. All the students are divided into small groups which are linked with groups of children. For a number of weeks the children come into college for short periods and work with the students on a range of activities. It allows our students to focus in depth on how children learn in both individual and group situations. The group dimension to this work is important and some time is spent analysing the dynamics of collaborative group activities and democratic processes. During these initial visits the students also work with the class teachers from the school to plan two full weeks of teaching which will take place during *School on Site*. They begin to learn ways in which teachers plan their curriculum within official requirements.

For the project fortnight, the students transform seminar rooms in college into fully equipped primary classrooms. They organise the learning environment and resources. This provides them with many practical opportunities to experience issues of democratic decision making, values and rights at adult level. For instance, as this is a group project, they have to negotiate teaching strategies and share responsibility. They can also make full use of college facilities such as computer rooms, drama studio and science laboratories in their work with the children.

One of the aims of the project is, therefore, to develop students' professional skills in collaborative group work both among themselves and within groups of children. This enables them to consider democratic teaching methods with colleagues and with pupils. The other aim is to extend their range of professional practical skills in a European context; for example the management of information technology.

Links with the ERASMUS project

In 1992 funding was obtained from the European Community under the ERASMUS programme for a curriculum development project entitled *Education for citizenship in a new Europe: learning democracy, social justice, global responsibility and respect for human rights*. Partners in this programme, which involved 22 universities, committed themselves to developing, the project within teacher education courses. The *School on Site* project provided an opportunity for developing this approach during the initial training of primary school teachers.

In 1994 and 1995 children from a local rural primary school worked with us in *School on Site*. The Manor School has about 170 children on roll, coming from the large village in which it is situated and from the surrounding countryside. Teachers, parents and governors were keen to develop the European dimension to the curriculum. As a first practical step we made contact with a headteacher of a cluster of village schools in the Marche region of Italy. She was keen to work with children and teachers in England and she was also leading a project which was looking at children's stereotypes and values in a number of European countries. We were thus able to undertake numerous approaches of developing understanding of teaching for citizenship in a new Europe.

Introducing the European dimension and citizenship to students

The majority of students working in *School on Site* had scarcely considered teaching on Europe. Only a few students had experience as part of a team. We intended to give them the opportunity to develop their confidence and to see how successful work can be achieved by building on small but sound starting points. We believe that democratic teaching methods and active learning are important and so we create an environment where students' experiences, skills and values may be included and developed. Some of them have studied Europe as part of their geography or foreign language main subject courses; others have studied in other European countries or spent time in them before coming to college; many have personal family, recreational or social contacts. We assessed the opportunities and relevance of this knowledge and experience in planning work for their children.

Many teachers find it hard to begin work on Europe with primary children because they believe they have no suitable contacts. In this particular project, the initial contact was provided but we discussed the principles of linking and evaluated the actual outcomes. For example, we concluded that such initiatives can begin on a small scale if they have a firm foundation. We also noted the importance of personal commitment and the need for close relationships between teachers in the participating schools. Students were made aware that our project was built up carefully over a two year period. Activities were carefully chosen to ensure that success would build upon success. Small scale activities in the first year were extended in the second. Between these two *School on Site* events children and teachers at the school continued regular contact with the Italian children and staff.

The personal links were indeed the key to success. In 1994 the head teacher in Italy was able to visit the Manor School. The children delighted in this and developed strong images of the enthusiasm she brought with her. By early 1995 it was agreed that a teacher from England would travel to Italy to collect resources to develop their European work. The friendship and help she received was discussed with the students who were then able to understand how such projects need to be built slowly and with commitment, a shared understanding and respect for everyone involved. A return visit by the Italian headteacher in 1995 visibly demonstrated this.

Introducing democratic approaches to students

School on Site provides important opportunities for student teachers to experience and analyse democratic teaching methods in the work they do with the children and with each other as beginning professionals. None of the teaching experiences provided by the college can be totally value free. While many teachers and schools provide an atmosphere in which students are allowed to develop personal approaches, students do appreciate that they are guests in a school and may be limited in some of the things they do. On the other hand in *School on Site*, where the students are the hosts, they can think creatively and with imagination. They start with teaching spaces in which they create learning environments of their own design. A range of high quality resources are provided and they must make decisions about how they are effectively used. Within the requirements discussed with the teachers, they must plan the timetable, prepare and teach the lessons and provide the professional framework to ensure safety.

Recent curriculum changes have required primary teachers to collaborate in much greater depth in the planning of learning experiences. New entrants to the profession need to bring with them a framework of skills and concepts which prepare them to make informed contributions to this school planning process. The *School on Site* ethos directly confronts students with the realities of demo-cratic decision-making and teaching methods. How will they arrange the teaching spaces? Who will use which resources and when? What are the group priorities? How can effective means of communication be created? How will the work be shared?

College tutors and the class teachers help the students to resolve these and other issues. These discussions often broaden out into questions of the social and political contexts in which schools work. It is important to refer to educational values, and in particular human rights values, which should underpin every primary school.

> For a primary school to operate successfully in a way which upholds human rights principles requires staff, pupils and parents to recognise the values which the school upholds, to agree with them and to promote them (Lyseight-Jones, 1991).

Numerous examples of this occur during *School on Site*: if a group of children need a quiet space to work effectively, how do students provide this? How can students help a group of children word processing together ensure that all their ideas are considered and valued? How can they plan activities for the children which are of interest and benefit both to the English and to the Italian children? Developing respect and empathy for the needs of everyone involved in the project is vital. If students have the practical opportunity within their course to experience issues of human rights and reflect upon them, then they will be able to take these into their careers and reflect on their own work as teachers.

The analysis of democratic teaching methods is also an important part of the group work activities prepared within *School on Site*. During their course students have the chance to develop skills in whole class, group and individual teaching methods. The *School on Site* course provides opportunities for all methods but in particular the students work with small groups of children to help their understanding of arranging a class into appropriate groups. They are confronted directly with group dynamics and the issues raised when considering democratic teaching methods. By focusing on the needs and learning strategies of individuals within groups, students examine ways of designing learning opportunities which allow children to make decisions, express their views and allow them to bring their experiences and ideas into the classroom. An effective example of this occurred when students prepared materials on the mountain areas of Italy where the cluster of schools with which they were connected were located. Tourism is an important means of employment but also has environmental implications. The children already had regular contact with children in the Italian locality and knew about unemployment there, just as they were aware of it among adults in their own locality. They also knew about positive and negative effects of tourism in the Oxford region. Building on this knowledge and experience, students and children developed empathy with their partner children in Italy.

From this basis some very effective geographical enquiry developed which included human rights issues about employment, leisure and making decisions about how our landscapes are used. All partners were able to learn that while they lived in contrasting landscapes in two countries, the underlying human concerns and needs were very similar. An example of this was discussion about the transport congestion created in part by tourism in Oxford being weighed against the employment opportunities created by the visitors. This led to ideas of world citizenship and a consideration of what skills children need if they are to travel widely during their lives. We then discussed the possible effects of global travel on the relationships between various parts of the world (D'Amore, 1988).

Children began to realise the need to understand peoples' lives in other countries in order to be more aware of the impact they might have on them as future travellers. Developing from this, students were able to work with the children on thinking about how landscapes in Europe may develop in the future. A relevant example for the Oxfordshire children is that Blenheim Palace is nearby: how might their locality be affected if more tourists come to their area? Will the roads be too congested? Where will cars be parked? How will the natural environment be affected? The Italian children were able to think about their more mountainous landscape and the ways in which it attracts visitors and sporting activities. These questions brought us into the sphere of futures education, as pioneered in the UK by Hicks:

'Education for the future' draws on two long-standing educational traditions. The first is the humanistic learner-centred tradition which focuses on the development and fulfilment of each individual. The second is concerned with building greater equality in society by highlighting and challenging existing inequalities of race, gender, class and disability (Hicks, 1994).

Work on futures education thus arose in a practical way which could be developed immediately with the children. Groups of students were able to adopt various teaching ideas and then compare them. For example, children were able to draw how they thought the landscape might look in twenty years time. They thought about what they would like to happen and what they felt was most likely. This approach, when linked with developing democratic teaching methods, allows students to develop ideas with children about how we are going to make choices in and for the future and who should be making them.

The project in action

The activities which took place in *School on Site* during 1994 /5 highlight many of the ways in which such a course offers opportunities for student teachers to have active experience of developing an understanding of European citizenship in children of primary school age. The examples which follow illustrate the approach and the effects of the project on students, children and teachers.

Empathy is an important concept when we are thinking about developing young children's understanding of how people in other countries live and the range of things which they consider to be important.

> Children need to build respect for themselves and others, value diversity, identify and feel comfortable with their own feelings and have respect for the feelings of others (Wiegand, 1992).

In the preparations for *School on Site* the teachers in Italy and England agreed to exchange sets of colour photographs of the school localities. One group of English children collected ideas from the class and then went into their locality with a camera to take thirty six photographs which they would send to Italy. Before the first picture had been taken, there was a great deal of discussion, sharing of ideas and taking other people's views into account. Three contrasting discussions highlight this. The local garage sold a particular make of Italian cars and the children were keen to show this link the village had with Italy. The village has a memorial to local people killed in the second world war. It was agreed not to include this because the children felt that as they were just developing their links with the Italian children it might be hard to include this element of previous historical links with their country. Nearly all the children thought it would be a good idea to photograph the sweet stand in the local shop so they could show their partners in Italy the types of sweets we have in England. They were very interested when they saw similar shopping pictures arriving from Italy. Children and sweets appear to include common values in both countries! Two sets of these photographs were made, laminated and numbered. Numbering allowed for easy cross-referencing in each country. Laminating the photographs allows them to be used in a range of creative ways. For instance water-based pens and post-its can be used on them. The same photos can be used in many curriculum areas. They were an important source of information when children were making models of the Italian landscapes.

Throughout *School on Site* the emphasis is on the quality of the learning environment and the resources available to children. Whilst it is important to select and use appropriate high quality resources, students also need to learn that resources are finite and must be managed in a professional way. Resource provision in schools varies enormously and students need to be aware of this and of its social implications for the relative degrees of opportunity which children have. Very often the children with the most pressing needs are also in schools where the quality of resources is most limited. Making democratic decisions together about how to use these finite resources is an important professional skill which student teachers need to develop.

The provision and use of teaching resources raised questions of comparative education. An important consideration within *School on Site* is the development of skills in information technology. It had been hoped to link the schools through e-mail and similar electronic means. While information technology has developed in English primary schools, this has not yet taken place to the same extent in Italy. Such links could not therefore be made. The extensive use of fax, video and traditional post made up for this. On the other hand, students learnt that the teaching of modern foreign languages in Italian primary education is far more highly developed than in England. The variation in priorities gave rise to many valuable discussions and a deeper understanding of the range of educational systems at work throughout Europe. Students preparing to teach in a new Europe need an understanding of these as they may not only have frequent contact with the various educational systems, but may also have the opportunity to work in them.

At a very practical level, the frequent use of information technology during *School on Site* provided many opportunities for those taking part to extend their understanding of new technologies and how they are affecting society. As citizens in a future Europe, both students and children need to be aware of these and possess the skills to be confident and critical in their use. It can also change the relationship between people. Students had been shown how to use fax machines and were pleased to be able to pass these skills on to the class teachers: a reversal of traditional student-teacher roles, but also important in beginning to develop an atmosphere of democracy and mutual learning in the school environment. Videos were made in Italy and England. Even the making of a five minute video involved children in many decision-making processes and provided excellent opportunities for students to consider how skills for democracy and equality can be developed in such active learning situations.

Developing European insight is often hampered by insufficient time and rigorous curriculum requirements. Another of our objectives within the *School on Site* programme is to introduce students to ways of planning which allow curriculum demands to be met by, for instance making a video or preparing a fax which they will send to their friends in Italy. Clear and effective communications are a formal objective in the English curriculum. This can easily be met by having the children writing an A4 sheet intended to be clear to Italian children who receive it on their fax machine. In a similar way, when they receive a video from Italy which tells a story through the use of pictures only, they learn important skills in analysing images and in understanding the ways in which various media allow us to communicate.

Further work on images was developed by the Italian head teacher who initiated an exchange of children's pictures of their families, hobbies and views about the environment as part of a Europe-wide project to improve our common social environment (Monachesi, 1994). Through these activities students also began to learn about working with children on issues of stereotypes, identities and nationalisms. The content of the children's letters revealed that they had many similar interests in sport. They talked about the importance of their friends and family. They shared some festivals and beliefs such as Christmas. These discussions and the personal contacts helped the children to go below the surface of national stereotypes and look at people's lives in more detail. Differences were also identified and students learned to discuss these with the children. For example, when the English children were comparing the cost of items in each country, they asked for the cost of a pet rabbit. The reply from Italy helped them to understand that rabbits were more often used for food rather than being kept as pets.

Extending the project

The importance of resources in all this work cannot be underestimated. In 1995 the Local Education Authority provided a grant to extend the work. Students saw how schools can develop initiatives and gain extra support for them. The funds were used for one teacher from the school to travel to Italy. This visit had two main objectives. The first was to reinforce and celebrate the personal contacts that were being developed between the schools. The second was the collection of resources which would be used in *School on Site* and eventually become an important on-going resource within the school. The resources were to have a strong geographical and social focus. The teacher undertook a short in-service course to consider the range of resources which would be useful, how they could be obtained and how they would be used within the geography curriculum. Finding first-hand sources of information is a common problem and on her return the teacher discussed her methods. It is usually a question of having ideas about where such resources may be found and making contact with those places. For example, the Italian headteacher had good contacts with the local town officials who, on learning that large scale plans of their villages would be of interest to English children, quickly found, copied and presented them to the teacher. Asking the right questions in the right places is an important skill for teachers intending to resource for active learning. All the resources collected meant a great deal to the children because they were about a locality in which their Italian friends lived and where their teacher had been, whereas geography textbooks may have little real meaning to them. It is not easy for children to visit these places as a part of their school work, but through working with a wide range of related materials, they were able to build up a picture of life in another locality.

Sensitive teachers encourage their children to reflect on such images, helping to show that children's experiences are valued. Nevertheless, it is vital that their understanding of other places be based on accurate information and good quality resources. On her return to England the teacher worked with students and other colleagues on developing ways in which the resources could be used with children. In addition to collecting maps, booklets and artefacts, she took many photographs. These provide a very rich source of evidence for the children to study. Through them children begin the process of understanding and interpreting images in an active and personal way, especially when able to compare them with the ones they sent to Italy (Kose, 1985). Students were able to work with children on environmental and citizenship issues when it was seen in photographs that villages in Italy and England had very similar recycling points for glass and paper. By using the fax link children were quickly able to find out more about how these facilities were used and why they were thought to be important. The opportunity to use technology to collect and assess information quickly was another important skill learned by both children and students.

While physical resources such as maps, photographs and artefacts are important in the development of such initiatives, the personal contacts can also provide many starting points for the promotion of citizenship through Europe within primary schools. These can occur in quite un-planned ways and it is necessary for student teachers to learn how to look for these opportunities and develop them within their teaching. Discussions about human rights, democracy and citizenship raise questions about laws and justice. During her stay in Italy, the visiting teacher met the local police officer for the Italian villages. He showed a great interest in the project and students considered possible ways in which links with him might be developed in future work. They were also able to see how the wider community can be brought into the educational process in a valid and relevant way.

The nature of *School on Site* demands that students and class teachers build close relationships. Through these and the many discussions they had, it became apparent to students that those involved with the link were fully committed to it and that many things happen within the 'hidden curriculum' as part of the every-day life of the school, in addition to the carefully planned curriculum. When an

Italian teacher faxed through a request for information, time was found to ensure that it was quickly responded to. At Christmas time a cake arrived through the post from Italy. These actions, by bringing in an affective aspect, are important in strengthening the relationships between people in different countries.

Before becoming involved in the work, many students thought that they needed fluency in other languages for such schemes to be a success. They quickly realised that enthusiasm and imagination were far more important. There was also some evidence from students that they had become aware of the importance of introducing modern foreign languages to primary school children and that children's enthusiasm for learning a language was a part of such linking activities. They experienced the success and enjoyment which young children get from beginning to learn and use a language.

The future

As we look with our students to the future of this work a number of possibilities emerge. Those involved in both Italy and England hope for exchanges of children to develop. New resources continue to be regularly exchanged. The school is also prepared to link with new partners and develop a matrix of relationships eligible for funding under the European Comenius scheme. Working with the Local Education Authority we will seek to develop examples of good practice in teaching for European citizenship. As teacher training becomes more school-based, this project can also serve as a model for developing the expertise of students, teachers and tutors in a practical and worthwhile way, with all those involved being able to contribute and learn from their joint experiences.

During 1994/5 *School on Site* set out to provide student teachers with first hand experience in developing work to promote a European citizenship with primary school children. We believe that if students can work in an environment where success is seen to be based on commitment, careful planning and enthusiasm, then they will be able to take these qualities with them into their work as qualified teachers. They also need an understanding of the key issues involved in such work, such as stereotyping, global responsibility, identities, empathy, bias in resources and the practicalities of organising a learning environment in which democratic teaching methods may be developed. It also involves them in being aware that

> Learning about places is about promoting understanding, developing a sense of commonality, harnessing embryonic tolerance and a sense of friendship, recognising similarities, and valuing and celebrating diversity (Catling, 1995).

If we can start to develop these qualities of thought and action within our primary school children, we may be laying many of the foundations needed to prepare them for citizenship in a new Europe.

References

Catling, S. (1995) Wider Horizons: the children's charter, *Primary Geographer,* 20, pp. 4-6.

D'Amore, L. (1988) Tourism — the world's peace industry, *Journal of Travel Research*, 27,(1), pp. 34-40.

Hicks, D. (1994) *Educating for the Future.* Godalming: WWF UK.

Kose, G. (1985) Children's knowledge of photography: a study of the developing awareness of a representational medium, *British Journal of Developmental Psychology*, 3, pp. 373-384.

Lyseight-Jones, P. (1991) Human Rights in Primary Education, in H. Starkey (Ed) *The Challenge of Human Rights Education.* London: Cassell.

Monachesi, D. (1994) *Education to Europe in Primaries: a way to improve our common social environment.* Paper presented at l9th conference of The Association for Teacher Education in Europe, Prague, September 1994.

Wiegand, P. (1992) *Places in the Primary School: Knowledge and Understanding of Places at Key Stages 1 and 2.* London: Falmer.

Chapter 18

Pupils' Views of the Future

Vilgot Oscarsson

Introduction

> The World could go under tomorrow, although it might be a bit better for
> Sweden. My own future will probably be OK, specially if I get good exam
> results. But in general there's not much I can do to influence the future.

This quotation epitomises the findings concerning the ways pupils look at the
future in the 1980s. It articulates pessimism, a sense of being overwhelmed,
powerlessness and passivity (Bjerstedt, 1986a, Bergstrom, Holmborg, 1985,
Escolona,1982). My own experience as a teacher led me to question these findings. Whilst I have encountered pupils whose views of the future seem quite
bleak and who seem at a loss to know what to do, the majority have had a quite
different attitude: 'we can influence the future, we want to do something, we
know what we can do'. This chapter reports on a research project conducted in
1992 which set out to discover how sixteen-year-old pupils in their final year of
compulsory schooling in Sweden think about the future. There are a number of
motives behind it.

Every new generation must be won over to democracy and thus it is important
to examine whether pupils feel they can influence their situation, if they have a
desire to, and whether they know what they need to do to accomplish this. Do the
pupils possess knowledge about the driving forces of change and development
and are they aware of their own role and responsibility in this process? Are their
views of the future as pessimistic as the research reports of the 1980s indicated?
To what degree are they socially engaged? However, perhaps the most powerful

motivation for studying pupil attitudes to the future can be found in school policy texts. The Swedish national curriculum states:

> The school has the responsibility for communicating values, knowledge and skills and for preparing pupils for living and working in future society

> In the teaching an historic perspective must be laid which amongst other things enables the pupil to develop a preparedness for the future.

To what degree do schools live up to these demands?

Main research problems and research purpose

About 900 pupils from grade 9 of the compulsory compre- hensive school sector responded to the national evaluation tests in global awareness in social and civic studies (SO) during the spring term of 1992. This chapter is based on their res- ponses. It describes and analyses the view of the future held by pupils and illustrates the role the school and its teaching can play in developing these views. It asks three main questions.

- **What are the pupils' views of the future?**
  What are the pupils' views about their own personal futures, about Sweden's future and a global future? What images of the future do the pupils hold and what forces do they see as significant for forming the future?

- **What possibilities are there for influencing the future?**
  Here we deal with the issues which pupils feel must be changed if they are to obtain the future they desire. What do they feel they need to do, can do and what do they want to do in order to obtain a future they believe in?

- **What have the pupils learnt in school which they feel is particularly important for the future?**
  Which knowledge and skills do the pupils see as most important for the future? Does the school and its teaching prepare them for the future as outlined in the national curriculum?

Methods

The context of the data collection

In the spring of 1992 the Swedish School Agency carried out a national evalua- tion of the compulsory comprehensive school. This set out to provide a view of the effects of nine years of compulsory schooling on pupil performances. A 10 per cent random sample of Swedish compulsory com- prehensive schools was drawn. This involved 101 schools and about 10,000 pupils and their teachers.

Almost 4000 pupils responded to a questionnaire concerning teaching in social and civic studies subjects (SO). Four groups, each of about 1000 pupils, answered questions and solved problems in groups, in pairs, and individually, using 13 different thematic booklets.

The selection and sampling of schools for social and civic studies fitted guidelines established by the Central Bureau of Statistics. Our sample can be considered representative of pupils in grade 9 of the Swedish school system.

The Questionnaire

One of the thematic booklets, *The Past and the Future*, included questions about the future (see Figure 1) and these were answered by approximately 900 pupils from 44 schools across Sweden. Their answers were analysed and our conclusions are presented below.

Three of the questions from the booklet were fixed response questions and seven were open-ended. For the fixed response questions the pupils were asked to record on a scale of 1 to 8 (1=not so good, 8=very good) how they felt the future would most likely be for them, for Sweden and globally. The results are tabulated in figures 2,3 and 4. A follow-up open-ended question was coupled to each of them. It read: *What did you think about and how did you reason when making your response?* Questions 13, 14, 15 were included with the aim of discovering what the pupils feel needs to be changed for a better future and their feelings about their capacity to influence change. We were particularly interested in question 12: *What have you learnt in school which is of particular importance for the future?*

We also used the results of questions from the common questionnaire to provide background variables such as level of self-reliance, political interest/activity and views of possibilities of influence in school and society. Details concerning the social, ethnic and regional background of pupils were also obtained from the national evaluation data.

How pupils see the future
Views of the future: bleak or optimistic?

In the beginning of the 1980s, several Swedish and international studies showed that pupils had a very pessimistic view of future societal development (Ankarstrand-Lindström, 1984a, 1984b; Raundalen and Finnoy 1986; Gould, Moon and van Horn, 1986; Chivian, 1988). The author of the report from a 1985 investigation summarised pupils' views of the future as follows:

> A real chamber of horrors greets the readers in these views of the future. Most frightening are the apocalyptic images of warfare, bombs, disaster, darkness, and cold. ..the time after the catastrophe when the survivors envy the dead. It would not suffice to say that these figures of horror are common, they are more or less general (Bjurwill, 1986).

Figure 1

The Questionnaire

These are the questions to the pupils starting with question no 6.

6. What does the future hold?
Place a tick in the box indicating how you feel the future will be.
Scale from 1 'not too bright' to 8 'very good'.
6 How will your personal future be?
Not too bright   very good
    1   2   3   4   5   6   7   8

7. What did you think about and how did you reason when forming your response?
I marked the above box because....
8. What will Sweden's future be like?
Not too bright   very good
    1   2   3   4   5   6   7   8

What did you think about and how did you reason when forming your response?
I marked the above box because....
10. What will the future for the World be like?
      Not too bright   very good
        1   2   3   4   5   6   7   8

What did you think about and how did you reason when forming your response?
I marked the above box because....
12. What have you learnt in school which will help you in the future? 13.
What stands in the way of the future you believe in?
What needs to be changed? For yourself? In Sweden? In the World?
14. Try to give some examples of how this can be done
15. Peace and freedom.
In your dreams of the future there may be ideas about the end of warfare and human oppression. What needs to be done to ensure this?

Pupil views of the future from the early 1990s

As can be seen from figures 2,3 and 4, whilst pupil judgements of their own personal futures are generally more positive than those about Sweden's and the global future, the majority of pupils choose the middle range of responses. In contrast to previous findings most pupils seem to feel the future will be pretty good, especially their own, but also for Sweden. Things are a little more negative concerning the global future. Approximately 30 per cent of the pupils responded on one of the 8 grade scale's three lowest levels whilst a little over 10 per cent responded on one of the three highest.

The pupil image of a global future is rather bleak but it is more optimistic than images found in investigations from the 1970s and 1980s. The more optimistic view of the future amongst our pupils compared to the 1980s, is also supported by the organisation of Swedish Physicians against Nuclear Weapons who note that whereas 13 per cent of older compulsory school pupils held an optimistic view of the future in 1984, in 1992 this had risen to 23 per cent. Over the same period pessimists fell from 44 per cent to 35 per cent (information leaflet Swedish Physicians against Nuclear Weapons 1992:50).

Who is optimistic?

Boys seem to have a more positive view of the future than girls. However, differences are not statistically significant in this respect. The differences arise because boys use the two extremes of scale more extensively than girls.

Previous studies have shown that social background is significant for views of the future amongst pupils, where pupils from the lower socio-economic classes were shown to have a bleaker view of the future than pupils from higher ones (Bjurwill, 1985, Bjurwill, 1986). No such relationship has been disclosed in our investigation. However, pupils from immigrant groups have a somewhat more negative view of their own personal future than do other pupil groups. Social background otherwise seems to have no importance in how optimistic or pessimistic pupil views of the future are.

Knowledge levels and views of the future

In debates concerning the role of the school with respect to the development of future orientations amongst its pupils, emphasis has often been placed on the need to provide pupils with insight into future issues, not least so that they may obtain a more positive view of their ability to influence societal development. Logically we might expect a relationship between knowledge and empowerment. However I know of no research which has demonstrated such a relationship.

Figure 2, 3 and 4

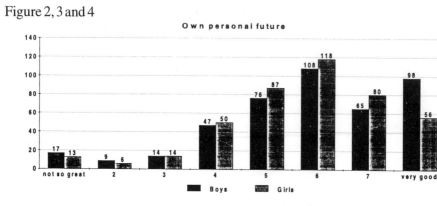

mean value, own personal future: **5,8**
correlation between own future and sweden's future: **r= +0.39**

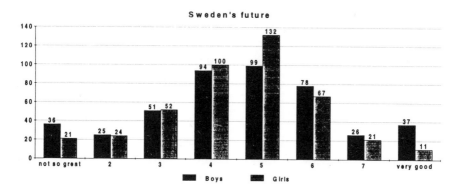

mean value, sweden's future: **4,6**
correlation between sweden's and global future: **r= +0.39**

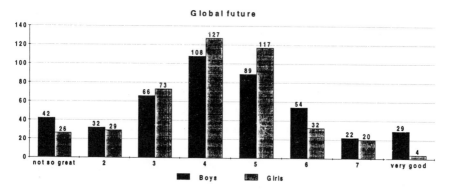

mean value, global future: **4,1**
correlation between own personal future and global future: **r= +0.39**

the diagrams show the total number of pupils at each scale score.

In our study we took school marks as an indicator of levels of knowledge. Surprisingly, we found that there is no relationship between school marks and degrees of optimism or pessimism with respect to the future.

The absence of a clear positive relationship between level of know- ledge and future view in our investigation cannot be taken to indicate that level of knowledge is irrelevant for future orientations. My experience as a teacher is that pupils with insight into key issues generally have a more positive view of the future than their peers. What our results may indicate is that the subject knowledge held by pupils might not be as decisive for their views of the future as has been indicated previously (Raundalen, 1986). Our data would indicate that other issues may play a more decisive role.

Self-reliance and possibilities of influence

The pupils who have a more positive view of their personal future are above all those who have strong *self-reliance*. Two indices were constructed from pupils' responses to questionnaire categories. *Social reliance* comprised 12 questions in which pupils were asked to indicate how they coped with various social situations, such as understanding other peoples' feelings and situations and accepting people who were in some way different from most others. Girls obtained higher ratings in social reliance than boys. Boys, on the other hand, obtained higher ratings in *political reliance*, the second index. The political reliance index concerned judgements about the pupil's views of his or her knowledge in making political decisions and influencing societal development. Social and political reliance show a positive correlation with pupils' views of their own future but not with respect to views of Sweden's or the global future.

A positive correlation was also found between pupils' views of their own future and their ability to influence the curriculum. Our results indicate that the school should, as far as possible, strive to support the growth of pupil self-reliance by providing pupils with ways of influencing their own educational situation in school. This might help them to a more optimistic view of their own future.

What do pupils think about the future?

Pupils' views about their own future, Sweden's future and global future were solicited by three fixed response questions, and the open ended question: *What did you think about and how did you reason when forming your response?*

Only a quarter of the pupils have answered the question with respect to Sweden's future and global future with more than one sentence. There is an absence of more reasoning answers. The pupils have given fuller responses about their own future (37 per cent gave more than a one sentence answer). However, most answers are short.

Girls answered the open questions more regularly than boys. They also gave longer answers and were more likely to give reasons for where they placed themselves on the optimism-pessimism scale. This distinct gender difference cannot only be explained by claiming girls are better acclimatised to school demands than boys are, or are more obedient and follow the teacher's instructions more closely. There appears to be a genuine difference in their interest in the future: girls appear more committed than boys and they more readily use emotional terms when expressing their images of the future.

How pupils describe their own future

I'm not sure what the future holds but I hope it will be good.

The above reflects the attitude which is most prevalent in pupils' responses concerning their reasoning about their future. A majority of the pupils (a little over 60 per cent) have a positive view of their future. Almost a third of responses however do express some *uncertainty* about personal futures. Girls express more uncertainty than boys.

These vaguely positive responses indicate that the majority of pupils appear to have interpreted the open question in terms of what they think and feel about a *desired future*. A number of pupils seem to have an image of an 'anticipated' future in their minds when they decide their position on the optimism scale, 'I will have a good life because I know that I will get a job' but the general picture we have obtained is that it is a view of a desired future they are responding to. In some cases a combination of desired and probable futures appear: 'I'm either going to be a pilot or take over my mother's chain of companies'.

The basis for views of personal futures

Views of personal futures might best be described with the term "uncertain optimism'. The answer to what lies behind these images can be found in the pupils' reasons for their responses. For instance, views are often coloured by their expectations of job possibilities.

I think I'll get a decent job.
I'm fairly positive toward the future, it looks like there'll be work and so on.

I think I'll get in on the upper-secondary course I want and that when I leave school the economy will be on the upswing again and I'll be able to get a job.

I'm a bit concerned that there won't be any work when I leave school.
I hope it it'll be OK but there'll likely be unemployment and that.
Unemployment just goes up and up. Where will it end?

When providing motivations for a positive view of their personal futures, it seems that in many cases (about a third of those responding to the question) pupils root their understanding in a belief in themselves; a belief in their own ability to obtain work in the future.

> I find learning things quite easy and hope to get a good job and a family.
> You have to aim high.

> I'm a bit selfish but you have to be to get by in today's society. In other words, things will go well for me.
> I'm aiming for the top.

Self-reliance appears to be the motto of these pupils. Thoughts about collective political solutions, collective effort or technological advances as a solution to future problems are most noteworthy by their absence. Future personal possibilities are firmly coupled to individual effort and capability: 'I have the ambition to succeed and hope to'.

But the majority of the pupils also seem to be aware that political and economic conditions are significant for their futures.

> My marks weren't that good and my family is not that rich so if I don't study further I'm not likely to get all that good a job.

> The rich people have businesses their kids can get work in but I haven't got rich parents.

What threats are there to personal views of the future?

Unemployment is the main threat to the realisation of the future in the eyes of pupils. However, pupils also mention environmental issues when discussing threats to the future. Environmental awareness amongst pupils has been demonstrated in a number of investigations, and this kind of awareness seems common amongst pupils in our sample (Jeger and Lindgren, 1992). Environmental problems are seen as threats to Sweden's and global futures. However, to some degree pupils also see environmental problems as a threat to their own futures.

About nine per cent of respondents gave environmental problems as a clear cause of pessimism with respect to personal futures:

> We are destroying our planet.
> The environment is just getting worse and worse.
> There's no clean water any more. No animals, no forests.

Girls seem more environmentally concerned than boys. 56 of the 82 pupils who gave a negative view of the future with an environment argument were girls. Girls also gave more extensive reasons for their responses than boys and used more emotionally loaded terminology.

An array of previous investigations have shown that pupils often account for negative views of the future by referring to threats of warfare, nuclear war, population explosions, famine in the third world and so forth (Ankarstrand-

Lindström, 1984a, 1984b; Utas-Carlsson, 1990; Bjerstedt, 1986b). Very few pupils, mainly girls, expressed these reasons in our investigation. Threats to personal futures tended to be coupled to economic and political conditions in Sweden. Current unemployment conditions appear to dominate pupils' thoughts concerning their own futures.

Gender differences

Girls expressed greater uncertainty toward the future than boys, provided fuller reasons for their views, more often included environmental issues and generally expressed themselves in more emotionally loaded ways. These are in accordance with findings from other investigations (Yebio, 1992; Brock-Utne, 1985). Girls also refer to children and family to a greater extent than boys do in their responses. ' My life will be fine. I'll get a good education, a good job, marry a nice man and have nice sweet children'. The idea of realising a positive future via family and children is exclusively found amongst girls in our investigation. Amongst boys, notions of a good future won through work and personal success predominated.

How pupils describe the global future

We have previously described the pupils' views of the global future as bleak compared with their views of their personal futures, but bright when compared to the images of the same emerging from research done during the 1980s.

> I believe that a lot of countries will sign a peace pact and that warfare will be less common. Environmental destruction will become more focused on, but it might be too late.

> The World is undergoing massive political change, the power blocs are standing up for little countries and new states are emerging. If we play our cards right the so called world peace might come before too long.

> Borders between countries are opening, walls are being torn down and it will become possible to travel freely between countries. And I hope the third world can be developed and get a better deal.

The above statements reflect the positive images of a global future amongst 40 per cent of the pupils' responses. The implications were that, despite present economic problems, developments are in the right direction. Other positive signals were found in references to European Community development and strengthened international co-operation through United Nations initiatives. Environmental problems were seen as difficulties being overcome, and disarmament treaties were cited as positive developments.

The pupils have knowledge about developments on the world political scene. It seems as though they have identified positive trends in the new world order and take these as their point of departure for an optimistic view of a global future. However, these pupils are in the minority. Sixty per cent of the pupils have a more pessimistic view of global futures than they have of Sweden's and their own .

The risk of environmental catastrophe is the commonest negative image of a global future. Of the 794 pupils who provided a reasoned negative image 30 per cent, mostly girls, cited environmental problems. Pupils are also clearly aware of local environmental problems in their home regions and in Sweden. However, only 10 per cent of them see these problems as a threat to their future. A sound economy and employment prospects are seen as keys to future security.

Warfare and threats of warfare also emerge as significant in pupils' accounts of future threats to global security. 173 pupils (somewhat over 20 per cent) cited war in their negative images of global future:

> I believe that there will be a new world war with all the terrible weapons there are. Racial antagonism is high and soon there'll be a new Hitler who will succeed in taking over the World.

This fear is rarely directly coupled to nuclear war. Indeed, very few pupils indicated an explicit fear of nuclear armaments and nuclear warfare. Our results differ significantly in this respect to findings from studies during the 1980s (Bjerstedt 1986b; Raundalen and Finnoy, 1986; Macy, 1983). The same applies to threats from starvation, poverty, over-population and the growing disparity between the industrialised and third worlds. Only a few pupils, mostly girls, provided these reasons for negative images of a global future.

Summary: children of our time

At the time the pupils responded to the questionnaire in the spring of 1992, environmental issues were featured in the media as were the end of the cold war and the beginnings of nuclear disarmament. Sweden's economic problems, global economic depression and mass unemployment were often covered. On the other hand, issues of nuclear armaments, relations between developed and third world nations, population growth, the distribution of global resources and the growing disparity between the industrialised and third world had slipped from the media agenda.

Pupils' judgements of Sweden's and global futures are influenced by media coverage. Global survival issues obtain the same unsatisfactory coverage in formal education as always. But education probably has less effect on the images generated by pupils than the media anyway.

The media also seems to a large degree responsible for influencing pupils' understanding of which forces and power relations are most significant for our global future. The pupils, like the media, attribute great significance to the United

Nations with respect to peace and disarmament negotiations and the reduction of threats of warfare. They also tend to personify 'evil', reflecting the media treatment of dictators such as Saddam Hussain. They seem to accept the media message that forces far beyond the local individual and her/his sphere of influence form our common future. This is a far cry from the aims of the national curriculum, which intends to make pupils aware of the possibilities of influence over local and global events and developments.

What preparations for the future are provided by the school and its teaching?

The third main question was: What do you feel you have learnt in school of importance for the future?

General knowledge

All school activities are in some sense future-oriented. This is also implied in the responses pupils gave. About a quarter of the pupils describe *general knowledge* as important. Here we have included responses such as 'everything is important', 'everything I have learned can be of use in some way', 'you need to be able to count, read and write'.

Subject knowledge

Social and civic subjects top the list of subjects which pupils regard as important for the future (25 per cent of pupils). This finding is in line with other data from the National Evaluation which indicates that pupils are more interested in these subjects than others and see them as important (The National Evaluation Report No 4, 1993). About 20 per cent of the pupils say the same about natural sciences and languages, whilst only 13 per cent give such indications for practical subjects such as cookery, woodwork, art and crafts, perhaps reflecting the general low status of these subjects in school.

Social development and acclimatisation to school

School should not only prepare pupils for the future. It also has a responsibility for the social and personal development of pupils. How are these facets reflected in the findings? About 15 per cent of the pupils provided responses which we categorised as *social and personal development qualities*. These are responses which express the pupils' conviction that school has contributed to their social and personal development for the future. For example, school has taught them: 'to function socially', 'to mix', 'cohesion', 'to make friends, 'to show respect, 'to show responsibility', 'to co-operate', 'to believe in myself'.

That only 15 per cent of the pupils give responses which are in line with the social and personal development aims of the school curriculum is disappointing. However, what is more noteworthy is again that girls are over-represented. Of the

135 pupils placed in the above category almost 65 per cent were girls. This result is in line with our earlier findings .

A similar number of pupils were placed in a category labelled *education competitive qualities*. This can be coupled to the school's personal development aims. Again, the responses express a positive view of the contribution of education to future needs. Such responses included: 'education and exams are important', 'you have to have an education', 'an education is always worth having', 'good marks, studies and education are important'.

Within this category we have also placed responses which express that the most important things pupils have learnt in school are strategies of accommodation or acclimatisation. Responses such as it is good to: 'adjust to time demands and sit still', 'take what you need', 'not to trust others', 'work hard', 'be more pushy', 'learn that you need to be best', 'learn how to get by and get a career', 'learn that life is tough and that there is no time for things other than school work during a school career', 'learn that your life depends on the grades you get from your teachers'.

Girls again dominate in this category (90 of 149 pupils), something which may be explained in terms of their being better adjusted to school than boys (Wernersson, 1988).

Starting from the aims expressed in the school curriculum, it is disappointing that so many pupils seem to feel that the important messages of schooling lie in the competitive orientation it has provided. However, school has a duty to prepare pupils for social reality outside. Pupils appear to understand this important function of the hidden curriculum.

Important knowledge and views of the future

The pupils who feel that school has mainly been good for helping them develop some kind of social competence (category *social and personal development qualities*: mainly girls) have a more positive view of the future in general than do pupils who emphasise subject knowledge. However, there is also a significant correlation between social competence and social reliance. Girls have higher scores than boys in both these variables.

A reasonable interpretation of the findings here is that girls are able to compensate for low self-confidence through developing greater levels of social competence. Both these qualities have been shown in our material to connect strongly to positive views of the future. Boys are generally more confident of their judgements than girls are (Brock-Utne, 1985; Wernersson, 1988).

Summary and conclusions

We found that the pupils involved in the evaluation of the social and civic subjects in the Swedish national school evaluation have a more optimistic view of the future than pupil groups in previous investigations. The material also shows that pupils seem to be politically aware and that many pupils have an action potential. The passive pessimism indicated in previous studies does not seem to apply to the same extent for these pupils.

The concept pairs, optimist-pessimist and active-passive, can be combined in a four-field table in the following way (Bjurwill, 1986):

Attitude		positive	negative
	Active	Development optimism plus Action optimism give **Active Optimism**	Development pessimism plus Action optimism gives **Active Pessimism**
	Passive	Development optimism plus Action pessimism gives **Passive Optimism**	Development pessimism plus Action pessimism gives **Passive Pessimism**

Table 1

Table 1 includes two forms of optimism and two forms of pessimism: development optimism and development pessimism depending on whether future developments are considered bright or bleak, and action optimism or action pessimism depending on whether action possibilities are seen as personally accessible or not. The first form of optimism- pessimism gives rise to *an attitude*, the second to an *outlook*.

The different fields in the table and the findings can be summarised as follows:

The majority of pupils can be located in the third frame of the table (passive optimism). That is, a slight majority of the pupils have a fairly bright view of the future (particularly their own personal future) but see very small possibilities of influencing developments on national or global levels. They see some possibilities for influencing their personal futures however.

The next largest group is formed by *passive pessimists*. This group comprises some 30-35 per cent and is surprisingly large considering explicit national curriculum aims yet surprisingly small considering the findings of previous studies, in which the group predominated.

Active pessimists are hardly to be found at all in our material. The pupils who would be located here are those who reason as follows: as the future looks so bleak you have to try to influence it as much as possible.

The group of ideal pupils, seen from a curriculum perspective, would be the group of active optimists. The size of this group is more difficult to ascertain. With respect to development optimism alone, the group could be as large as 50 per cent. However, with respect to manifest active political involvement and the exertion of influence it might be as small as five per cent. From pupils' responses to our questions, we estimate its size as of the order of 10-15 per cent of the total sample.

Promoting active optimism

One of the tasks of the school is to develop pupils into active citizens who have the desire and capability of influencing societal development. What can the school do?

A common point of view is that increasing the emphasis in schooling processes on subject type knowledge is important for enabling the development of active optimism. This may be the case to some extent, at least with respect to the promotion of greater insight into central future issues. However, our material does not indicate that extensive subject knowledge is an adequate or perhaps even necessary basis for developing future orientations. What seems more important is the social role played in the cultivation of democracy.

We can support this in a number of ways. For instance, if subject knowledge had been most significant, then passive pessimists would be expected to comprise an overwhelmingly proportion of the 'poor' performers in school subjects. But this is not the case. There are no distinct differences between categories in these respects. What does seem to be significant for the group of passive pessimists though, is the relatively high proportion of boys who have a negative view of the possibilities of obtaining secure future employment on the national job-market, who have low values of self-reliance and social competence, and who feel they have little possibility of influencing the school curriculum.

We conclude that if pupils are given the opportunity to practise democracy in school, for instance through becoming actively involved in its curriculum development processes, and are given the opportunity to develop social competence, the chance of increasing their positive view of the future is enhanced as is the possibility of their being able to influence future societal development by taking an active part in its democratic processes.

Girls appear to have a greater social competence than boys. However, they also appear to have less self-confidence. If our conclusions are reliable then the message is clear. School should enhance the self-confidence of girls and aid the development of social competence of boys. We believe that in this way schools can improve their capacity to prepare for a positive and democratic future.

References

Ankarstrand-Lindström, G. (1984a) *Skolelevers upplevelser av framtid och skola. Enkätstudier.* Pedagogisk-psykologiska problem, nr 432, Lärarhögskolan, Malmö.

Ankarstrand-Lindström, G. (1984b) *Framtidsperspektiv i gymnasieundervisningen: Några skolfösök på temat 'Fred i framtiden"?* Pedagogiska hjälpmedel, *Malamö* Lärarhögskolan, nr 36.

Ankarstrand-Lindström, G. (1992) *'Lån grynmgs fard mot dag?' Internationalisering av undervisning (Fredsundervisning). Utvärdering av erfatenheter från skolförsök i åk 8 i Malmö.* Pedagogisk-psykologiska problem, nr 570, Institutionen för pedagogik och specialpedagogik, Lärarhögskolan, Malmö.

Bergström, A. Holmborg, P-O. (1985) *How Swedish teenagers think and feel concerning the nuclear threat. Impact of the Nuclear war on Children and Adolescents.* Proceedings of an International Research Symposium, Internate Psysicians for the Prevention of Nuclear War, Boston, USA

Bjerstedt, Å. (1986a) *Lära för framtid: En läsguide.* Pedagogisk orientering och debatt 73, Institutionen för pedagogik, Lärarhögskolan, Malmö.

Bjerstedt, Å. (1986b) *Lära för framtid.* Stockholm, Liber Utbildningsförlaget.

Bjurwill, C. (1985) *Framtidsföreställningar hos skolbarn: Studier med hjälp av semantiska differentialer.* Pedagogisk-psykologiska problem, nr 456. Institutionen für pedagogik, Lärarhögskolan, Malmö.

Bjurwill, C. (1986) *Framtidsföreställningar hos skolelever: Studier med hjälp av uppsatsanalys.* Pedagogisk-psykologiska problem, nr 459, Institutionen för pedagogik, Lärarhögskolan, Malmö.

Brock-Utne, B. (1985) *Education for peace: A feminist perspective.* Oxford: Pergamon Press.

Chivian, E. et al. (1988) American and Soviet teenagers' concems about nuclear war and the future. *New England Journal of Medicine*, 1988, 319, pp 407-413.

Escolona, S. K. (1982) Growing up with the threat of nuclear war. Some indirect effect of personality development. *American Journal of Orthopsychiatry.* 37, pp 18- 23.

Gould, B. B., Moon, S.and van Hoorn, J. (1986) *Growing up scared? The psychological effect of the nuclear threat on children*, New York, Open Books.

Hicks, D. and Holden, C. (1995) *Visions of the future; why we need to teach for tomorrow* Stoke on Trent, Trentham Books

Informationsblad för svenska lakare mot kärnvapen 1992 50

Jegers, I. and Lindgren, M. (1992) *Morgondagens värderingar.- för dig som tanker vara med bortom sekelskiftet.* Stockholm, Konsultförlaget AB

Macy, J.R. (1983) *Despair and personal power in the nuclear age.* Philadelphia, PA: New Society Publishers.

The National Evaluation Report No 4, (1993) *Den Nationela Utvärderingen av grundskolan våren 1992* (1993) En första resultatredovisning. Skolverkets rapport 4, Vårnamo

Raundalen, M. and Raundalen, T.S. (1986) *Barn i atomåldem.* Oslo: J.W. Capelen, 1984 (svensk översättning, Stockholm, Prisma 1986).

Raundalen, M. and Finnoy, O.J. (1986) Children's and teenagers' views of the future. *International Journal of Mental Health.* 15, pp.114-125.

Utas-Carlsson, K. (1990) *Samtal om fred och krig med elever i årskurs 5.* Pedagogisk-psykologiska problem, nr 534, lärarhögskolan, Malmö.

Yebio, B. (1990): Ungdomars tankar om krig, fred ock framtid: Intervjuerfarenheter från årskurs 8. Särtryck ock småtryck från Institutionen för pedagogik och specialpedagogik, nr 684, lärarhöskolan, Malmö

Wernersson, I. (1988) *Olika kön samma skola? En kunskapsöversikt om hur elevernas könstillhörighet skolsituation.* Skolöverstyrelsen, Stockholm

Index